CANADA AT THE POLLS

CANADA AT THE POLLS

The General Election of 1974

Edited by Howard R. Penniman

American Enterprise Institute for Public Policy Research
Washington, D. C.

ISBN 0-8447-3178-1

Foreign Affairs Study 24, October 1975

Library of Congress Catalog Card No. 75-24771

Printed in the United States of America

CONTENTS

PREFACE

Canada at the Polls: The General Election of 1974 is another in the series of studies of national elections in selected democratic countries published by the American Enterprise Institute for Public Policy Research (AEI). Volumes covering the two 1974 British parliamentary elections and the French presidential election of the same year have already been published. Studies of the 1974 House of Councillors election in Japan and the national elections in Denmark, Norway, and Sweden in 1973 are in progress.

On 8 July 1974, Canadian voters gave the Liberal party 141 seats of a possible 264 in the federal House of Commons—the largest number received by any party in the last six national elections. The unanticipated magnitude of the Liberal triumph reduced the representation of each of the remaining parties. The Progressive Conservative party, Canada's second major party, fared badly. The party began the campaign with high hopes of gaining some seats and possibly even becoming the largest party in the House of Commons. Instead, its share of the seats dropped to ninety-five, from 107 in 1972. Party leader Robert Stanfield retained his seat in Parliament, but a month after the election announced plans to give up his party position prior to the next elections. The New Democratic party (NDP) lost fifteen seats, including that of David Lewis, the party leader, who has since been replaced. The Social Credit party's representation (all from Quebec) fell from fifteen to eleven, but the party leadership has remained unchanged.

Minority governments, as William P. Irvine notes in his overview of the 1974 election (Chapter 2 of this volume), have been a frequent occurrence during the seventeen years from 1957 to 1974. During this period, Canadian voters have, in five of eight elections, failed to give any party an absolute majority of the seats in the House of

Commons. During the same years third party and independent candidates have won between 20 and 28 percent of the votes in every election except the one in 1958, when the Progressive Conservatives won 54 percent of the popular votes and 208 seats in Parliament. The five minority governments, dependent upon the support of two parties to remain in power, have generally been short-lived—remaining in office an average of only two years, far less than the full term of five years allowed under the constitution.

Canadian parties are "disciplined," that is, all members of each party in Parliament are expected to vote as a unit. This makes it virtually impossible for two parties to satisfy the varied demands and interests of more than 22 million Canadians spread across a huge continent, with differing and sometimes conflicting economic interests, who speak two official languages, and who are divided by a federal system into ten provinces with independently elected governments whose powers are increasing. Because those who support third parties have often been concentrated in the western provinces, they have gained a respectable number of seats for their relatively small vote. Their situation, then, has been comparable to the national parties of Scotland, Northern Ireland, and Wales in recent elections and very different from the plight of the British Liberal party, which won nearly 20 percent of the votes in both 1974 elections but only 2 percent of the membership of the House of Commons. Perhaps because it has happened more frequently in Canada, voters there seem less disturbed by the possibility of electing a minority government than do the voters of Britain. Whatever the fears of some, it may be expected that as many as a fourth of the voters in both countries will frequently vote for candidates named by third parties.

At a time when traditional modes of financing party campaigns are increasingly under fire in many democracies, readers may find Khayyam Z. Paltiel's examination (Chapter 7) of developments in Canadian campaign regulation of special interest. Paltiel describes the rather minimal controls that have long characterized Canadian campaign financing. He notes that in 1974 only 75 percent of the candidates filed legally required reports of monies received and expended during the campaign. As in previous years, no one was prosecuted for his failure to file, and the reports that were filed were not audited. In 1974, however, Parliament enacted legislation which went into effect in August (after the election) that may sharply change this situation.[1] "The new law aims to reduce spending by parties and

---

[1] Initially the law was to go into effect 1 July 1974, but that date fell in the middle of the campaigns, so the effective date was moved back one month.

candidates by setting limits to certain expenditures, imposing overall spending ceilings, and transferring some costs to the state. . . . [It] requires full disclosure of donors, contributions, and costs higher than a specified minimum, and provides mechanisms for reporting, checking, and publicizing the declarations made by parties and candidates." The impact of these drastically changed rules on the financing of campaigns will be of interest to all concerned with the problem.

In addition to the essays contributed by Irvine and Paltiel, John Meisel discusses the nature and development of the Canadian party system and the "civic culture" within which the parties operate; Stephen Clarkson, George Perlin, Jo Surich, and Michael B. Stein separately contribute chapters on the campaigns of the Liberal, Progressive Conservative, NDP, and Social Credit parties; Lawrence LeDuc describes Canadian opinion polls and the results of the polling during the campaign; and Frederick J. Fletcher discusses the role of the media in Canadian elections. The electoral data in the appendix were provided by Richard M. Scammon.

Howard R. Penniman

1
THE PARTY SYSTEM AND THE 1974 ELECTION

John Meisel

Party systems in complex societies provide the key to an understanding of how the demands of the population are converted into
governmental outputs. This is not to say that interest groups,
bureaucracies, and nonpartisan territorial or ethnic configurations may
not exercise mighty influences on public decisions; but the interaction
among the various power centers is orchestrated by the party system.
To evaluate an election, therefore, it is necessary to study its consequences not only for the legislative period immediately following,
but also for the long-run interaction among political parties and
between the respective parties and their publics.

Although they are in part shaped by a series of specific election
outcomes, party systems reflect and respond to a broad spectrum
of influences which transcend elections and go to the very roots of
society. This discussion of Canada's party system at the time of the
country's thirtieth general election, therefore, begins by noting the
more or less fixed, nonpolitical constraints within which the parties
have been shaped and within which they breathe; from here it moves
to more narrowly political but largely nonpartisan influences. The
system's nature is then described and, in the final section, evaluated.

Fixed Constraints on the Party System

Canada's social institutions are influenced in crucial ways not only
by its immense extent and topographical variety, but also by its
pattern of settlement. Strung out, as they are, over three thousand
miles along a narrow, seemingly interminable, east-west sliver lining
the southern border, the 22 million Canadians lack a natural geographic center around which their social interactions can be said to

1

cohere. This dispersal is exacerbated by the degree to which the country's regions differ from one another in their physiographic and economic character. Like its southerly neighbor, Canada is comprised of Atlantic and Pacific coastal regions, gigantic lakes and rivers, majestic mountains, and rolling plains, but it also contains barren northlands, colossal island provinces, and its Arctic hat. This heterogeneity has made for striking economic differences between and within Canada's ten provinces, and is no doubt reflected in the psychological make-up of the inhabitants of its diverse regions. Another psychological influence is the fact that Canada is a small country in terms of population, only recently emancipated from its imperial ties, and thrust into inescapably intimate proximity with the world's greatest power. Geography has endowed Canada lavishly, but among its legacies is a dazzling variety of regional disparities and an economy under constant pressure from that of the United States. Much of Canada's economic history in fact centers around problems associated with the production of minerals and staples depending on foreign investment and fluctuating world markets and prices. Under these circumstances it is not surprising that Canadian governments, and with them, of course, Canadian parties, have been much more preoccupied than their U.S. counterparts with developing and regulating economic activities, mitigating centrifugal economic, social and political forces, and promoting national systems of communication and transportation. In the absence of national and nationalizing nonpolitical institutions, therefore, parties and the party system have become important factors in nation building and in the evolution and preservation of national unity.[1]

Politics cannot escape the traditions, styles, and memories bequeathed by the past. The dominant historical antecedents of Canada link the population and its institutions to the British and French regimes which colonized the territory now known as Canada. The legacies of the "mother countries" are, of course, complex and pervasive, but the most important elements for our purposes are the sense of community and unity—as well as the isolation—of the French and the parliamentary institutions and political style of the British. The cultural traditions of the few original French settlers were reinforced and modified by their position in North America, where they were an abandoned, nearly leaderless minority. They also predisposed the *canadiens* towards an exceptionally strong sense of

---

[1] John Meisel, "Recent Changes in Canadian Parties," in Hugh Thorburn, ed., *Party Politics in Canada*, second edition (Scarborough: Prentice-Hall, 1967).

cohesion and a political style dominated by the need for national survival.[2] The pivotal role played by the Catholic Church in this struggle has linked it to the politics of French Canada. The British legacy included not only the institutional framework of a parliamentary system, but also the values that evolved with it, such as a strong emphasis on property and civil rights, the rejection of doctrinaire parties, and distrust of minority governments.

Canada's British and French antecedents thus endowed the country with two diverse political traditions, and, perhaps even more important, two founding ethnic groups capable of independent survival on Canadian soil. Their vital interests have to be reconciled at the risk of undermining the very viability of the state.[3] The demographic make-up of Canada is a third inescapable environmental condition affecting the operation of the party system. While the history and the key decisions in Canada have been dominated by the two "charter groups," the French and the English, a third, less homogeneous grouping of the population has also become important. Non-French and non-English people of European origin comprise a little under one quarter of the population and, although they are proportionately still less powerful and influential than the other two groups, they have become a political factor to be reckoned with, particularly in the West and in the large cities.

Finally, the propinquity to the United States, already mentioned, is so important as to merit being identified as the fourth fixed constraint on Canadian parties. The crushing economic, political, and cultural influence of its neighbor disposes many Canadians to adopt attitudes and values similar to those prevalent in the United States and, more important perhaps, restrict the capacity of Canadian governments to pursue certain policies. But Canadians do not, of course, respond uniformly to the American presence; many, particularly among the middle class, resent Yankee influences. The party system, then, must cope with conflicting attitudes to Canada's large neighbor and to policies designed to deal with the consequences of its ubiquitous presence.

---

[2] Pierre Elliott Trudeau, "Some Obstacles to Democracy in Quebec," in Pierre Elliott Trudeau, *Federalism and the French Canadians* (Toronto: Macmillan of Canada, 1968), p. 107; John Meisel, "Political Styles and Language-use in Canada," in J. G. Savard and R. Vigneault, eds., *Multilingual Political Systems: Problems and Solutions* (Quebec: Presses de l'Université Laval, 1975).

[3] John Meisel, " 'Cancel Out and Pass On': A View of Canada's Present Options," in John Meisel, *Working Papers on Canadian Politics*, second revised edition (Montreal and London: McGill-Queen's University Press, 1975), pp. 184-185.

Political Constraints on the Party System

Institutions. Among the political arrangements greatly influencing the functioning of the Canadian party system are the method of conducting elections, parliamentarianism, federalism, and the role played by the public service. For purposes of electing the House of Commons, Canada has in the recent past been divided into about 260 federal constituencies.[4] Each of the ridings sends one member to the Ottawa legislature, elected by the plurality or "first-past-the-post" principle.[5] There has been some controversy about the effects of this method of choosing members of Parliament on the success and character of the parties.[6] It is sufficient to note here that the existing way of conducting elections and counting ballots has enabled so-called third parties to arise and survive, and that it has led to some parties receiving sizeable electoral support in certain regions without securing corresponding representation in the legislature.

Candidates are normally chosen in conventions organized by local riding associations and, in safe seats, to secure the nomination is tantamount to election. There are no primaries and a potential candidate must normally present himself for election to a meeting of party members. Nominating conventions have no legal status and the degree to which they are organized formally varies considerably; it ranges from large-scale, meticulously structured gatherings of constitutionally selected delegates to casual backroom encounters of a few party cronies. In some instances, the name of the candidate is simply announced by the party organization. The critical point is that a parliamentary aspirant has almost no chance of being elected unless he is a standard-bearer of one of the parties.[7] Acceptability to those who have power at the constituency level of the parties is thus one of the necessary conditions for a successful federal political career— a condition which has obvious implications for the ease with which innovators or mavericks can win national audiences and attention.

---

[4] The number has varied slightly; it was 264 in 1974.

[5] For more detail on the electoral system, see T. H. Qualter, *The Election Process in Canada* (Toronto: McGraw-Hill Co. of Canada Ltd., 1970) and W. E. Lyons, *One Man–One Vote* (Toronto: McGraw-Hill Co. of Canada Ltd., 1970).

[6] See Alan C. Cairns, "The Electoral System and the Party System in Canada, 1921-1965," *Canadian Journal of Political Science*, vol. 1, no. 1 (March 1968); J. A. A. Lovink, "On Analysing the Impact of the Electoral System on the Party System in Canada," *Canadian Journal of Political Science*, vol. 3, no. 4 (December 1970), and Alan C. Cairns, "A Reply to J. A. A. Lovink . . . ," *Canadian Journal of Political Science*, vol. 3, no. 4 (December 1970).

[7] The case of Lloyd Jones's win in Moncton in 1974 as an independent, mentioned below, and the presence of one or two unattached members in most Parliaments, do not weaken the general validity of this observation.

Legislators are bound by the collective decisions of their party caucuses, which assures a reasonable degree of predictability and responsibility in the whole system. Voters can form fairly accurate impressions of how a candidate will behave if elected, since his behavior is dictated by a stable process of collective decision making strongly influenced by the long-standing positions of the parties. The executive is not elected by the public as such, but holds office by virtue of commanding the support of the House of Commons, of which it is an integral part. Its power flows from its capacity—guaranteed by traditional party loyalty—to command a majority of the members, either because the government party holds a majority of seats, or because it has the support of members of other parties who agree, for a while at least, to back the government.

One of the consequences for a parliamentary party system in a highly heterogeneous society is that regional, ethnic, and social compromises cannot be worked out by executive-legislative interaction and bargaining. Legislators cannot take idiosyncratic, independent positions to protect the special characteristics of their districts, as they sometimes do in the United States. Instead, compromises are arrived at largely through the working of the multiparty system and the intricate interrelationship between the federal and provincial organizations within the political parties.[8] The upper chamber—the Senate—is not as useful as its United States counterpart in hammering out national compromises, either, although its composition reflects the regional character of the country. Senators are appointed by the government and usually owe their sinecures to their financial or other contributions to the party holding office when they were appointed. The Senate is relatively powerless, but the existence of this channel for fancy patronage nevertheless contributes something to the capacity of parties to construct consensus and majority support. Leaders lucky enough to hold office can use Senate appointments to retire honorably cabinet colleagues who might expediently be replaced with others or to reward and recognize services and spokesmen for diverse interests and points of view.

The Senate's usefulness here is, however, rather limited; it is possible that its much greater potential will be realized in the future as the federal-provincial arrangements undergo significant constitutional change. At present, the federal structure of Canada—the division of powers and the working arrangements which have evolved

---

[8] John Meisel, "Cleavages, Parties and Values in Canada," *Sage Professional Papers in Contemporary Political Sociology*, vol. 1, no. 06-003 (London and Beverly Hills: Sage Publications, 1974), pp. 20-23.

between the federal government and the provinces—is among the most important political constraints affecting the party system. Each province has a parliamentary system of its own, serviced by a party system only tenuously related to the national party battle. This situation has a number of consequences. It leads to a certain division of labor according to which issues which might otherwise become national controversies are handled at the local level and kept out of the more complex country-wide arena. The presence of provincially oriented political parties, whether quite distinct from or independent of the national parties, or whether linked to them, also provides for considerable maneuverability within the national parties and the national party system. And it removes the necessity of federal parties becoming implicated in some acutely contentious, relatively localized issues.

Most important of all, the great and increasing power of provincial governments in relation to certain economic and social problems has meant that some extremely critical political decisions in Canada have been reached through federal-provincial negotiations.[9] Many of these are conducted and concluded by officials and then given "political" approval by the governments concerned. Federal-provincial conferences at the ministerial level have become important sites for top level "federal-provincial diplomacy" and although they are subject to ultimate partisan approval in the sense that the governments involved are in the final analysis accountable to their respective legislatures, it would be a rash party caucus that would repudiate its leaders (government) after they had reached agreements with other governments.[10] The result of this aspect of Canada's federal ways is that in some vital areas of decision making the parties are left with merely plebiscitary powers to accept or reject agreements made by high-powered ministers and permanent officials.

The last political constraint on the party system to be mentioned here concerns the well-established and excellent public service which reaches from its Ottawa fortress to every nook and cranny of the country. Each department is technically under the control of a minister and the service as a whole is collectively responsible to the cabinet, which, in turn, depends on the confidence of Parliament. Like most large bureaucracies, however, the public service has acquired

---

[9] Richard Simeon, *Federal-Provincial Diplomacy: The Making of Recent Policy in Canada* (Toronto and Buffalo: University of Toronto Press, 1972).

[10] Instances are known however, particularly in Quebec, in which the consent to federal-provincial agreements by provincial premiers was withdrawn after the latter confronted public reactions to them in their own provinces.

immense knowledge and skill, and hence independent power. There is some debate in Canada, as elsewhere, over whether anyone can really stop the bureaucracy from being a law unto itself, regardless of democratic appearances. Whatever the answer to this conundrum, there is little doubt that the government departments strengthen the party in office by making available to it resources far exceeding those available to the opposition. The party battle is thus affected by the frequency and recency with which each of the major parties has had the advantage of partnership with the public service.

Political Culture. Regional, economic, and ethnic differences are so pronounced in Canada that it is in some ways misleading to talk of a nationwide Canadian political culture; it would be more appropriate to consider a variety of subcultures.[11] We have neither the knowledge as yet, nor the space here, to indulge in that luxury, however. Instead we must proceed by making generalizations about the country as a whole. The reader should, however, bear in mind that substantial variations exist, particularly insofar as French and English Canada are concerned, and also with respect to regional economic differences.

Interest in politics is fairly high in Canada but it cannot be said to reach fever pitch. In terms of electoral turnout, Canada ranks well above the United States, slightly below the United Kingdom, and some distance behind communities endowed with a high sense of civic duty, like Finland, the German Federal Republic, or the Netherlands.[12] Around 75 percent of the eligible voters have bothered to vote in recent elections, but it is, of course, uncertain whether voting reflects concern about the outcome or merely, as appears to be the case in

---

[11] Mason Wade, ed., *Regionalism in the Canadian Community, 1867-1967* (Toronto: University of Toronto Press, 1969); Richard Simeon and David J. Elkins, "Regional Political Cultures in Canada," *Canadian Journal of Political Science*, vol. 7, no. 3 (September 1974), pp. 397-437; John Wilson, "The Canadian Political Cultures: Towards a Redefinition of the Nature of the Canadian Political System," *Canadian Journal of Political Science*, vol. 7, no. 3 (September 1974), pp. 438-483; Mildred A. Schwartz, *Politics and Territory: The Sociology of Regional Persistence in Canada* (Montreal: McGill University Press, 1973); Donald E. Blake, "The Measurement of Regionalism in Canadian Voting Patterns," *Canadian Journal of Political Science*, vol. 5, no. 1 (March 1972), pp. 55-81; Meisel, "Cleavages, Parties and Values."

[12] Walter Dean Burnham, "The United States: The Politics of Heterogeneity," pp. 697-700; Richard Rose, "Britain: Simple Interactions and Complex Realities," pp. 493-494; Pertti Pesonen, "Finland: Party Support in a Fragmented System," pp. 277-285; Derek W. Urwin, "Germany: Continuity and Change in Electoral Politics," pp. 142-145; and Arend Lijphart, "The Netherlands: Continuity and Change in Voting," pp. 233-238, all in Richard Rose, ed., *Electoral Behavior: A Comparative Handbook* (New York: The Free Press, 1974).

Germany, a sense of duty to "live right" as a citizen.[13] Canadians, as one would expect of a people living in a large, affluent land, are more preoccupied with private than with public pursuits. Politics tends to be considered by most people as a marginal activity. On television political programs cause less of a stir than the games of the so-called National Hockey League or even so "American" an institution as the World Series.

The low-key interest in politics no doubt reflects the view, widely held, at least until recently, that redress for personal misfortune, and avenues of economic betterment, can most effectively be sought through private efforts of individuals rather than through governmental action. On the other hand, this emphasis on self-help has not prevented Canadian governments, particularly after the Second World War, from embarking on massive welfare and redistribution programs. Another factor in the relatively low level of politicization is the almost universal practice of conducting municipal elections without the formal participation of parties. Canadians, nevertheless, show a widespread identification with parties. At least 80 percent of the respondents in the two available national postelection surveys conducted by academics indicated that they thought of themselves as Liberals, Conservatives, NDPers or identifiers with some other party.[14] This puts Canada ahead of the United States, where the proportion identifying with parties is around 70 percent but behind Britain and Australia, where around 90 percent identify with political parties.[15]

Canadians also seem to occupy a position somewhere between the British and the Americans with respect to another important aspect of political culture: the degree to which they are deferential. Hard data on this topic are scarce but certain inferences can be made. Unlike Americans, Canadians have never experienced Jacksonian democracy, their system does not provide for the popular election of a large number of executive and judicial officials, they are not

---

[13] Urwin, "Germany," p. 143.

[14] The 1965 survey (N = 2,125) was conducted by Philip E. Converse, John Meisel, Maurice Pinard, Peter Regenstreif and Mildred Schwartz, and that of 1968 (N = 2,767) by John Meisel.

[15] Burnham, "The United States," p. 714; David E. Butler and Donald E. Stokes, *Political Change in Britain: Forces Shaping Electoral Choice* (London: Macmillan, 1969), p. 38; Don Aitkin and Michael Kahan, "Australia: Class Politics in the New World," in Rose, ed., *Electoral Behavior*, p. 451. These crossnational comparisons must be interpreted with caution: the data from the various countries tend to be elicited in response to differently worded questions. It nevertheless seems likely that fewer Canadians are attached to political parties than people in the United Kingdom, but that a larger proportion of Canadians than Americans feel themselves linked more or less stably to a given political party.

accustomed to seeing their leading politicians subjected to searching scrutiny by legislative committees before their appointments are confirmed, and so on. For these and many other reasons, Canadians appear to adopt a more deferential position than Americans towards people in authority, whether in the private or the public sector. While this tendency is not as pronounced as in Great Britain, it has permitted a characteristic feature of the British political system to emerge in Canada: the excellent and powerful career civil service mentioned above, which has helped the federal government provide strong national leadership over the years. However, Canadians have not mirrored Americans in bestowing respect and adulation on their military heroes. Deference to authority is related to respect for law and order, which is also greater in Canada than in the United States. The incidence of violent crimes is lower, citizens do not have nor claim the constitutional right to carry arms, and there is no effective "gun lobby."

No country, alas, is free of ethnic and religious bias, or of the feeling on the part of most groups that they are somehow superior to others. Canada is no exception but Canadians are, as a whole, remarkably tolerant of various minorities. The educational systems in the various provinces have not instilled in children a powerful feeling of national pride, as their American counterparts have, possibly because the country has lacked a strong sense of national identity. Tensions between French and English-speaking Canadians, and, in the past, between Catholics and Protestants, have been acute, but both major ethnic groups have been reasonably hospitable towards other groups. Few countries have been so tolerant of foreigners working on their soil, so ready to employ them in their public services, or so willing to allow them to become citizens. It is immaterial that some of this tolerance was born of necessity in a country often badly in need of manpower. Unlike the United States, Canada has never formally espoused a "melting-pot" policy, but on the contrary, has encouraged the survival of the cultures of its ethnic minorities.

The absence of an aggressive "Canadianism" is accompanied by a lively sense of regional loyalty. This attachment to one's own area is by no means confined to Quebec, among whose Francophones it is of course greatly reinforced by ethnic loyalty, but is evident in all regions. The province of Ontario, possibly because it has played a dominant role in so many aspects of Canada's life, is the place in which regional loyalty appears to be most tempered by a highly developed sense of Canadianism. Ontarians tend to assume that what is good for their province is good for Canada, and, not without reason, that what is good for Canada ends up being pretty good for Ontario.

The people's sense of civic efficacy and trust has become an important component of political culture in the eyes of most scholars, largely as a result of the suggestive work of Angus Campbell and his Michigan associates, and of Almond and Verba in their exploration of civic culture.[16] Substantial regional variations exist with respect to these two aspects of the political perceptions and feelings of Canadians. In Ontario and British Columbia, and to some extent in Manitoba, as well as among English-speaking Quebeckers, these indicators of civic competence are high, comparable to those recorded by Almond and Verba for countries like the United States. The Atlantic provinces, on the other hand, resemble countries like Italy, where the sense of civic competence is comparatively low.[17] Since it is often argued that Canada is free of significant class distinctions, it is important to note that the citizens' sense of competence varies substantially not only according to region, but also according to class and education. There is, in fact, considerable evidence to suggest that, insofar as one can speak of a national political culture in Canada, it is shared primarily by the better-educated, better-off members of the population.[18]

The dominant political culture, then, appears to be sustained by a nationwide elite which reinforces its value system through constant interaction with fellow members in occupational, professional and leisure associations. It is probably broadly correct to characterize these values as strongly individualistic, favoring a free enterprise system, and placing great confidence in the virtues and efficacy of brokerage politics in a pluralistic system. Despite its stress on the desirability of the pursuit of private goods, the value system is com-

---

[16] The measures were developed by Angus Campbell, Gerald Gurin and Warren E. Miller, *The Voter Decides* (Evanston, Ill.: Row, Peterson, 1954). They defined political efficacy as: "the feeling that individual political action does have, or can have, an impact upon the political process, i.e., that it is worthwhile to perform one's civic duties. It is the feeling that political and social change is possible, and that the individual citizen can play a part in bringing about this change." (p. 187) The series of questions was used by Gabriel Almond and Sidney Verba in their five-nation study, *The Civic Culture* (Boston: Little, Brown, and Company, 1965), and they have been replicated in many other studies, including those done in Canada in 1965 and 1968.

[17] Simeon and Elkins, "Regional Political Cultures," pp. 408-409; Samuel H. Barnes, "Italy: Religion and Class in Electoral Behavior," in Rose, ed., *Electoral Behavior*, pp. 207-208; John Meisel, "Some Bases of Party Support in the 1968 Election," in Meisel, *Working Papers*, p. 24.

[18] Simeon and Elkins, "Regional Political Cultures," p. 431.

patible with the acceptance of a substantial participation by the state in the economic life of the country, including the outright ownership of railways, airlines, broadcasting systems, and industrial and mining complexes. At the same time, while popular support for democratic socialist parties has only seldom exceeded 20 percent nationally, it has been substantial in some regions and has permitted the mildly socialist New Democratic party to form governments in three provinces.

The Nature of the Party System

The Players. There are both federal and provincial parties in Canada. All of the parties that contest elections for the House of Commons in Ottawa also seek office in at least some of the provinces. But the relationship between the organizations in the two jurisdictions varies a great deal, even when the federal and provincial units bear the same party name. Thus the National Liberal Federation of Canada is legally, and in a very real sense also in practice, quite separate from *Le Parti Liberal du Québec*. In some instances, the relations between the national and provincial organizations are quite close and the distinctions are minimal: in others the two are at loggerheads and maintain only the most tenuous and formal links. In some instances there is no provincial equivalent of a federal party: the Conservatives have had to fight elections without a Quebec organization since the mid-thirties, although the Union Nationale party normally provided strong organizational support for them in that province. Now that the Union Nationale is virtually defunct, the Conservatives lack a provincial organization in the French Canadian stronghold—an area where, as we shall see, they are in sore need of help.

Since this chapter is concerned exclusively with federal politics, it will deal with the party system and parties only at the national level, although occasional reference will be made to the interaction between the national and the provincial organizations.

The Conservative party.[19] The Canadian Dominion came into being in 1867, forged out of a number of British colonies in central and eastern North America largely as a result of the diplomatic skill and political acumen of Sir John A. Macdonald, leader of the Conservative party. Heading a loose alliance of eastern commercial interests, conservative elements among French Canadians (supported by the Roman Catholic Church), Ontario Tories, and "ministerialists"

---

[19] The Conservative party is officially called the Progressive Conservative party. The two names are used interchangeably in this volume.

(M.P.s prepared to support any ministry, at a price),[20] Macdonald established a party and an administration strongly committed to nation building and centralizing policies. It was a party reminiscent of Hamilton's Federalists, favoring the interests of the propertied classes; it was allied with and supported the entrenched commercial, social, and religious institutions of the times. Among its greatest assets (apart from Macdonald himself) were its capacity to enlist the support of substantial groups among both French and English Canadians and its attractive and unifying program of creating a viable political community north of the United States, stretching from the Atlantic to the Pacific.

Towards the end of the century the hegemony of the Conservative party was challenged successfully by the Liberals. Under a French Canadian leader, Laurier, they succeeded in replacing the Conservatives as the favorite of French Canada, while at the same time securing significant levels of support in English Canada. Hereafter only extremely rarely did the Conservatives manage to put together a national majority that included substantial English and French support. They had assumed the unenviable role of playing second fiddle to the Liberals, despite being the only viable alternative to them as a potential government party. During this century the Conservative party has held office only from 1911 to the early twenties, during the worst of the Depression from 1930 to 1935, and from 1957 to 1963, seven years marked by the meteoric rise of John G. Diefenbaker, under whose leadership it won the greatest majority anyone had ever mustered in the House of Commons. Diefenbaker frittered away his national support by conducting his government (admittedly in difficult times) in a capricious, vainglorious manner which ultimately alienated not only French Canada (to which he had made a successful appeal in 1958), but also the large urban centers, business and industrial interests, and the intellectual community.

Diefenbaker, a westerner, nevertheless changed the traditional nature and image of the party by extending its support to his own region and thereby increasing the voice of agrarian populism, as well as that of the new wealth of the West, derived primarily from oil and agri-business. At the same time, the traditional domination of the party by the financial and commercial interests of Toronto and English Quebec diminished substantially. Recently the Conservative party has received its most important support from the West, particularly

---

20 Escott M. Reid, "The Rise of National Parties in Canada," *Papers and Proceedings of the Fourth Annual Meeting of the Canadian Political Science Association*, vol. 4 (Toronto: May 1932), p. 188.

the prairies, the Atlantic provinces, particularly after Diefenbaker was replaced as party leader by the former Nova Scotia premier, Robert Stanfield, and in rural and small-town Ontario. The bulk of its voters are English-speaking and Protestant. The party appeals more to older than to younger voters, to electors with fewer rather than more years of schooling, to those with lower incomes, and to unskilled rather than skilled labor. The only major occupational group preferring the Conservatives to any other party are the farmers.[21]

Both the style and the postures of the party reflect the basis of its support, although the leadership is also influenced by other factors—the source of funds, tradition, the party's position in the various provinces, and so on. The Conservative party is committed to the preservation and strengthening of the private enterprise system and in this regard is much closer to the Liberals than to the NDP. It differs from the Liberals in being less sensitive to the position of Francophones and less active in proposing policies designed to equalize the economic and other disparities between French and English Canada, less centralist, more wary of United States influences, and still a little more "pro-British," more responsive to rural and agricultural interests, somewhat more hospitable to anti-intellectualism and to authoritarianism on issues like the death penalty. It would be dangerous to make too much of these differences, however, since they are very much a matter of degree. Within both the Conservative and Liberal parties there are individuals who do not fit these generalizations.

During Stanfield's leadership a group within the party did, in fact, attempt to take positions not unlike those adopted by the Liberals with respect to some of these matters, for instance, language policy. Characteristically, however, serious dissension developed and once again revealed the Conservative party as an uneasy alliance between basically conflicting regional and ideological interests. The appearance of disunity was heightened during the Stanfield era by Diefenbaker's sometimes mischievous and disloyal behavior after his unceremonious dismissal as leader of the party. The party leadership has recently had to reconcile the demands of the prairie M.P.s, who generally followed Diefenbaker's lead on national issues, the objectives of the powerful Tory interests in Toronto, and the ideas of an articulate group of progressives. In 1972, when the Liberals had obviously antagonized an impressive collection of groups and individuals, Stanfield was able to present a reasonably credible picture

---

[21] Meisel, "Some Bases of Party Support," pp. 3-5; Mildred A. Schwartz, "Canadian Voting Behavior," in Rose, ed., *Electoral Behavior*, pp. 543-617.

of a party likely to provide an alternative government, but two years later new divisions, this time over the wages and incomes policy, contributed to many voters' renewed preference for the Liberals.

The Liberal party. In the 1860s, at the time of Confederation, the Liberal party was a disparate and ineffective alliance of populist reformers, anticlerical Francophones, western Ontario frontiersmen and provincially minded elements in the maritimes. They strongly resented the centralizing and commercially minded policies of Macdonald's government, especially a protective tariff and the building of a railway at virtually any financial or moral cost. After Laurier assumed the Liberal leadership the support base of the party broadened, particularly in Quebec, where the Liberals won the approval of the powerful clergy. Laurier in fact completed one critical phase in Canada's process of nation building by fashioning a national party capable of providing an alternative to the Conservatives. In the course of doing this, Laurier adopted policies which resembled those of the Conservatives and also added a major innovation: the encouragement of large-scale immigration from Europe. On the whole, however, the Liberals found themselves compelled to govern in a manner similar to that of their rivals. In the words of one historian, they "had to combine Jeffersonian principles with Hamiltonian practices."[22] Laurier was defeated in 1911, largely because of his espousal of reciprocity with the United States, and it was the Conservatives who formed the government during the First World War and had the onerous responsibility of imposing military conscription on reluctant French Canada. Although many English-speaking Liberals joined and supported the war-time Union Government, the Liberal party as such survived and reinforced its image as the friend and champion of French Canada. This aspect of the party was a cardinal preoccupation of Mackenzie King, Laurier's successor, and the Liberals' fundamental concern for the survival of the English-French partnership has been maintained ever since, under St. Laurent, Pearson, and Trudeau.

The modern Liberal party was also influenced by being in office during an immensely long and very crucial stretch of time—for most of the period since the twenties. This was the era when a competent, professional, public service was becoming a necessity for adequate administration, and when Canada was gaining increasing independence from Britain and slipping ever more firmly into the American orbit.

---

[22] F. H. Underhill, "The Development of National Political Parties in Canada," *The Canadian Historical Review*, vol. 16, no. 4 (December 1935), p. 385.

These circumstances are among those shaping the current pattern of Liberal party support. French Canada and English Quebec are its apparently unassailable fortresses, and it also does extremely well among so-called "new Canadians"—immigrants who have arrived since the Second World War. Urban centers, particularly the huge metropolitan agglomerations, also furnish disproportionately strong support for the Liberals. Although the party has tended to attract substantial proportions of voters in all sectors of the population (with the exception of farmers), it has been particularly favored by younger voters, those enjoying better-than-average incomes, individuals with many years of formal education, and those in high-status occupations. Intellectuals and what might be termed the business eggheads have shown considerably greater enthusiasm for the Liberals than for the Conservatives in recent years, although the former have also displayed some affinity for the NDP. If Quebec is the party's stronghold, the prairies and British Columbia are its Achilles heel: in these regions its candidates have failed to arouse much enthusiasm.

The priorities of the Liberal party are, of course, linked to its support pattern and to its definition of itself. It assumes that it is the only party capable of governing Canada, since it alone has continued to have something resembling national support. Also, partly as the result of its unique bicultural appeal, it considers the demands of English-French accommodation the *sine qua non* of any acceptable Canadian governmental program. In the degree to which it responds to these demands and draws on the advice of leaders from both ethnic groups, it is unique. Its foreign, economic, and other policies, while recently a little more responsive than previously to Canada's rising nationalism, have been less guarded than those of the other parties with respect to the dangers of United States domination, and its general posture has consequently been more continentalist.[23] With respect to Canada's other major continuous preoccupation, the nature of its federal arrangements, Liberal governments have been inclined to be centralizing. Although cognizant of the special position of Quebec, Liberal governments have not encouraged the centrifugal forces which, in recent years, have enhanced the powers of the provinces, particularly those enjoying economic development and rapid growth.

Liberal politicians have enjoyed close ties and a relationship of easy trust with the federal civil service, particularly its upper echelons, and have therefore been in constant touch with advisors disposed to

---

[23] George Grant, *Lament for a Nation: The Defeat of Canadian Nationalism* (Toronto and Montreal: McClelland and Stewart, 1965).

view the governmental apparatus as an instrument of national policy. Nevertheless, in recent years they have retreated somewhat from the use of state-owned corporations—a device previously employed by both Liberal and Conservative administrations. While the tendency for the government to participate in the economic life of the country has not diminished in recent years, Liberal governments have consistently encouraged private competition with public enterprises, and have permitted private interests to grow at the expense of the latter. This trend is no doubt related to the party's strong support among the upper-income voters and business and industrial interests, and to the credibility accorded by civil servants to interest groups representing the private sector.[24] The party's electoral style has been typically North American, resembling that associated with the campaigns of John F. Kennedy: heavy reliance has been placed on surveys and all the other paraphernalia of public relations firms, lavish sums of money have been spent on campaigns, contributed largely by corporate and other business and professional donors; inspiration has been derived from the advice of trusted experts in the universities and in the business world. The difference between the two old parties in these matters is small, except that the Liberals' long years in office have given them a decided advantage and have left their mark on their style of operation. Their relations with the intellectual community have been much closer than those of the Conservatives, and they have established, as noted above, a special and unique relationship of trust with the mandarinate in the federal public service. Despite operating according to the dominant practices of North American parties—being financed by corporate donations, freely deploying both individual and group patronage, spending prodigious amounts in campaigns—the Trudeau Liberal government has recently introduced reform legislation intended to limit and publicly subsidize electoral expenditures and compel parties and candidates to publish the sources of their financial support.

The New Democratic party. The New Democratic party is the lineal descendant of the Co-operative Commonwealth Federation (CCF), Canada's major social democratic party, which emerged in the thirties partly as a western regional protest movement and partly as the instrument of labor.[25] There was a CCF government in Saskatche-

---

[24] Robert Presthus, *Elite Accommodation in Canadian Politics* (Toronto: Macmillan of Canada, 1973).

[25] Seymour Martin Lipset, *Agrarian Socialism* (Garden City, N.Y.: Anchor Books, Doubleday and Company, 1968); Walter D. Young, *The Anatomy of a Party: The National CCF 1932-61* (Toronto: University of Toronto Press, 1969); Kenneth

wan from 1944 to 1964, but, like its successor, the CCF was never able to gather sufficient electoral support to be viewed as a possible alternative federal government party. Its influence has, nevertheless, been great. Many progressive measures introduced by successive Liberal administrations resulted from or were accelerated by the prodding of the CCF and the NDP.

The NDP's greatest strength is in the West (at the time of the 1974 election it held office in British Columbia, Saskatchewan, and Manitoba) and in Ontario; it has made no impact on Quebec and has been weak in the Atlantic provinces, except in a small number of working class constituencies. People in manual occupations, particularly skilled ones, form its main support, and the party does well among teachers, Protestant clergymen and other individuals who can loosely be described as the urban intelligentsia. In its program it resembles Clement Attlee's British Labour party: it favors greater governmental control over private enterprise, the heavy taxing of business and industry, massive social welfare programs, and strong measures designed to curb American influence in Canada. The party has enjoyed effective leadership throughout its history and has played a role in Parliament often far exceeding its numerical strength there. Like many other left-wing parties, it has suffered from doctrinal schisms and has become more conservative and electorally opportunistic as it has changed from a socio-political movement to a power-seeking party.

The Social Credit party. The national Social Credit party is now based in Quebec, but originally it grew out of two quite separate roots: one was the Social Credit movement, which arose in Western Canada in the thirties and dominated Alberta politics for thirty years; the other was the *Union Créditiste des Electeurs,* in Quebec, and its successor, *Le Ralliement des Créditistes.*[26] Now the party has lost its western wing and is the spokesman *par excellence* of rural protest in Quebec. Its influence is minimal, except on those rare occasions when a minority government may wish to rely on its vote—as Diefenbaker once did—in efforts to avoid a Commons defeat. In terms of parlia-

McNaught, *A Prophet in Politics: A Biography of J. S. Woodsworth* (Toronto: University of Toronto Press, 1959).

[26] Michael B. Stein, *The Dynamics of Right-Wing Protest* (Toronto: University of Toronto Press, 1973); C. B. Macpherson, *Democracy in Alberta: Social Credit and the Party System,* second edition (Toronto: University of Toronto Press, 1962); J. A. Irving, *The Social Credit Movement in Alberta* (Toronto: University of Toronto Press, 1959); Maurice Pinard, *The Rise of a Third Party: A Study in Crisis Politics* (Englewood Cliffs, N.J.: Prentice-Hall, 1971).

mentary seats, it has been the only serious federal competitor of the Liberals in Quebec, ever since its resurgence there in the early sixties.

The Game. At least four parties having played active and sometimes critical roles on the national scene since the thirties, Canada must be recognized as having a multiparty system. It is referred to as a two-party or a two-plus-party system on the grounds that none of the minor parties has ever formed a government, but this reasoning fails to do justice to the delicate interplay between the parties at the parliamentary and electoral levels and its consequences for government policy. There are regions where the party battle is not a contest between the Liberals and the Conservatives, but between one of these and either the NDP or the Social Credit party. More important, the so-called third parties influence the positions taken by the other parties and by governments. Finally, to pretend that only two parties are full-fledged members of the system is to deflect attention from the endemic presence of minority governments.

But Canada's multiparty system is obviously quite different from that of a country like Israel or Italy, where there are so many contestants that every government is a coalition. There are only two ministerial parties at the national level in Canada, and of the two the Liberals are so much the stronger that their position is unique. It is responsible for Canada having a one-party dominant party system. As we have seen, only one party has consistently drawn support from both the major ethnic groups and, in this sense, has a national constituency. This party has held office so much longer and more frequently than its rival that it dominates the whole system, which responds to its initiatives and fortunes.

The chief consequence of the multiparty, one-party dominated configuration is that in recent years Canada has alternated between majority and minority governments. The strength and dominance of the Liberals, as well as the ideological concerns of the minority parties, have so far forestalled the establishment of coalition governments. The practice has been, instead, for one party to form the government in hopes of being able to muster enough strength in the House of Commons to avoid defeat on any of its major legislative initiatives. Thus the Conservatives formed minority governments in this way in 1957–1958, and in 1962–1963, the Liberals in the years 1963–1965, 1965–1968, and 1972–1974.

It is too soon to make confident generalizations about the consequences of this pattern for policy making, but certain observations are at least plausible. It is reasonable to assume that minority governments will adjust their programs to suit the opposition parties on whom they depend for support, and that minority governments therefore pursue less coherent and more opportunistic programs than administrations in full command of the legislature. Minority governments have, in fact, appeared to be more responsive to causes normally championed by the minority parties; the Liberal government's sensitivity to NDP pressure from 1972 to 1974 is a good example. On the other hand, governments not dependent on minority support have found it easier to resist the pressures of regional or other minority groups and to develop broad policies that further the overall, national interest.

It is sometimes alleged that majority governments are more likely to push for policies evolved by experts within the Ottawa public service, which tend to be pan-Canadian and centralizing in conception, whereas the programs of minority cabinets are prone to reflect the interests of regionally based, more selectively supported minor parties. Minority governments may also be particularly disposed to accommodate the requests of provincial governments and of the provincial wings of their own parties, since they put a high premium on any support likely to improve their precarious position.

It has been suggested that in the United States the main impetus for leadership shifts between the President and Congress, and that the periods of presidential leadership are the more innovative.[27] Presidential leadership has also been regarded as more centralizing. It is intriguing but, alas, premature to consider whether a similar alternation between centripetal and centrifugal styles can be observed in Canada, as governments commanding parliamentary majorities alternate with minority governments. Whatever the answer, Canadian experience has shown that minority governments can produce effective legislative programs and that majority status in a one-party dominant system may tend to make the majority party arrogant and insensitive.

The consequence of Canada's multiparty, one-party-dominant party system, insofar as governmental outputs are concerned, is that the various administrations which govern the country pursue policies over the long run which are sensitive to both special interests, even those outside the normal orbit of the two major parties, and to the national interests which override those of subgroups within the

---

[27] James MacGregor Burns, *The Deadlock of Democracy: Four-Party Politics in America* (Englewood Cliffs, N.J.: Prentice-Hall, 1963); Arthur M. Schlesinger, "Tides of American Politics," *Yale Review*, new series, vol. 29, no. 2 (December 1939), pp. 217-230.

society. This judgment, which in some measure, no doubt, idealizes the manner in which the party system performs, assumes that the minority parties do in fact reflect interests which would be overlooked if these parties did not exist. The most pressing interests are thus taken into account when governments formulate and execute their policies. It has been argued that some widespread and deep-seated elements of Canada's political value system have led to neglect of the really critical issues confronting the country. Specifically, the suggestion has been made that the emphasis on ethnic and regional disparities and exigencies has contributed to the serious down-playing of ultimately more critical interests: those associated with class and with certain intellectual positions normally ignored by political parties.[28] A consideration of this charge takes us into the final section of this chapter—an evaluation of Canada's party system.

Evaluation of the Party System

There are two usual methods for evaluating political systems. One concerns itself with stability and survival. It tests the capacity of existing arrangements to survive without cataclysmic challenges to law and order, and to assure a reasonable level of predictability about the future. The other, somewhat more nuanced, tests the degree to which the needs of those who, in the eyes of the critic, ought to benefit from the operation of the system are satisfied. The "test cases" may be some proportion of the total population, certain threatened groups—minorities or the poor, for instance—or groups deemed to play a particularly critical role in the life of the community—innovators, perhaps, or custodians of traditional values.

By the first method, Canada's party and political systems rate remarkably well. Despite the enormous difficulty of maintaining a viable political community in so vast and heterogeneous a country, despite the profound differences between French and English Canada and the strains imposed by major economic crises and two world wars, the state of Canada has not only survived but has provided a high level of personal freedom and continued economic growth, which are shared, to some extent at least, by most groups in Canadian society. At one level, therefore, Canada's performance compares extremely well with those of other countries and must be rated a success.

It is, however, not unreasonable to argue that the test criteria employed above are not stringent enough. Any performance should

---

28 John Porter, *The Vertical Mosaic* (Toronto: University of Toronto Press, 1965), pp. 366-385.

be judged in relation to the opportunities available for even better achievement. On these grounds one can argue that Canada's immense potential wealth, its geographical position, and the conditions prevail-- ing in the world during the first hundred years of its existence provided opportunities for a much better performance than that actually attained.

In three domains Canada's party system deserves less than top marks. They are the improvement of French-English relations, the reduction of disparities in living standards, in particular with respect to the native peoples, and the defense of a Canadian identity inde- pendent of that of Canada's giant neighbor. More than 200 years after the conquest of the French by the British in 1759, the French Canadians are still a clearly disadvantaged group. The Pearson and Trudeau governments have attempted to remedy the situation but the medicine appears inadequate, given the extent and intensity of the malady. Cultural attrition of Francophones continues: the propor- tion of French-speaking Canadians is still declining according to the 1971 census,[29] although an index of mutual intelligibility between French- and English-speaking Canadians is rising by infinitessimal amounts, and has just surpassed the mark it had reached in 1941![30] The French are proportionately less numerous than before, not only in provinces where they constitute important minorities (Ontario and New Brunswick), but in Quebec itself. In this province, while the majority of the population, even the French population, still rejects the separatist political option, the independentist *Parti Québécois* won 30 percent of the popular vote in the 1973 provincial election, and surveys show a small but steady increase in support for separation at the rate of about 1 percent a year.[31] At the same time, such measures as have been taken to equalize job opportunities in the federal public service, and to ameliorate the position of Francophones generally, are beginning to create a backlash among Anglophones, particularly in the public service. The notorious 1974 capture of a Conservative seat by the aggressively anti-French mayor of Moncton, New Brunswick, running as an independent, is a straw in the wind, although the ethnic aspects of the case were blurred by other factors

---

[29] Canada, Ministry of Industry Trade and Commerce, *Canada Year Book 1973* (Ottawa: Information Canada, 1973), Table 5.18, p. 215.

[30] Ronald Manzer, *Canada: A Socio-political Report* (Toronto and Montreal: McGraw-Hill Ryerson, 1974), p. 105; see also, Stanley Lieberson, *Language and Ethnic Relations in Canada* (New York: Wiley, 1970), pp. 31-32.

[31] Maurice Pinard, "Separatism and the Polarization of the Quebec Electorate: The 1973 Provincial Election," Paper presented at the Canadian Sociology and Anthropology Association meeting, Toronto, 25 August 1974, p. 27.

(the mayor's local popularity, resentment of the Conservative leader's interference in the nomination of a local candidate, the splitting of the "tolerant" vote between the official Conservative and Liberal candidates, and so on).

Although the average standard of living of Canadians is extremely high, domestic disparities are enormous. Criteria of poverty are difficult to establish and tend to be subjective, but it is probably no exaggeration to conclude from the various studies of the subject that at least one out of every five Canadians lives in poverty.[32] Indicators of welfare, infant mortality rates, for instance, show substantial regional variation and astronomical levels of deprivation among groups like Indians and Eskimos.[33]

Finally, Canada has been drifting, unrestrained, into a state of dependence on the United States which raises serious questions about the degree of its political, economic, and cultural independence. This is not the place to sort out the complex arguments and data touching on what has been called the "integrity" of Canada,[34] but we must fleetingly examine some of its aspects in our effort to evaluate the party system. Formally, Canadian governments are, of course, completely independent of the United States. But the ownership and control of so much of the Canadian economy, particularly some of its most critical sectors, by American individuals and corporations, and the domination of all aspects of Canadian culture by American influences raise doubts about the extent to which Canadian governments are really capable of independent action. Like the United States, Canada has, as we have seen, accepted brokerage politics, which depends on extensive consultation with those affected by decisions and policies. Insofar as economic policies are concerned, this

---

[32] Manzer, *Canada*, pp. 57-62; Canada, Special Senate Committee on Poverty, *Report: Poverty in Canada* (Ottawa: Information Canada, 1971), pp. 1-55; Ian Adams, William Cameron, Brian Hill and Peter Penz, *The Real Poverty Report* (Edmonton: M. G. Hurtig, 1971), pp. 1-23.

[33] Manzer, *Canada*, p. 34.

[34] Kari Levitt, *Silent Surrender: The Multinational Corporation in Canada* (Toronto: Macmillan of Canada, 1970); Canada, Task Force on the Structure of Canadian Industry (Melville Watkins, chairman), *Report: Foreign Ownership and the Structure of Canadian Industry* (Ottawa: Queen's Printer, 1968); Abraham Rotstein and Gary Lax, eds., *Independence: The Canadian Challenge* (Toronto: The Committee for an Independent Canada, 1972); Government of Canada, *Foreign Direct Investment in Canada (The Gray Report)* (Ottawa: Information Canada, 1972); James Laxer, *The Politics of the Continental Resources Deal* (Toronto and Chicago: New Press, 1970); A. E. Safarian, *Foreign Ownership of Canadian Industry* (Toronto: McGraw-Hill, 1966); Canada, Royal Commission on Canada's Economic Prospects (Walter Gordon, chairman), *Final Report* (Ottawa: Queen's Printer, 1957).

means spokesmen for foreign-owned and controlled enterprises whose priorities and constraints are by no means necessarily determined by Canadian needs. At the same time, much of Canadian popular culture —television programs, periodic literature, book and magazine publishing and distributing, films, advertising, architecture, sports, and the artifacts of daily living—are American-dominated. Clearly, critical Canadian decisions are taken with the direct participation of American interests (often speaking through Canadian mouths) and in a setting saturated by American values. Even the field of foreign policy, where many Canadians pride themselves on having exhibited some independence of the United States, Canada's unquestioning acceptance of American definitions of the cold war, refusal to risk any serious alienation of its neighbor, and naive belief that good-boy status brings influence in Washington, have led Canada to play America's game, while ostensibly pursuing an independent course.[35]

Most fundamentally, it must be recognized that the United States's value system presents a highly confused picture. Americans have demonstrated time and again that their culture greatly prizes honesty, decency, generous humaneness, and generally activities ennobling the individual. On the other hand, anyone who has eyes to see and ears to hear and who is within reach of American television and the other mass media cannot escape the impression that there is also a less pleasant side to the coin. America is revealed as a society in which influence-peddling, police brutality, perversion of the prescribed procedures of administering justice, officially engineered character assassination, defoliation of impoverished lands, and the use of torture and murder as instruments of public policy, have become not yet the norm, but so widespread and commonplace as no longer to astonish, and hence to become acceptable and tolerable parts of the human condition. The processes which culminated in the Vietnam War and Watergate have, to a significant measure, threatened to insensitize the moral conscience of America. Nevertheless, criticism of these developments has been nowhere more strident and telling than in the United States itself, indicating that many Americans are profoundly appalled by them.

This essay is not a moral tract and the issues raised here cannot be discussed as extensively and carefully as they deserve. They are, however, relevant to our theme, for it is impossible to evaluate the

---

[35] Charles Taylor, *Snow Job: Canada, the United States and Vietnam (1954 to 1973)* (Toronto: Anansi, 1974); James Eayrs, "North Atlantic Torturers' Organization," pp. 266-276, "Weapons and Pushers," pp. 247-266, in James Eayrs, *Greenpeace and Her Enemies* (Toronto: Anansi, 1973).

Canadian party system without noting that it has done little to protect Canadians against the subtle but pervasive shifts which have vitiated America's value system. On the contrary, by fashioning and participating in a party system in which the principal actors depend, when meeting their astronomically rising costs, on contributions from large corporate donors who are the members, imitators, and hangers-on of North America's military-industrial complex, politicians have powerfully assisted the penetration of the Canadian consciousness by the lowest common denominator in American culture.

Developments in the field of broadcasting, among others, illustrate this situation.[36] Broadcasting was originally considered a public trust in Canada, to be deployed as a means not of making profits but of enriching the cultural life of the community and the level of political discourse. Increasingly, however, Canadian governments have allowed interests which had made heavy contributions to party war chests to invade the airwaves and fill them with programs, the overwhelming majority of which are anything but edifying. The exploitation of murder, brutality and violence, perpetrated by American television networks, has permeated Canadian viewing, only to be interspersed at frequent intervals with exhortations on the part of advertisers to mindless consumption of products, many of questionable benefit, some even harmful. Even the once excellent publicly owned Canadian Broadcasting Corporation has been allowed to follow the example of the American networks. It has actually become the fabulously tax-supported purveyor of many dubious American programs. Thus the Americanization of Canadian minds and the insensitivity to uniquely Canadian problems which it implies, have occurred in part because political parties have preferred the gifts of private broadcasting interests to the public-spirited and indigenous use of the limited channels and airwaves. Similar patterns can be observed in the fields of book and magazine publishing, hotel chains, sports, and so on. Efforts, in recent years, to stem the tide of irresponsible commercialism and of Americanization have come much too late in the game and have so far met with less than striking success.

It is fair to ask what all this has to do with our present concerns. One can argue, of course, that it is far-fetched to hold the party system responsible for sweeping cultural developments. And no doubt this is in part correct. For, while political parties influence in some measure the evolving value system, they are even more pro-

---

[36] Frank Peers, *The Politics of Canadian Broadcasting 1920-1951* (Toronto: University of Toronto Press, 1969); E. Austin Weir, *The Struggle for National Broadcasting in Canada* (Toronto and Montreal: McClelland and Stewart, 1965).

foundly shaped by it. It would have been impossible for parties single-handedly to reverse trends growing out of economic, social, and cultural conditions in all of North America. It is nevertheless the case that had twentieth-century Canadian politicians had anything like the kind of conviction that motivated Macdonald and his "national policy"—had the party leaders, in other words, put a high priority on the Canadian society and polity maintaining and developing an identity and a character different from that of the rest of English North America—and had they had the courage to act accordingly, they could have evolved and pursued policies to that end. They had no such vision or daring and repeatedly ignored opportunities for encouraging a Canadian value system that could have modified and complemented that of the United States. The fact that efforts in this direction are now being made, when it is probably too late, indicates that politicians are at last becoming aware of their opportunities and that they were too slow to perceive the earlier dangers and too timid to act in response to them.

Similarly, the party system should not be held solely responsible for unresolved English-French tensions and the sense of cultural threat which terrifies so many of French Canada's intellectual and artistic leaders, any more than it can take sole blame for income and welfare imbalances or the failure to preserve and develop values drawing on the country's own past and particular position. Nevertheless, it is still necessary to conclude that political leadership has failed to exploit the fantastic opportunities Canada has provided. The party system has confronted its problems and opportunities in a competent but pedestrian way. It has provided conditions in which Canadians could fashion a pale reflection of many of the strengths and weaknesses of their more dynamic neighbor to the south. Because of its particular nature, French Canada has escaped these influences somewhat better than the rest of the country, but without thus gaining a sense of confidence in its own survival and without infusing much of its own genius into Canada's socio-political fabric.

Consequences of the 1974 Election

The principal results of the 1974 election for the party system were the reinstatement of a majority government and the restoration of the Liberal party to its accustomed dominance. The election thus halted the realignment of electoral support that had seemed to be emerging in 1972.

Electoral patterns in Canada indicate that the one-party-dominant status of the Liberals results in part from certain deeply rooted partisan attachments which endow the party system with a certain virtually unalterable structural rigidity. A recent exploration of the link between religious affiliation and party choice, surprisingly strong in an era when religious issues are no longer salient in federal politics, reveals the Liberal party as enjoying an advantage over its opponents, seemingly perpetuating its dominant status in the party system.[37] The study in question, based on the 1968 election but concerned with continuities, shows that the Liberal party attracts more or less uniformly high support from Catholics, whether they be rich or poor, progressive or reactionary, young or old. Protestant voters, on the other hand, while generally much less attached to the Liberals than Catholics, vary much more among themselves in this respect, depending on their particular characteristics. Thus Protestant voters who come from metropolitan areas are young, well educated and well off, hold progressive views or have an above-average interest in world affairs, tend to display about the same level of Liberal attachment as Catholics. The pattern of party support with respect to Catholics and Protestants is, therefore, that Catholics are overwhelmingly and uniformly Liberal, whereas Protestants vary much more and only certain subgroups among them approximate the degree of Liberal preference displayed by Catholics. When deciding difficult policy options, then, Liberal leaders can count on the unwavering support of a very high percentage of Catholic voters (about half the population is Catholic) and on a proportion of Protestant voters among whom the most progressive, liberal, conciliatory and up-to-date will be strongly overrepresented. Conservative policy makers, on the other hand, know that they enjoy only very limited Catholic support, and that among their Protestant voters, the great majority is old-fashioned, set in its ways, and less disposed to compromise on many contemporary political issues. It is therefore easier for Liberal leaders to propose policies likely to cement the country's cleavages, particularly in religious or ethnic matters. Conservatives like Robert Stanfield, who have attempted to adopt conciliatory policies—the new language legislation, for instance—or progressive measures like the guaranteed annual income, have had to contend with heavy flak from some of their own backbenchers, responding, no doubt, to what they knew to be the views of a substantial proportion of their constituents.

This seeming digression is relevant here because on rare occasions the structural advantage of the Liberals has been lost in realign-

---

[37] John Meisel, "Bizarre Aspects of a Vanishing Act: The Religious Cleavage and Voting in Canada," in Meisel, *Working Papers*, pp. 266-273.

ments of the electorate. This happened in 1958 when Diefenbaker made an effective appeal to a great many Catholics, and again, to a lesser degree in 1972, when the monolithic attachment of Catholics to the Liberals was shaken. Both deviant elections were followed by the Liberals' success in reestablishing their previous support pattern. This is not the place to determine how far this was due to the political skill of the Liberals or the ineptitude of the Conservatives and the NDP, but we must note that in 1974 the Conservatives failed to hold the Catholic beachhead captured in the previous election, and that 1974 thus reinforced the structural predisposition of the system towards the one-party-dominant role of the Liberal party. Whoever is chosen as Stanfield's successor will have to contend with a Conservative party the support of which is overwhelmingly Protestant, a party in which even the Protestant support is weighted towards certain reactions and policy positions exacerbating the party's problems in achieving genuine national appeal.

At the same time, in 1974 Conservative support was proportionately no less than it had been in 1972 (over 35 percent of the vote), and the third parties succeeded in attracting better than one out of every five voters (over 21 percent). The basis for a multiparty system is thus preserved and the likelihood persists that minority governments will continue to be part of the Canadian scene.

Turning to the consequences of the election for the themes we discussed in our evaluation of the party system, we must also conclude that few major changes are likely.

As a result of the 1974 election, both Stanfield and Lewis are being replaced. The NDP succession has passed without crisis to Edward Broadbent, but the struggle for the Conservative leadership is mobilizing the various inconsistent elements in the party and will engage its energies at the expense of its capacity to provide vigorous and single-minded opposition. The tiny Social Credit contingent in Parliament cannot seriously challenge the Liberals, who are basking in their comfortable parliamentary majority. Under these conditions the principal opposition to the Ottawa government is likely to emanate from the provincial governments, of various partisan stripes, pressing for what they see as their provincial rights against federal encroachments, and, as a consequence, political decision making will be very much influenced by the federal nature of the country. At the present time the chief issues are control of natural resources, taxation, and various aspects of communications, all matters of considerable provincial concern. A critical range of political issues, then, is in the process of being resolved by bargaining among governments, not parties, although the partisan complexion of those governments inevitably has some influence on their strategies.

Insofar as the decisions within sole federal jurisdiction are concerned, the strong position of the Liberals after the 1974 contest and the weak position of the opposition are likely to promote continued accommodation between French and English Canada (at least so long as a *Parti Québécois* government does not rule Quebec). Cautious attention to welfare requirements providing a cushion for the most needy sector can also be expected from the government, but there will be no massive effort to narrow the huge gaps between rich and poor. The most blatant and threatening cultural and economic inroads from the United States will probably be opposed, and the most exposed Canadian interests protected, but the crushing consequences of past inactivity in the face of American influence will probably not be reversed. In summary, the government elected in 1974 can be expected to carry on in a "business as usual" manner, tackling the country's problems piecemeal, in the reasonably competent, incrementalist style of its predecessors. The crises visited upon Canada by the world's food and energy shortages, by unprecedented pressures on its economy and environment, and by international tensions, are not likely to be met with innovative, daring, or drastic responses. As the results of the 1974 election show, the complacency of Canada's leaders in the face of dramatic challenges reflects an unwillingness to be disturbed, evident in the population as a whole.

2

AN OVERVIEW OF THE 1974 FEDERAL ELECTION IN CANADA

William P. Irvine

For most of Canada's history, the calling of elections has been fairly routine, occurring at four- or five-year intervals. As Canada moved into a period of successive minority governments, however, the life span of a Parliament became more problematical. To understand the circumstances of the calling of the 1974 federal election, it is necessary first to understand the source of the executive's claim to office, that is, the executive's legitimacy, in a parliamentary system.

In a democratic presidential system, as in the United States, the executive's claim to office depends, directly or indirectly, on popular election. At fixed terms, the president is obliged to seek a renewal of his popular mandate. The extremely grave measure of removing him from office legally before the end of his term can only be accomplished through a deliberately difficult process. In a parliamentary system, by contrast, voters do not, in theory, vote for an executive at all. Rather, they elect members of a legislature, and an executive is chosen from the legislature. In a constitutional monarchy such as Canada or Great Britain, the choice is made by the monarch or his representative. The monarch is constrained, however, to choose an executive which can command the voting support of a majority in the legislature. Although there may be an outside bound to the life of a legislature (in Canada elections must be called at least every five years), there is no maximum or minimum term to the life of the executive. The executive remains in office as long as, and only as long as, it continues to command the support of a majority of the legislature. Thus, a single legislature may be asked to ratify several governments in turn. An executive might be formed, govern successfully for a while, suffer defeat in the Parliament, and be replaced by another government, that to be later replaced by a third, and so on—all without the calling of new elections. A "vote of confidence" from the legislature is all that is required to sustain the executive's claim to office. The party to which the executive belongs need not be the largest party in the legislature, nor need it have won the largest popular vote in the preceding election.

In legal fiction, therefore, Canadians do not choose their government. This is determined not by their votes, but by the votes of the members of the legislature. In fact, of course, the votes of Canada's legislators are quite predictable: all are party men and, generally, parties vote as blocs. To know the majority party in the legislature is to know the executive.

The situation becomes more complicated, however, when no single party holds a majority in the legislature. As we see in Table 2-1, this has been true for five of the eleven Canadian parliaments elected since 1945, including the 1972 Parliament which governed until just before the most recent elections. In such cases it is not immediately obvious which party might form an executive capable of commanding the support of a majority of the legislature, and, in the short run, a change of government generally does not occur. When an election is called, the Parliament is dissolved and most members of Parliament become private citizens, but the executive does not automatically resign. The prime minister and his cabinet colleagues remain in office until dismissed by the Parliament. Even if their party loses badly in the election, they are under no obligation to resign until actually defeated by the new Parliament. Usually, if the election-night loss is decisive, the government accepts the verdict in good grace and immediately hands in its resignation to the monarch's representative, the governor general. With a decisive verdict, his task is routine. He calls on the leader of the largest party in the new Parliament to form a government, which assumes office before Parliament meets. Again, given the nature of party discipline in Canada, the Parliament invariably confirms this government. When the election verdict is indecisive, the prime minister has the option of remaining in office and awaiting the verdict of Parliament, or resigning and recommending to the governor general that the leader of some party, usually the largest in the Parliament, be asked to form a government.

In 1972 Prime Minister Trudeau chose the former course. He had led a majority government in the 1968 Parliament, and had recommended that that Parliament be dissolved in 1972. He had not, of course, resigned as prime minister, but remained in office until Parliament, by its votes, might compel him to resign or to seek a new dissolution. On election night, it was unclear whether his Liberal

Table 2-1

CANADIAN FEDERAL PARLIAMENTARY ELECTION RESULTS, 1945–1974

Election Year	Seats Required for Majority	Seats for					Votes for				
		Liberal	Progressive Conservative	New Democratic	Social Credit	Other	Liberal	Progressive Conservative	New Democratic	Social Credit	Other
1945	123	125	67	28	13	12	41%	27%	16%	4%	12%
1949	132	193	41	13	10	5	49	30	13	4	4
1953	133	171	51	23	15	5	49	31	11	5	4
1957	133	105	112	25	19	4	41	39	11	7	2
1958	133	49	208	8	0	0	34	54	9	2	1
1962	133	116	100	19	30	0	37	37	14	12	0
1963	133	129	95	17	24	0	42	33	13	12	0
1965	133	131	97	21	14	2	40	32	18	9	1
1968	133	155	72	22	14	1	45	31	17	6	2
1972	133	109	107	31	15	2	38	35	18	8	1
1974	133	141	95	16	11	1	43	35	16	5	1

a The size of the House of Commons has varied periodically with the decennial redistributions. It was 245 in 1945, 262 in 1949, 265 from 1953 until 1968, and 264 from 1968 on.

Source: For 1945–1968: H. G. Thorburn, ed., *Party Politics in Canada*, 3rd edition (Scarborough, Ontario: Prentice-Hall of Canada, 1972), p. 249; for 1972–1974: *The Toronto Star*, 9 July 1974, p. 1.

party would win the largest number of seats in the Parliament. Ultimately, the Liberals won both the largest number of seats in the Parliament and the largest popular vote (though not a majority of either). Technically Trudeau's claim to office rested upon neither of these, however. He was in office because he had never been defeated by Parliament. His job was to make sure that he wouldn't be.

Minority Government in Canada: The 1972 Parliament

Trudeau wasn't defeated by Parliament until 1974. The reasons for his defeat then and for the calling of the federal election have to do with the career of his 1972 minority government, which, therefore, must be examined here in some detail.

The major contenders for office in 1972, as in almost every election since Canada became a nation, were the Liberal party and the Progressive Conservative party, led by a former prime minister of the province of Nova Scotia, Robert Stanfield. As had happened more often than not since 1957, neither was a majority party so neither could choose a prime minister by itself—nor were they likely to choose one jointly, despite being strikingly similar in many of their policies. Each, when in office, has initiated or broadened social welfare programs, and each has established government enterprise in areas where it felt private business would not, or ought not, operate. Nevertheless, the two parties are historic opponents. In this century, for example, the Liberals have been more sympathetic to French Canadian views than the Progressive Conservatives, though the current pronouncements of the two parties differ less than their past positions. But, except possibly in the face of an overwhelming foreign threat, they would not combine to choose a prime minister between them. To get parliamentary ratification in 1972, both Trudeau and Stanfield would have to turn to the smaller parties.

One of these, the Social Credit party, can be ignored in this discussion as it must have been in prime ministerial calculations. With fifteen parliamentary seats, this party could not contribute enough votes to give either the Liberals or the Progressive Conservatives a majority. There was, in 1972, only one swing party: the New Democratic party (NDP). This is a democratic socialist party much akin to the British Labour party, and it commanded thirty-one votes in the 1972 Canadian Parliament. Although Liberals tend to refer to the NDP and its predecessor, the Canadian Commonwealth Federation (CCF), as "Liberals in a hurry," there is, in fact, so little difference between the social philosophies of the Liberals and the Progressive Conservatives that the NDP could have supported either.

Whichever party did get NDP support to sustain a government would have to do so without the benefit of any formal coalition agreement. The NDP is sufficiently distinct in social philosophy from either the Liberals or the Progressive Conservatives that it would be an uncomfortable minor partner in a government dominated by either. Its position was that the Liberals, having the opportunity to meet Parliament first, should bring in their program and have it voted on, item by item.

It was in this sense that Prime Minister Trudeau's government, after the 1972 election, was a minority government. He never, with his own party, commanded a majority of parliamentary votes, and he never had a formal alliance which would guarantee him the additional votes he required. Rather, he was forced to piece together the necessary support as each issue came before Parliament. While this is not unlike the task facing an American president, the stakes are infinitely higher. For a prime minister to lose a single important vote is probably to lose his legitimate claim to office. Because of their potential instability, minority governments usually have a bad press in modern parliamentary democracies. Apart from the incongruity of the tail wagging the dog, minority governments are held to be unable to plan for the long term, unlikely to take unpopular decisions to meet economic or other problems, and unlikely to resist embarking on major spending programs. To be sure, minority governments have their defenders, and it is interesting that the defense is different in Britain and Canada. In Britain, minority government is held to be better because it is more moderate. There the Liberal party with policies somewhere ·between those of the Labour and Conservative parties can compel its opponents to abandon the most extreme items in their programs. In Canada minority government is held to be better because it is more socially conscious. Left to themselves, it is claimed, both the Liberals and the Progressive Conservatives would tend to favor the middle classes. When they are dependent on NDP support, on the other hand, they adopt measures beneficial to poorer Canadians.

On the whole, the legislation adopted by the 1972 Parliament was more immediately responsive to public demands than had been the programs of majority governments and would seem to corroborate the Canadians' concept of minority government as more socially conscious. In the immediate aftermath of the 1972 election, the NDP began to publicize the conditions for its support of either a Liberal or a Progressive Conservative government. These included the government's taking measures to combat unemployment and the increasing cost of living, introducing more effective legislation to deal with foreign ownership in the Canadian economy and reform of inequities in the tax system. As noted above, the Liberals had the first opportunity to respond, and respond they did. The election had been held on 30 October 1972, the Parliament was recalled, and the speech from the throne (a statement of the government's legislative priorities similar to a state of the union message) was read on 4 January 1973. This was followed by a budget on 19 February 1973. In these two major statements of policy, the Liberal minority government committed itself, among other things, to personal income tax cuts and heightened exemptions, increases in the old-age pension and family allowance payments, housing development legislation, a parliamentary inquiry into food prices and tougher curbs on foreign investment in Canada.

The cause and effect relationship between NDP demand and Liberal policy is, however, not as clear as it might seem from the foregoing. Quite apart from the government's protestations that these things would have been done in any case, it is possible to interpret Liberal policy in 1973 as an extended act of contrition, given the Liberals' near defeat by the electorate and their prospects of being forced to seek a new mandate before long. One indication that Liberal policy was not designed exclusively to woo the NDP was the announcement of other policies, some of which were inconsistent with NDP philosophy. The 1972 election campaign had revealed strong dissatisfaction with a number of Liberal policies which had been innovative in conception if not always deft in execution. Among these were language policies, attempts to offer summer employment to youth, more liberal penal policies, and programs of immigration and unemployment insurance, which the public thought were widely abused. It had also revealed, once more, the alienation of the West of Canada, arising not only from such policies as those enumerated above, but also from what westerners perceived as the Liberals' essential disregard for western needs. In announcing their policy after the election, Liberals sought to respond in some measure to western alienation by promising changes in freight rates, more regionally based financial institutions, and a conference on western economic opportunities. None of these promises could be expected to win over many parliamentary votes, given that most of the West had voted solidly for the Progressive Conservative party. Similarly, the Liberals' promise to review and tighten up regulations dealing with unemployment insurance was more popular with the electorate than with the NDP, whose main concern was the possibility of legitimate claims being denied in any sweeping reevaluation.

There is another argument against the thesis that the NDP was particularly crucial in the government's thoughts. The strategic position of the NDP was not as strong as it appeared on the surface because it really had only one party to bargain with. The Progressive Conservative party clearly felt that an early election would be to their advantage. Hence, they would make no bargains designed to prolong the life of even their own minority government. Also, the NDP's position was powerful only in a minority Parliament. If they provoked an election that led to a majority for either of the large parties, they would find themselves in a much less enviable parliamentary position. The NDP and the Liberals had a common interest in postponing an election until the apparent Progressive Conservative tide had ebbed. Both had to avoid situations where they would be obliged to vote against each other and provoke what neither wanted. In politics, the rational course of action is not always the easiest to follow. It was important that the Liberals concede at least symbolic victories to the NDP, while the Progressive Conservatives, for their part, sought to inflict symbolic defeats on the NDP. This they did by criticizing the Liberal government for various sins of omission or commission to which the NDP might be expected to be especially sensitive. For example, the Progressive Conservatives criticized the decision of the Liberal government to sell a wholly government-owned corporation to a large umbrella corporation that would be mainly in private hands. Similarly, they introduced several motions condemning the Liberals' handling of the economy, and one expressing lack of confidence in some 1972 Liberal proposals to make tax concessions to corporations. These had not been passed and were not before Parliament, but the Liberals had promised to reintroduce them. They were precisely the sort of measure the NDP had campaigned against in 1972, yet for the NDP to support the Progressive Conservative motion would be to bring down the Liberal government.

It was extremely difficult for the NDP to justify its failure to support these motions (and many others in this spirit) to its own faithful. The leadership of the party sought refuge in two lines of defense. On the one hand, they could argue that, on balance, Liberal policy as announced in the throne and budget speeches was good for Canadians and that the government ought to be given a chance to enact these promised measures. On the other hand, they argued that the Progressive Conservative motions were frivolous and self-serving, motivated not by philosophy or policy, but simply by desire for office.

In this way Parliament in 1973 picked its way between governmental measures designed to attract third-party votes and opposition motions of want-of-confidence designed to split the de facto alliance between the NDP and the Liberal minority government. Perhaps the most tense period came about four months into the session, when the Liberals did reintroduce their corporate tax proposals. Before the 1972 election the government had promised substantial tax concessions to spur capital investment by industry, including a diminution in tax rates for manufacturing and processing corporations from 49 to 40 percent, and accelerated depreciation write-offs. The calling of the election prevented the enactment of these measures. During the 1972 election campaign, the NDP exploited a theme designed as a counterfoil to the charge that social welfare was being abused, with which the Progressive Conservatives were belaboring the government. This was the theme of the "corporate welfare bum," the large enterprise receiving subsidies and concessions from the government without producing much expansion in return. Having so strongly committed itself to this theme, the NDP could not, with even the subtlest reasoning, justify supporting the corporate tax proposals when the Liberals felt committed to reintroduce them. This seemed to be the issue most likely to topple the government, but ultimately the Progressive Conservatives felt that they could not oppose the tax concessions. On 21 March 1973 Stanfield announced that his party would accept the corporate tax measures with a one-year time limit, appearing to be generous to the government while robbing the proposal of any value as a stimulus to expansion. The government put the ball back in his court by offering to include in the measures provisions for their parliamentary review in a year, provided such review was demanded by at least sixty members of Parliament, that is, by at least some members of the Progressive Conservative party. On this basis, the year-old budget proposals were passed, and one of the more tense periods of the 1973 session came to an end.

Although one could never be sure that the Progressive Conservatives would not eventually word a motion of confidence in such a way as to compel NDP support, the life of the Liberal government was not again seriously in question until December 1973. As a result of the energy crisis provoked by the October War and the quadrupling of oil prices, the Liberal government had adopted new export controls, export taxes, and voluntary price controls in an attempt to insulate the Canadian consumer from the full impact of the price increases. The price control agreement was due to expire at the end of January 1974. The NDP opposed its expiration, or at least immediate adjustment of Canadian prices to world levels, and began to make threatening speeches about the beginning of December. Finally, on 6 December 1974 the prime minister announced that the price controls would be extended until the end of the winter heating season. In so doing, he may also have extended the life of his government. A "tension barometer" installed in the Canadian House of Commons would have recorded several feverish peaks in 1973 and early 1974, but the general tenor of the readings would have been encouraging: the Parliament was workable, important legislation was being passed, and the government was able to stick by its important commitments and priorities, even though not always in the straightforward, automatic way characteristic of majority government. It certainly would not have seemed impossible that the de facto alliance with the NDP might last for another year or two.

The Achilles heel of this alliance seems to have been extraparliamentary. Although the NDP could convincingly point to considerable government activity and legislation reflecting its point of view and its direct influence, it could never completely dispel the unease that many of its supporters felt with the arrangement. There was always the fear that, with the passing months, the NDP would become indistinguishable from the Liberal party in the eyes of the electorate, and this would mean sharing not only the credit for popular legislative proposals, but also the blame for the government's shortcomings. The most menacing prospect electorally was having to support the government during a prolonged period of double-digit inflation.

At the time of the 1972 election, the major economic problem had been unemployment, which had been high throughout the year and which, during the election campaign, had reached a level of 7.1 percent on a seasonally adjusted basis, an increase of 0.4 percentage points over the previous month. At the same time, the annual rate of inflation was 5.3 percent. Unemployment kept mounting during 1972, but began a fairly long-term retreat in January 1973 which lasted until July of that year when the unemployment rate was down to 5.2 percent. Except in September and October 1973, the rate never exceeded 5.6 percent in any month up until the 1974 election. Indeed, figures released just after polling day showed that in June 1974, 4.9 percent of the Canadian labor force was unemployed. In September 1972, the annual rate of increase in the consumer price index had been much lower than the rate of unemployment. The trend, however, had been wholly different. Canada managed to maintain an annual rate of price increases under 6 percent until March 1973. From there the rate increased almost without respite, and by March 1974 had reached 10.4 percent. The food and housing components of the index were growing even more quickly. The prime lending rate of the Bank of Canada was increased seven times between April 1973 and May 1974, going from 4.75 percent at the beginning of the period to 8.75 percent at the end. Home mortgage rates were in excess of 10 percent by April 1974.

It seemed inevitable that the government would be the focus of the discontent engendered by the escalating prices, and that the NDP would feel pressed to dissociate itself from the government. The Liberals could argue, and did, that much of the increase was generated by trends in the world economy from which Canada could not be isolated, that the Canadian experience was better than that of many other economies and not substantially different from the American, and that the only thing that could be done was to attempt to mitigate the effects of inflation.

The restiveness of the NDP became evident when they combined with the Progressive Conservatives to force the government to withdraw an adjournment motion, effectively canceling the usual Easter recess for members of Parliament. Later in April the NDP made known the price for its continued parliamentary support of the Liberal government. This included a "two-price system" (that is, one price for exports and a lower price for domestic sales) for such basic commodities as lumber and copper, a 6 percent ceiling on home mortgage rates, a national price control board with the power to roll back what it considered to be unjustified price increases, and an excess profits tax on corporations. The government was willing to go some way towards meeting the last demand, but opposed the rest as unworkable or counter-productive. This was viewed as a totally inadequate response by the NDP, who made it clear that when the budget was brought in on 6 May they would vote to defeat the government.

Thus it was that, after nineteen months in office, the Liberal government was defeated by 137 to 123 on the nineteenth vote of confidence it had to face. The Progressive Conservative party and the New Democratic party had combined to defeat the government for failing to aid those on low fixed incomes, deal with a housing crisis, and eliminate inequities in the tax system. Given this parliamentary defeat, the government could have simply resigned and allowed the leader of the Progressive Conservatives to assume office and try to govern. They chose instead, not surprisingly, to remain in office and to recommend the dissolution of the Parliament that had rejected them. That way, at least, they would be able to fight the election with the resources of office at their disposal. The governor general acceded to the recommended dissolution, and an election was called for 8 July.

The 1974 Election

The Issues. The central feature of the campaign is neatly summed up in the slogans of the major parties. The Liberals asked Canadians to decide whom they wished to entrust with the office of prime minister: "The issue is leadership, and the (current) problem is inflation." To this the Progressive Conservatives retorted, "The issue is inflation, and the problem is leadership." They attempted to focus the campaign on the stewardship of the governing party (as non-governing parties tend to) and highlighted galloping inflation as an indication of what they considered to be general mismanagement. As the second part of the Progressive Conservative slogan suggests, that party also felt that the Liberals were cheating the Canadian electorate by failing to explain the very difficult measures that would have to be taken to curb inflation. After much soul-searching, the Progressive Conservative leader, Robert Stanfield, and his closest advisors had decided that wage and price controls were the only effective way to handle the problem. Stanfield committed his party to this position right from the beginning of the campaign, and argued that the Liberals were too cowardly to take, or admit that they would take, steps to legislatively control prices and incomes.

This was a courageous stand to adopt. Prime Minister Trudeau said as much in his victory remarks the night the votes were counted. It was not, however, auspicious ground from which to fight a campaign as leader of a conservative party. Progressive Conservative support consisted of a hard core of prairie agricultural and petroleum producers, to which Stanfield, since taking over the leadership in 1967, had sought to reattract the traditionally Progressive Conservative Ontario business community. Neither of these elements was enthusiastic about wage and price controls, nor were many of the candidates for Parliament who sought to appeal to them. Consequently, contradictory statements were made by Progressive Conservative spokesmen throughout the campaign, statements which gave the impression of a party fundamentally divided over what was supposedly their central program.

The division in the party had several consequences. In the first place, it meant that the leader, who had become convinced in mid-1973 of the necessity of price and income controls had to devote his energies to getting his party to accept it in principle when he might better have been commissioning studies of how, precisely, to make it work. Inadequate consideration and the continued division in his party made Stanfield appear to retreat on the policy during the course of the campaign, by forcing him repeatedly to admit that exceptions would be made to the control program: prices at the farm gate were to be uncontrolled, as were sales of houses, and so on. Poor preparation meant that Stanfield could make no convincing reply to Liberal claims that controls would be constitutionally unworkable in Canada, and that they would be impracticable in any case in an economy as dependent on world trade as the Canadian.

To fight the election on wage and price controls was probably a poor decision strategically for the Progressive Conservatives, whatever the merits of the policy in dealing with Canada's economic problems. By choosing to commit himself to a policy, rather than simply attack the government's record, Stanfield in effect changed places with the government, inviting the Liberals to attack him. This they did on all the grounds mentioned above: the policy was unworkable, Stanfield's own party was not united behind it, and it allowed so many exceptions that major items of popular concern would not be subject to controlled prices. Moreover, it opened Stanfield to attack on a second front.

The Canadian Labour Congress (CLC) opened its tenth anniversary convention in Vancouver the week after the defeat of the Liberal government in the House of Commons. At that convention, the leader of the CLC made a strong speech condemning wage, though not price, controls. This stand was then taken up by the leader of the New Democratic party, David Lewis. On 9 May, the day after the defeat of the government, Lewis had said that the central issue of the coming campaign would be inflation and he would be blaming the Liberals for it. When Lewis spoke to the CLC convention a week later, however, he devoted most of his speech to an attack on Stanfield and his policy of controlling both wages and prices. In a more typical election campaign, the NDP would have been attacking the failings of the government of the day, and simply asserting that the leading opposition party was too beholden to the same interests as controlled the government to do anything about these problems. In this campaign, the NDP spent at least as much time in direct attack on the Progressive Conservatives as it did in criticism of the government's record.

Stanfield's charges notwithstanding, the Liberal government did have a policy for dealing with inflation, a policy based on a radically different conception of the problem from that of the Progressive Conservatives. While the latter thought inflation was fueled largely by domestic forces and hence likely to respond to controls and reductions in government spending, the Liberals considered inflation in Canada to be a manifestation of a worldwide phenomenon. It followed that inflation could only be mitigated and not controlled. Consequently the Liberal government had sought to ease the burden on low income groups through tax reductions, increased family allowances, and pensions indexed to the cost of living. At the same time, the Liberals sought to stimulate supply by allowing producers to pass on to the consumer virtually all their increased costs and to take (except in the case of oil) maximum advantage of the increased world price levels. The Liberal minister of agriculture was able to boast of exceptionally high returns on farm investment (as compared to usual returns from farming) and to claim that, in the long run, this was the best defense against inflation. In this view, price controls simply meant shortages. Producers would go out of business if they were not allowed to pass on the increased world price of fertilizer or animal food—or if the returns on their investment became so small that they might better sell their land and leave the proceeds in the bank.

As the debate between these two conceptions of the problem proceeded, it was not clear that the Progressive Conservatives had picked the losing strategy. All the polls showed that concern with inflation outweighed everything else, and the Gallup poll of Canada found that 70 percent of Canadians felt that inflation could be controlled by government, which suggested considerable dissent from the central Liberal premise.[1] What they thought ought to be done, however, was less encouraging to Progressive Conservative strategists. Only 15 percent opted for both price and wage controls, while 30 percent wanted price controls alone, the solution advocated by the NDP. However, during the campaign, the regular releases of Statistics Canada appeared to confirm the Progressive Conservative charges that the Liberal policy of increasing supply was totally ineffective. Although Statistics Canada is a government agency, it has a regular schedule for the release of its monthly statistics, and it adheres to that schedule regardless of whether there is an election

---

[1] Canadian Gallup Poll Ltd., release of 19 June 1974.

campaign in progress. During the 1972 campaign, as we have noted, Statistics Canada reported a seasonally adjusted unemployment rate of 7.1 percent, the highest for eleven years. Its cost of living release in the middle of the 1974 campaign was just as devastating. It reported that prices in May had increased by 1.7 percentage points over April, the largest monthly increase since the Korean War, bringing the consumer price index to a level almost 11 percentage points higher than it had been a year before. Food prices had increased by 3 percentage points in the month, and stood 18 percentage points higher than a year before. Somewhat earlier in the campaign, banks had increased mortgage interest rates to 11 or 11.5 percent, and limited mortgages to 75 percent of the purchase price. A little later in the campaign, Statistics Canada released its quarterly figures on profits and sales, showing industrial profits up over 45 percent, with sales up only 24 percent. This provided rather better ammunition for the NDP than for the Progressive Conservatives. Even the latter, however, were able to point to the figures as evidence that business would be able to absorb the raw materials prices left uncontrolled at the farm gate and at the Canadian border and still make a reasonable profit despite controls on the prices at which they could resell processed or imported material.

The Progressive Conservative campaign was further aided by the leaking, in the *Toronto Star* of 29 June, of the fact that the Liberal government had a contingency plan for wage and price controls. After the release of this information, Stanfield could argue both that the Liberals were deceitful in attacking his plan as entirely unworkable and that they were totally insensitive if they felt that current conditions had not made life sufficiently bad for sufficiently many Canadians to justify the imposition of this contingency plan.

If these developments were to have promoted the Progressive Conservative campaign, they would have had to be exploited to push the Liberals onto the defensive. But the Liberals refused to be pushed. They continued to stress the strength of their leadership, pointing to the Progressive Conservatives' disunity over inflation policy and other issues, and to highlight the contrasting styles of Trudeau and Stanfield to the former's advantage.

The candidates had become leaders of their parties within a few months of each other at the end of 1967 and the beginning of 1968, and from the beginning Trudeau had had the more resonant image. Like the Kennedys in the United States, he was thought to have "charisma" and a capacity to move youth. Trudeau was a cosmopolitan bachelor, heir to substantial wealth, educated at the best

American and European universities, a world traveler and intellectual. He had stood up to an authoritarian provincial regime in Quebec in the 1950s and had only seriously entered politics in 1965. Thus he could appear, in 1968, to be a man above the compromises and routines of the politico and the bureaucrat. Stanfield, by contrast, was a seasoned politician who, before moving into national politics, had been prime minister of his province for eleven years. To achieve that office he had had to overturn one of the most strongly entrenched political machines of Canadian politics. He was a deeply honest and sincere man, but without much public presence. By contrast to Trudeau, he seems to have struck the Canadian people as conventional and unexciting. When asked to attribute qualities to their national leaders, Canadians interviewed after the 1968 election tended to ascribe honesty and fairmindedness to Stanfield, but intelligence, progressive-mindedness, and the ability to resolve English-French differences, to Trudeau.[2]

By 1972 Prime Minister Trudeau had become a much more controversial figure. He was identified both with a set of policies and with a style of governing which seemed to anger many Canadians. In particular, his style of governing suggested that he was arrogant, unconcerned about the feelings and values of others, and technocratic rather than liberal in his approach to social problems. Nevertheless, his sharply defined image was in itself an advantage. If Stanfield moved fewer Canadians to passionate hatred, he was also less successful in attracting strong commitment. A study carried out after the 1972 election showed that Trudeau had again been, on balance, an asset to his party.[3] This is quite remarkable given the style of his campaign—aloof, above politics, a dialogue with people who had no fundamental problems or grievances.

Liberal strategists were convinced that Trudeau's image as a leader was their major asset, and ought to be made the most of in the campaign. Furthermore, the opposition to Trudeau appeared to have softened since 1972. His most divisive policies had been relegated to history, his arrogance attentuated by the experience of working with a minority Parliament. To cash in on this asset, the Liberals had to turn the focus of the campaign away from any particular issue, to a general concern with who would be best to rule

---

[2] These figures are taken from the codebook to the 1968 survey of the Canadian electorate designed by Professor John Meisel of Queen's University and supported by the Canada Council.

[3] Peter Regenstreif et al., "Partisan Stability and Change in the 1972 Election" (unpublished paper presented at the 1973 annual meeting of the Canadian Political Science Association).

Canada and to confront the unknown challenges of the future. They hoped to portray Trudeau as intelligent and toughminded, his opponent as weak and vacillating. The Progressive Conservatives' disarray over wage and price controls could be used to make precisely that point. Other circumstances discussed below helped the Liberals remain on the offensive and keep the Progressive Conservatives on the defensive.

At least in terms of the attention devoted to it by party leaders and the media, the inflation/leadership debate dominated the 1974 campaign. No other themes were fully developed, although many were mentioned. One of these was the issue of English-French relations which has been present in Canadian politics since the 1960s. To his credit, Stanfield has always avoided making a party issue of this problem, but it remains sufficiently divisive that it cannot easily be kept under the rug, and it surfaced in 1974. Early in the campaign, a local mayor in New Brunswick who was strongly identified with opposition to the spread of bilingualism (that is, the use of both English and French) in Canada, sought and won the Progressive Conservative nomination for his constituency. He was immediately repudiated by the party leader. Stanfield's position was strong and courageous, but it further pointed up the divisions in the Progressive Conservative party.

Just before the opening of the campaign, the government of Quebec had announced its intention to pass legislation affecting the use of English as a language of instruction in the school system. Among the provisions was the requirement that immigrants to Quebec send their children to French language schools. Such a proposal contravened the spirit of the federal Official Languages Act which many felt had been imposed on English Canada. Characteristically, Stanfield did not press this issue in his federal campaign. Towards the end of the campaign the issue emerged again when it was rumored that three of the French Canadian terrorists who had kidnapped the British trade commissioner in Montreal in 1972, and who had been exiled to Cuba in exchange for his safe release, had managed to leave Cuba and were currently in Paris. If the rumor were true (and their presence in Paris was confirmed in August 1974), it opened the possibility of extraditing them to Canada for what could only be an extremely emotion-charged trial. Many Progressive Conservatives including Stanfield began to press for their extradition and prosecution. The minister of justice was, at first, inclined to agree, but the prime minister announced that the terms of the agreement with the kidnappers required only their exile from Canada and, apart from precluding their traveling on Canadian documents, did not necessarily confine them to Cuba. Trudeau took the position that to press for extradition would violate the understanding that had secured the safe release of the trade commissioner. It is a tribute to Stanfield that he did not press the issue beyond that point. It would have been easy for a less scrupulous party leader to have sought to portray the Liberals as soft on terrorists, and French Canadian terrorists at that. Such a line may have been taken in some local contests, but was eschewed nationally.

Related to the English-French problem is the question of the alienation of Western Canada, which has already been mentioned. Early in 1973 the Liberals had attempted to improve their image in the West, but the energy crisis of late 1973 and 1974 led to a new confrontation between central Canada, where most of the industrial and domestic consumers of energy are located, and the West, particularly Alberta, where the major production occurs. The energy crisis had led to export limitations, a domestic price fixed substantially below the world price, and a federal export tax which prevented oil companies and oil-producing provinces from fully benefitting from the escalating world price even on the oil they did export. Subsequent federal tax proposals dealing with raw materials, although they affected virtually every province, added to the anger in the West against the Liberal party.

Regional identification is strong in Canada, and many issues of purely local importance, though they escaped the attention of the national media, must have influenced substantial numbers of votes. Fishermen on both coasts, for example, had discovered that whole species were being fished to extinction by foreign trawler fleets, and reproached the government with having failed to protect them. Aboriginal rights may have been significant in some of Canada's far northern constituencies. Election returns suggest that in British Columbia votes were affected by provincial developments that are not matters of federal responsibility at all. The NDP government of the province had adopted controversial legislation dealing with rent control, the sale of farmland, and the taxation of mining companies not long before the federal election in which NDP representation for British Columbia fell to its lowest level since the Second World War.

In order to understand the overriding importance of the inflation issue (and some regional ones in Alberta and British Columbia) it is useful to consider what did *not* become national issues. Except in the instances noted above (whose significance we have not yet the data to assess), one is tempted to conclude that even relations between

English-speaking and French-speaking Canadians were not an issue. Neither was corporate taxation, though both had figured in the 1972 campaign. The nonpartisan Committee for an Independent Canada tried to persuade the parties to take stands on the general issue of American control over the Canadian economy and the specific issue of the building of a Mackenzie River oil and gas pipeline but was rebuffed. This issue, too, had received more attention in 1972. Advertisements designed to make voters concerned about cruelty in the Gulf of St. Lawrence seal hunt were similarly unsuccessful in arousing the interest of the electorate.

Indeed, about half way through the campaign a group of churchmen representing Canada's seven leading denominations denounced the campaigns of all the party leaders for moral blindness—in particular, for their insensitivity to domestic and world poverty, the victims of famine in Africa, and the crippling effect on developing economies of worldwide inflation. This charge was largely justified. If the 1974 campaign was impressive in the way it focused attention on a real issue and significant policy alternatives, it was unsatisfactory in its absence of moral tone and vision. Canadians were not asked to decide what kind of country they would like to have, or even what kind of country it would be possible to have given Canada's extremely privileged position in the world community.

The Course of the Campaign. The preceding section has presented the terms of the election debate but has permitted only a side glance at the strategies of the parties and the constraints under which their leaders operated. It has been suggested that the Progressive Conservatives committed a tactical error in advocating wage and price controls, rather than simply criticizing the Liberal record and referring only vaguely to plans to combat inflation. The Progressive Conservatives had, in a sense, taken the place of the governing party and had exposed themselves to attack. At the same time, not being the party in power, they needed media exposure for their leader. In the course of a fifty-day marathon by chartered DC-9, Stanfield crisscrossed the country and made several campaign appearances each day. He spent considerable time with reporters, holding press conferences and appearing on open-line talk shows. Given his central theme of the need for economy in government and elsewhere, Stanfield could not make promises, and his media strategy simply opened him to continual probing of the wage and price scheme: the exceptions to it, his party's divisions over it, dissent in his party in other areas.

By contrast, Prime Minister Trudeau avoided the media almost entirely. He took on almost as heavy a schedule of public appearances, though, and at each appearance, he would make some new promise, particularly in the areas of transport, housing, and agriculture. There were, literally, daily announcements of mortgage subsidies for low-income earners, more government backing to mortgages for low-cost homes, cash grants to first-time home buyers, new policy for freight rates, government ownership of a fleet of box cars to move prairie grain, government takeover of rail passenger service, a quarter of a billion dollars for urban mass transit, and so on.

Trudeau was able to keep Stanfield continually reacting to his initiatives and to bury the criticisms of one announcement in the avalanche of publicity generated by the next. By refusing to debate either representatives of the media or his political opponents, Trudeau was able to avoid the hard questions about his policies (mainly, how much they would cost and their inflationary impact) which were plaguing Stanfield in connection with his own wage and price control scheme.

As indicated above, external events did intrude into the campaign. There was the announcement of the May cost-of-living figures, the exposure of the Liberal contingency plan, an OECD report showing Canadian inflation to be only slightly worse than that in the United States and well below the average for OECD countries, and the rumored presence in Paris of the Quebec terrorists. In the closing days of the campaign, a scandal over government appointments, which had been simmering through the preceding months, came to a boil when the Royal Canadian Mounted Police confiscated some documents relating to the 1972 election campaign of the minister of labour. No development or tactic of Stanfield's, however, had enough public impact to seriously deflect the Liberals from the strategy they had chosen. They continued to capture the headlines with the prime minister's announcements and with the campaigning of his wife and, occasionally, of his young children. His party had been in power for eleven years and he, himself, for six, yet Trudeau managed to preempt the usual campaign role of the leader of the opposition. He continually attacked his opponent's pledged program and outbid him with campaign promises.

The Progressive Conservative strategy had been to put the prime minister on the defensive and keep the pressure on him until he made mistakes of judgment or public outbursts of arrogance and temper. This strategy was undermined by party disunity and seemed to have been conceived in complete ignorance of what the Liberal riposte might be. In exposing himself to attack, Stanfield was taking a principled stand, directed by his own conception of how elections ought to be fought in a democracy. This choice severely crippled his chances of victory.

It was commonplace in the media to describe the 1974 campaign as dull. Here again, data are lacking as to the true extent of public interest. However, the timing and content of the campaign were not such as to maximize public attention. Summer elections are usually avoided in Canada since many voters are away from their usual places of residence and following the media less regularly than usual. Summer reruns are not auspicious vehicles for political advertising, and people at vacation addresses may or may not continue to read major urban newspapers. More fortuitously, the planting season in many parts of Canada had been seriously delayed by bad weather in 1974, and, if crops were to be planted at all, they would have to be planted in a very short period that coincided with the opening of the campaign.

Given that country cottages are still luxuries and that Canada is an increasingly urban nation, however, these factors are not enough to explain the apparent apathy of the electorate. Another factor was the low profile of the prime minister. He elicited neither the positive nor the negative feeling in this campaign that had marked his previous ones. But perhaps most responsible for the apparent disinterest was simply public perplexity generated by the central issue. Both strategies for dealing with inflation—mitigating its consequences and attacking the thing itself through more stringent legal controls—were under severe attack. Moreover, to the extent that Canadians had found some shelter from inflation, either in government assistance or in new wage agreements negotiated by unions, inflation had become far less immediate a menace than the Progressive Conservative threat to delay implementation of new wage agreements for ninety days.

The Outcome. The election of a Liberal majority government on 8 July 1974 was a surprise to everyone, except the pollsters, and no doubt some of them would not have bet on what their data seemed to be telling them. Experience with preelection polls in previous campaigns had suggested two things: first, Liberals tended to lose support in the polls in the course of a campaign; and second, many people who intended to vote for the Progressive Conservatives would not declare their intention to opinion surveyors, so polls tended to underreport Progressive Conservative support. Drawing on their experience, commentators had felt the Liberals would have a hard time even retaining their minority position. The Liberals had entered the campaign with slightly less support than they had had in the polls taken forty-five days before the 1972 elections, and they had lost ground in that campaign, apparently over the unemployment issue. It was generally expected that the same thing would happen in 1974 as the Progressive Conservatives pressed the inflation issue, insisting that Trudeau was responsible. Instead, the polls reported that, within the limits of sampling error, the Liberals were at least retaining, if not adding to, the strength with which they had begun the campaign. The national preelection survey by the Canadian Institute of Public Opinion, and an Ontario poll commissioned by the *Toronto Star* were both almost perfectly accurate.[4]

How are we to explain the Liberal party's success in increasing both its parliamentary representation and its popular support, despite having been in office during a period of increasing inflation and despite having had to fight an election at a time when inflation crossed the 10 percent barrier? While this chapter is being written, official vote figures have not yet been released by the government and detailed survey results are not yet generally available. Hence it is clearly premature to offer explanations. We can, however, begin to examine three hypotheses. Two of these have been current in the press since the election. First, some people have argued that Prime Minister Trudeau did succeed in shifting the focus of the electorate from inflation to leadership. Second, others have taken a diametrically opposite position, that inflation was important, but not in the way the Progressive Conservatives had hoped it would be. Instead, the prospect of wage and price controls so alarmed the working class, particularly the organized workers, that they abandoned their traditional allegiance to the NDP and voted Liberal. A third explanation for the Liberals' success, which was not current in the press but which had convinced the author of this study even before the election, casts inflation as such a complex and perplexing issue that the average voter has difficulty in deciding for himself how government ought to treat it. When the voter is at sea in this way, he tends to fall back on his basic commitments. If he is a Progressive Conservative, he will probably think that wage and price controls are the right approach; if he is a Liberal, he will tend to like Pierre Elliott Trudeau, and so forth. These three explanations are sufficiently different that, with reliable evidence, it should be possible to choose among them. In the

---

[4] Peter Regenstreif, "The Poll's Message: A Liberal Win but Not a Romp," *The Toronto Star*, 6 July 1974, pp. 1-2.

absence of evidence, we can at least get some clues from data such as the percentages set forth in Table 2-2.

Table 2-2

FEDERAL ELECTION RETURNS OF MAJOR PARTIES, BY PROVINCE, 1962–1974

(in percents)

Province/Party	Election Year					
	1962	1963	1965	1968	1972	1974
Newfoundland						
Liberal	59	65	64	42	47	47
Progressive Conservative	36	30	32	53	47	43
Prince Edward Island						
Liberal	44	47	44	45	41	46
Progressive Conservative	51	51	54	52	52	49
Nova Scotia						
Liberal	42	47	42	38	34	41
Progressive Conservative	47	47	49	55	53	48
New Brunswick						
Liberal	45	47	47	44	44	48
Progressive Conservative	46	40	43	50	44	39
Quebec						
Liberal	40	46	46	53	48	54
Progressive Conservative	30	20	21	21	18	21
Social Credit	26	27	18	16	25	18
Ontario						
Liberal	42	46	44	46	38	45
Progressive Conservative	39	35	34	32	38	35
New Democratic	17	16	22	21	22	19
Manitoba						
Liberal	31	34	31	41	29	27
Progressive Conservative	41	42	41	31	44	47
New Democratic	20	17	24	25	26	25

Table 2-2 *(Continued)*

Province/Party	Election Year					
	1962	1963	1965	1968	1972	1974
Saskatchewan						
Liberal	23	24	24	27	24	31
Progressive Conservative	50	64	48	37	38	36
New Democratic	22	18	26	36	36	32
Alberta						
Liberal	19	22	22	35	24	25
Progressive Conservative	43	45	47	50	59	61
Social Credit	29	26	23	2	5	5
British Columbia						
Liberal	27	33	30	42	29	33
Progressive Conservative	27	23	19	20	32	42
New Democratic	31	30	33	33	36	23
Social Credit	14	13	17	5	3	2

Source: For 1962–1968: Thorburn, ed., *Party Politics in Canada*, pp. 238–249; for 1972 and 1974: preliminary Canadian press estimates of the vote as published in *The Toronto Globe and Mail*, 1 November 1972 and 10 July 1974.

It is commonly accepted by Canadian political scientists that at least a partial realignment of political forces occurred between 1957 and 1962. In English Canada the dominant force was John Diefenbaker, who established his Progressive Conservative party as the party of Atlantic and Prairie Canada, and of older and rural Canadians elsewhere. Indirectly, he may also have weakened the Liberal grip on Quebec sufficiently to allow a French Canadian version of the Social Credit party to become established. In any case, by 1962 the realignment had emerged, and we may take the 1962 to 1965 election results as indicating a general baseline vote for each party in each province, with which to compare the 1974 results. This, of course, is very crude, not only because we are dealing with such large, often heterogeneous, groupings of people, but also because we are ignoring the fact that, in the nine years since 1965, many Progressive Conservative supporters have died and many new Liberals have come of voting age. Despite these limitations, the comparison is instructive.

Throughout Canada's Atlantic provinces of Newfoundland, Nova Scotia, New Brunswick, and Prince Edward Island (with the partial exception of the latter), there was a "native son" effect after the accession of Stanfield to the Progressive Conservative leadership. In the 1968 election the Progressive Conservatives improved markedly on their baseline. The initial surge was not retained in 1972, however, despite the fact that this region suffers more severely from unemployment than any other. Progressive Conservative fortunes continued to ebb into 1974 (when, we hypothesize, they had not even the short-term advantage of unemployment going for them). By 1974 both the Liberal and the Progressive Conservative parties were nearer their 1962–1965 averages than to their 1968 vote when party leadership had been a determining influence. A partial exception to this generalization is Newfoundland, where the Liberals have not regained the ample majority they enjoyed before 1965. In part, this is because the effect of the Liberal provincial prime minister, Joseph Smallwood, was sufficient to insulate Newfoundland from the Diefenbaker realignment. Since Smallwood's departure from politics, it is not obvious what any party's "normal" vote would be.

The figures for Quebec conform less well to the hypothesis of reversion to basic party commitment but are consistent with the hypothesis that emphasizes Prime Minister Trudeau's leadership, though in this case we may suppose that the operative factor is his ethnic background rather than his personality. The Liberals had dominated Quebec politics from 1896 to 1958, always obtaining at least 51 percent of the vote and averaging nearly 60 percent during the whole period of their dominance. In 1958 they were pushed below the 50 percent mark to 46 percent and lost more ground in 1962, though this further slippage was temporary. A benchmark of 46 percent for the Liberal vote would seem reasonable for the post-Diefenbaker era. In 1972 the Liberals attracted slightly more than their hard-core support, while in both 1968 and 1974 they did much better, thanks to their strong French-Canadian leadership. It appears that the leadership factor may have been neutralized by the impact of unemployment in 1972, but it would seem that the impact of inflation was insufficiently strong to offset Trudeau's appeal in 1974. After slipping ten percentage points between 1962 and 1963, the Progressive Conservative vote has stabilized in Quebec at a level only slightly ahead of that of Social Credit and about half that of the Liberals. It is testimony to the strength of Social Credit support, established only in the previous decade, that press reports of Social Credit demise in 1974 were seriously premature. Social Credit fought the election under the handicap of an ailing leader and an ignominious defeat in the 1973 provincial election, and still managed to hold its vote at the level achieved in 1965–1968.

Ontario provides good evidence for the reversion to basic-commitment thesis. No party's vote series shows much movement except in 1972, when the Liberals lost and the Progressive Conservatives gained (though not necessarily directly to and from each other). The 1974 election returned to the normal 1962–1965 pattern.

The evidence for western Canada is slightly more mixed, though it still supports the author's hypothesis. It is evident in both Manitoba and Alberta that Trudeau's impact was felt only in the 1968 election; the Liberal vote returned to normal immediately thereafter. In Alberta, normal partisanship has yet to firm up after the decision of Social Credit to cease contesting federal elections in that province. Consequently, the Progressive Conservatives are gaining even over the levels achieved when the party was led by a westerner, Diefenbaker. Similarly, it is possible to interpret the Manitoba results as indicating that the Liberals are being squeezed to extinction. If this is true, a new norm may be in the process of being established.

In Saskatchewan, the Liberal vote was quite stable from 1962 to 1972, and the 1974 result shows an even stronger upturn than had occurred in 1968, Trudeau's first election. The most revealing point of comparison with the Saskatchewan vote, though, might be the price of wheat on the Chicago Exchange. The Progressive Conservative and New Democratic parties are clearly seeking new norms since the departure of Diefenbaker, a Saskatchewan resident, from the leadership of the Progressive Conservative party. The Liberal vote did increase in 1974 apparently at the expense of the NDP, but it is doubtful that this had much to do with the issues.

In British Columbia, the pattern for the Liberals is very much like that in Alberta. In every election except 1968, the Liberals won roughly one-third of the vote. The collapse of Social Credit as a federal party helped the 1968 Liberal upsurge but has left a number of voters uncertain of their sympathies in federal politics. The Progressive Conservative results in 1972 and 1974 were well above the norm for recent years and the NDP 1974 result well below. In the latter case there must have been some powerful short-term forces at work, although whether these were fear of wage and price control, or anger at the provincial NDP, or, for that matter, appreciation of the prime minister's attractive wife, a native of British Columbia, cannot be discerned on the basis of these data.

The evidence in this rapid overview of province-by-province election statistics is thus ambiguous. There is little indication of massive support for Trudeau's leadership, however. Only in two of the ten provinces, Quebec and Saskatchewan, is the Liberal vote substantially above its 1962–1965 norm. Similarly, it is not clear (at least when the data are aggregated to the provincial level) that the NDP lost much of its traditional support in a bid by trade unionists to block wage and price control. Although the NDP suffered declines from its 1972 levels of support in many provinces, it only dropped substantially below its 1962–1965 norm in British Columbia, where, as we have seen, local issues were probably decisive. At this juncture, the best explanation of the 1974 election results is that Canadians, in their confusion, were returning to their long-standing partisan commitments. This seems to hold quite well in five of the ten provinces: Prince Edward Island, Nova Scotia, New Brunswick, Ontario and (for the Liberals) Alberta and British Columbia as well. Where the evidence is inconsistent, the problem is less one of contradictory results than of the fluidity of some provincial electorates. There is considerable flux and possible realignment occurring in Newfoundland and the four western provinces. As was noted before, only Quebec is clearly inconsistent with this hypothesis.

It would be premature to attempt to assess the meaning of the 1974 election in this paper. Commanding, as they do, majority support in the House of Commons, the Liberals are in a position to give the election any of several meanings. On the one hand, they could construe it as a mandate to govern on their own, from an electorate that wanted leadership, not the uncertainty of minority government. (We have already cast doubt on the leadership interpretation, and the data necessary for a serious assessment of the "vote-against-minority-government" view are simply not yet available.) [5] If this course is taken by the Liberal cabinet, it will undoubtedly strengthen the conservative wing of the party. The opposite interpretation of the results is also plausible: the Liberals were not punished for inflation because they had done their best to alleviate its impact through tax, social welfare, and other concessions. This view would counsel the continuation of these policies, even though they are no longer dictated by parliamentary strategy as they were under Trudeau's minority government. Whichever implications are read into the election result, a majority government will find it easier to adopt stringent belt-tightening measures in the event of continued

---

[5] This issue has been shown to have had some impact in previous elections. Larry LeDuc, "Public Opinion and Minority Government" (unpublished paper presented at the 1974 annual meeting of the Canadian Political Science Association).

rapid inflation. Those measures might even go as far as price and wage controls, though at the price of Liberal credibility.

Elections also tend to take in meanings in the public mind that are largely independent of the intentions of politicians. In Quebec the 1972 election was widely interpreted as an anti-French vote, despite the weight of evidence to the contrary. Only the most paranoid could persist in such an interpretation of the 1974 results. More plausible this time is the western fear of isolation. Of forty-five members of Parliament from the prairies, four will sit on the government side of the House, and thirty-six will sit with the Progressive Conservatives. The Liberals would be unlikely to view this as a mandate to ignore western interests. Nevertheless, it is simply the case that those interests are not represented in the Liberal government, which has an assured four-year term of office. Though no politician now intends to isolate the West, the popular view can only be confirmed unless the government deliberately decides to give it the lie. If it does, it will have to adopt a positive economic policy, rather than simply rely on international price movements. This will be especially true if the government is determined to shelter Canadians, at least partly, from these price movements, as it did in the case of oil prices. No talk of community solidarity will reconcile western producers to price controls unless these are part of a larger policy which will shelter the West from dependence on products traded in commodity markets.

It will be unfortunate if this majority government overemphasizes the interests of central Canadian business, for the task of building a Canadian community is still unfinished. The differences between English-speaking and French-speaking Canadians are not definitively bridged, and the equitable distribution of economic development throughout the country has not yet been undertaken. If Canada is to become a more liberal community, the public must be educated to accept more humane penal and immigration practices domestically and more generous assistance for the underdeveloped world beyond Canada's borders.

3

PIERRE TRUDEAU
AND THE LIBERAL PARTY:
THE JOCKEY AND THE HORSE

Stephen Clarkson

The 1974 federal election in Canada was both a mind-boggling puzzle and the most straightforward event a political analyst could hope to study. In a time of world upheaval, international monetary disasters, national bankruptcies, coalition governments, and, on the domestic front, worsening economic dilemmas, the unruffled Canadian voters returned to power the very party that had presided over the country's fortunes and misfortunes for the previous decade, the party presumably identified with the alarming inflation over which the election campaign was fought. Or—to shift the focus slightly—they returned to office a strong, attractive leader who commanded an efficient and experienced political machine with a tradition of governmental dominance.

Another facet in this scenario of political stability amidst international and domestic tension is the Canadian electoral process itself. For a few weeks, from Newfoundland in the East to British Columbia in the West, the public consciousness is dominated by campaigning. The citizenry is bombarded with conflicting messages broadcast over radio and television, printed in the news media, sent through the mail and voiced over the doorstep. Signs and billboards clutter the roadsides. Pledges are made and refuted, statements published and attacked, policies proposed and opposed. Yet through all the bedlam an unusual institution, the political party, is the vehicle for translating thousands of hours of intensive campaigning and millions of separately cast votes into a final decision—victory and the reins of power or defeat and the task of opposition.

Furthermore, while it may help precipitate a clear result at election time, the Liberal Party of Canada is itself an enigma. To a small extent this could be because it is unique among the Liberal parties of the world in that it is in power.[1] Even to political scientists, the federal and provincial Liberal parties remain little documented and poorly analyzed. Indeed, it is an unwritten law of Canadian party studies that their quality and quantity vary inversely with the size and success of the party under analysis. As the biggest Canadian party and the one most successful at maintaining its grasp on the levers of power in Ottawa, the Liberal party has been the object of the least scholarly research.[2]

Election time is when the political parties come out into the light of day. The whole political stage is handed over for them to occupy in proud and high relief for a few frantic weeks, while the governing process goes into temporary hibernation. Analysis of the Liberal party will not reveal much that is new about the 1974 election, but a study of the election campaign can lay bare some of the hidden realities of the Liberal party. While the election campaign itself may have been atypical, the Liberal party's role was archetypal. Despite a number of obstacles, both internal and external, the party succeeded. How this happened and what this means is the subject for this chapter. The extent to which any party has been a nation-building agency in Canada is subject to dispute, among academics as well as partisans, but there is no doubt that the Liberal party has dominated Canadian national politics in living memory. By 1974 it had held office in Ottawa for fifty-two years in this century. Two factors stand out in explaining this Liberal predominance in federal politics: the party's leadership and the country's electoral system.

Prime Ministerial Imprints

The origins of the Liberal party are found in nineteenth-century radical and reformist groups, in particular the anticlerical *Rouges* in French Canada and the antiestablishment "Grits" in Upper Canada.[3] Nevertheless, during its long years in power since the turn of the

---

[1] So much is it the norm for Liberal parties in countries other than Canada *not* to control the government that the Liberal Party of Canada did not become a member of the International Liberal Union until 1974.

[2] The one complete book on the Liberal party is partisan and insubstantial: Jack W. Pickersgill, *The Liberal Party* (Toronto: McClelland and Stewart, 1962). Apart from what can be gleaned from the major biographies, memoirs, or diaries of the Liberal prime ministers, information must be sought in the specialized articles of the professional political science journals.

[3] William Christian and Colin Campbell, *Political Parties and Ideologies in Canada: Liberals, Conservatives, Socialists, Nationalists* (Toronto: McGraw-Hill, 1974), Chapter 3.

century the Liberal party became, in a real sense, the creation of its leaders, each of whom made his mark as prime minister. Wilfred Laurier's achievement for his party, as the first French-Canadian prime minister, was to reconcile the Catholic Church with the Liberals, win Quebec's support, and so wrest power decisively from the Conservative party in 1896. Laurier's fifteen years in office (1896–1911) confirmed the Liberals as the less pro-British and more pro-American of the two national parties.

Mackenzie King's long tenures as party leader (1919–1948) and prime minister (1921–1930 and 1935–1948) included years of emerging class conflict, disastrous depression, and war mobilization. Where Laurier had had to do battle with only one rival party, the Conservatives, King saw new, more radical regional and national parties emerge on both his left and his right. King's legacy to his party was a style of politics at once conservative and reformist: reluctant to make new departures and take bold steps in policy matters, he was, nonetheless, ready to undermine electoral threats from the left by adopting the forward-looking social-justice planks of the social democrats. Laurier had been opposition leader during the racially divisive years of World War I. King was prime minister throughout the Second World War, but he managed to avoid seriously antagonizing French-speaking Quebeckers, unlike the Conservatives whose imposition of conscription in 1917 caused serious partisan damage. This feat kept Quebec in the Liberal fold, while identifying the Liberal party with patriotism, both pro-British (Canada declared war on Germany the day after Great Britain did) and pro-American (King eagerly entered into continental military planning agreements with U.S. President Franklin D. Roosevelt).

The concerted integration of Canada into the American economy, which was begun by King in the military sphere, was vigorously extended into resource exploitation and secondary manufacturing by his French-Canadian successor, Louis St. Laurent. With the Americans clearly acknowledged as the country's best friends in their role as cold war defenders of the Atlantic world, the massive influx of American capital into the Canadian economy was heralded not with despair but with delight by St. Laurent's trade minister, C. D. Howe. His policies were traditional, encouraging the export of staple resources and the establishment of branch plants in Canada by foreign— mainly American—corporations.

Lester "Mike" Pearson, who won a Nobel Peace Prize for his work as secretary of state for external affairs under St. Laurent, was party leader from 1957 to 1968 and prime minister from 1963 to

1968. He kept Canada on the path of collective security in foreign policy, which, in practice, meant close collaboration with the United States, primarily in the Atlantic Alliance but also in such disastrous operations as the Vietnam War.[4] At home Pearson's attainments were similarly ambiguous. The broad system of social welfare first proposed by Mackenzie King was completed, but at the cost of further concessions to the increasingly demanding provincial governments who, more and more, were calling the tune for Ottawa. Meanwhile the economy, increasingly dominated by American multinational corporations, continued on its path of satellitic integration, its vast resources a supply hinterland for American industry and its manufacturing sector a vulnerable, inefficient assembly line and distribution network for American exports.

Though it is always difficult to encapsulate the ideology of a party at any particular time, two academic assessments succeed rather well in summarizing the position of the Liberal party before the 1968 change of leadership:

> The Liberal Party has continued to speak the language of King: ambiguous and ambivalent, presenting first its radical face and then its conservative face, urging reform and warning against hasty, ill-considered change, calling for increased state responsibility but stopping short of socialism openly, speaking for the common people but preaching the solidarity of classes.[5]

> Looking at Canada from the outside, the Liberal Party is notable for its sympathies with the United States and for its willingness to accept the increasing integration of Canada in the English-speaking part of the North American community. . . . At the same time the Liberals have shown an unmistakable enthusiasm for collective security in international politics, based on vigorous participation in the United Nations and in regional pacts like NATO.[6]

The selection of Pierre Elliott Trudeau as Pearson's successor by the Liberal party convention of 1968 at first appeared to be a radical departure for the governing national party. But the change of style in leadership masked continuity of substance. The selection

---

[4] Charles Taylor, *Snow Job: Canada, the United States and Vietnam (1954 to 1973)* (Toronto: Anansi, 1974).

[5] Gad Horowitz, "Conservatism, Liberalism and Socialism in Canada: An Interpretation," in Hugh G. Thorburn, ed., *Party Politics in Canada*, 2nd edition (Toronto: Prentice-Hall, 1967), pp. 68–69.

[6] John Meisel, "Recent Changes in Canadian Parties," in Thorburn, *Party Politics in Canada*, p. 48.

of a Quebecker was a recommitment of the Liberal party to the Francophone electorate whose support was so crucial to its national dominance. The choice of Trudeau, former radical, albeit millionaire, intellectual, reaffirmed the Janus-like stance of a center party with a record of co-opting personalities and policies from the left while maintaining a conservative continentalism in its actual performance.

Electoral Foundation for Liberal Dominance

Although there can be no doubting that the Liberal party's leaders have set their mark on Canada's political and economic physiognomy in the twentieth century, it can be argued that their impact has been as much a consequence as a cause of Liberal party success at the polls. For the Liberals have been the chief beneficiary of an electoral system that so favors the party in power that their preeminence has been christened "one-party dominance." [7] Whether the single-member constituency with election by plurality has determined the shape of the Canadian party system has been a matter of some debate.[8] There is, however, no doubt that this electoral system has worked to the benefit of the Liberal party. As can be seen from Figure 3-1, the Liberal party received a higher proportion of seats than votes in eighteen out of twenty-three elections since 1896, getting over ten percentage points more seats than votes in eight of those contests. Aggregating the returns from all the regions of the federation, however, the discrepancy between votes cast and seats won is considerably smaller than it would be in a unitary state.

As can be seen from Figure 3-1, the average federal Liberal vote since 1896 has fluctuated within a range of eighteen percentage points, from a low of 34 percent in 1958 to a high of 52 percent in 1900 and 1904. Its share of seats in Parliament has varied over fifty-five percentage points, from 18.5 percent in 1958 to 74 percent in 1949.

At the regional level, results vary even more widely, particularly in the small provinces. The Liberal record in British Columbia, for

[7] Donald V. Smiley, "The Two-Party System and One-Party Dominance in the Liberal Democratic State," *Canadian Journal of Economics and Political Science,* vol. 24 (August 1958), pp. 312-322.

[8] Alan C. Cairns, "The Electoral System and the Party System in Canada, 1921–1965," *Canadian Journal of Political Science,* vol. 1, no. 1 (March 1968), pp. 55-80, and J. A. A. Lovink, "The Impact of the Electoral System on the Party System in Canada," *Canadian Journal of Political Science,* vol. 3, no. 2 (December 1970), pp. 497-516.

Figure 3-1

TOTAL SUPPORT RECEIVED BY LIBERAL PARTY

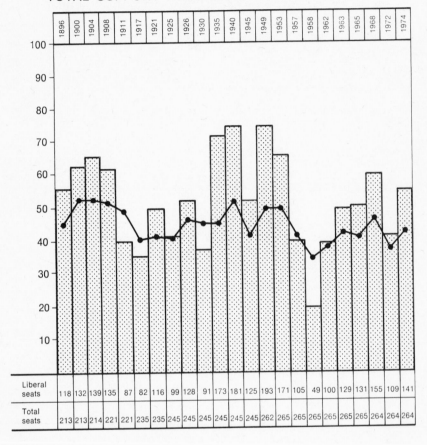

	1896	1900	1904	1908	1911	1917	1921	1925	1926	1930	1935	1940	1945	1949	1953	1957	1958	1962	1963	1965	1968	1972	1974
Liberal seats	118	132	139	135	87	82	116	99	128	91	173	181	125	193	171	105	49	100	129	131	155	109	141
Total seats	213	213	214	221	221	235	235	245	245	245	245	245	245	262	265	265	265	265	265	265	264	264	264

▒ Percentage of seats held by Liberals

●—● Percentage of votes received by Liberal party candidates

Source: Hugh Thorburn, ed., *Party Politics in Canada*, 3rd edition (Toronto: Prentice-Hall, 1972); *Toronto Globe and Mail*, 2 November 1972 and 10 July 1974, appendixes.

example, has shown a fluctuation of 100 percent in seats, from 100 percent in the election of 1904 to zero percent in the election of 1911, even though the votes received by the party's candidates have fluctuated by only twelve percentage points, as can be seen in Figure 3-2.

Figure 3-2

SUPPORT BY BRITISH COLUMBIA FOR THE FEDERAL LIBERAL PARTY

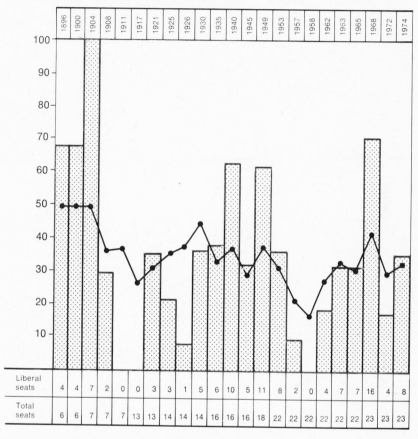

	1896	1900	1904	1908	1911	1917	1921	1925	1926	1930	1935	1940	1945	1949	1953	1957	1958	1962	1963	1965	1968	1972	1974
Liberal seats	4	4	7	2	0	0	3	3	1	5	6	10	5	11	8	2	0	4	7	7	16	4	8
Total seats	6	6	7	7	7	13	13	14	14	14	16	16	16	18	22	22	22	22	22	22	23	23	23

Percentage of seats held by Liberals

Percentage of votes received by Liberal candidates

Source: Thorburn, *Party Politics in Canada; Toronto Globe and Mail,* 2 November 1972 and 10 July 1974.

The combined impact of exaggerated wins or losses resulting from the electoral system and of the fragmentation of the Canadian political system along geographical, historical, and even ethnic lines, has been to increase the unevenness of political party representation in the federal Parliament. As Figure 3-3 shows, the prairie provinces

Figure 3-3

SUPPORT BY PRAIRIE PROVINCES FOR THE FEDERAL LIBERAL PARTY

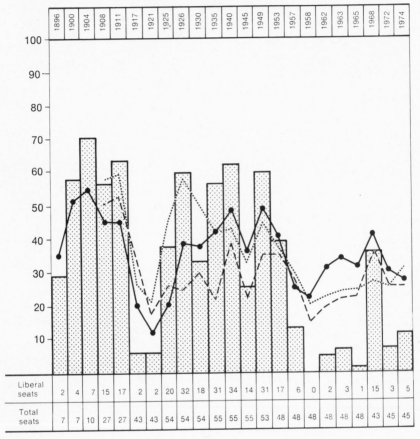

	1896	1900	1904	1908	1911	1917	1921	1925	1926	1930	1935	1940	1945	1949	1953	1957	1958	1962	1963	1965	1968	1972	1974
Liberal seats	2	4	7	15	17	2	2	20	32	18	31	34	14	31	17	6	0	2	3	1	15	3	5
Total seats	7	7	10	27	27	43	43	54	54	54	55	55	55	53	48	48	48	48	48	48	43	45	45

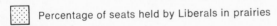 Percentage of seats held by Liberals in prairies

●—●— Percentage of votes received by Liberal candidates in Manitoba

— — — Percentage of votes received by Liberal candidates in Saskatchewan

·········· Percentage of votes received by Liberal candidates in Alberta

Source: Thorburn, *Party Politics in Canada; Toronto Globe and Mail,* 2 November 1972 and 10 July 1974.

Figure 3-4

SUPPORT IN MARITIME PROVINCES FOR THE FEDERAL LIBERAL PARTY

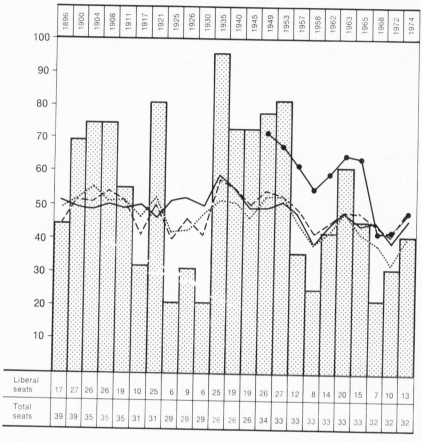

	1896	1900	1904	1908	1911	1917	1921	1925	1926	1930	1935	1940	1945	1949	1953	1957	1958	1962	1963	1965	1968	1972	1974
Liberal seats	17	27	26	26	19	10	25	6	9	6	25	19	19	26	27	12	8	14	20	15	7	10	13
Total seats	39	39	35	35	35	31	31	29	29	29	26	26	26	34	33	33	33	33	33	33	32	32	32

 Percentage of seats held by Liberals in maritimes

●—● Percentage of votes received by Liberal candidates in Newfoundland

——— Percentage of votes received by Liberal candidates in Prince Edward Island

········· Percentage of votes received by Liberal candidates in Nova Scotia

— — — Percentage of votes received by Liberal candidates in New Brunswick

Source: Thorburn, *Party Politics in Canada; Toronto Globe and Mail,* 2 November 1972 and 10 July 1974.

have fluctuated from an area of strength to, in recent decades, a zone of continuing weakness. The existence of solidly entrenched third parties in the provincial legislatures of the prairies has worked against a Liberal comeback. In these provinces the Liberal party suffers from the electoral system as if it were a "third party" itself, receiving on average only 9 percent of the seats, despite retaining about one-quarter of the vote. Like the New Democratic party elsewhere in the country, it has a continuing base of electoral support with no prospect of winning corresponding representation in Parliament.

The number of seats gained by the Liberal party has varied even more greatly in the four maritime provinces, though the spread of votes is narrower here than in the three western provinces. Whereas the Liberal vote has varied with ranges of up to forty-four percentage points, the number of seats has varied by as much as eighty-six, ninety and eighty-eight percentage points in Alberta, Saskatchewan, and Manitoba respectively, the range in the Atlantic provinces goes from thirty percentage points in Newfoundland through twenty-two percentage points in Nova Scotia and twenty percentage points in Prince Edward Island, down to seventeen percentage points in New Brunswick. These smaller swings in the votes received have not prevented the range of seats won by the Liberal party from vacillating enormously: From 100 to 14 percent in Newfoundland, from zero to 100 percent in Nova Scotia and Prince Edward Island, and from 9 to 90 percent in New Brunswick.

When aggregated, however, the pattern appears more stable than the figures would indicate. As Figure 3-4 demonstrates, the Liberal party has received a fairly constant level of voter support, averaging high in the fourth decile. The absence of a strong third party leaves the Liberal and Conservative parties vying with each other in a classic two-party "ins and outs" system and, consequently, maintaining high levels of support.

The most powerful illustration of the advantage given the winner by the single-member, simple-plurality electoral system is the Liberals' record in the province of Quebec, where, as Figure 3-5 shows, the Liberal party has received voting support generally within the fifth decile, yet has generally made off with some 70 percent of the seats. Only once in the course of twenty-three elections have the Liberals received a smaller proportion of the seats than of the votes from the province, and that was 1958, the year of the great Diefenbaker sweep. Also of interest is the level of voting support for the Liberal party in 1958: 46 percent, which, in an adverse national swing, only yielded the party twenty-five of the province's seventy-five seats, whereas two and three elections later, the same 46 percent of the provincial vote yielded forty-seven and fifty-six seats—63 percent and 75 percent of the total from the province. This simple illustration points out how unpredictable are the returns in seats from a given level of votes, and how the fortunes of a party often depend more on a shift of a few thousand votes in key marginal ridings than on large swings of the whole public. It is the party leaders' awareness of how small a shift in the vote may determine their parties' fates that accounts for much of the intensity of election campaigns. A two percentage-point shift of the popular vote can lead to a thirteen percentage-point gain in seats, as it did in Ontario in 1968, and these thirteen seats can make the difference between minority and majority government.

Figure 3-6 depicts the Liberal party's struggle to establish itself firmly in Ontario with a level of voting support under 50 percent. With its low return of seats from the prairies and only moderate returns from British Columbia and the maritimes, the danger that threatens the Liberal party is being restricted to its Quebec fortress. Except for the 1957 and 1958 Diefenbaker successes, Ontario has, in fact, been a successful hunting ground for the Liberals since the mid-1930s. Although even 60 percent of Ontario's seats was not enough in 1963 and 1965 to secure an absolute majority for the party, it did confirm its credentials as the only party with a firm foot planted in both of the country's central, highly urbanized, highly populated areas. Equally clear, however, is the fact that an adverse swing of opinion in Ontario could knock down one of those two foundations of the Liberals' claim to being the most "national" of the country's political parties. The gaping hole in representation from the prairie provinces notwithstanding, the Liberals' near monopoly in Quebec, their generally good position in Ontario, their moderate hold in the maritimes, and their fair to poor situation in British Columbia do make them the most credibly national of the Canadian political parties.

Social and Organizational Foundations of the Liberal Party

Good distribution of voting and representation support from coast to coast and a long record of dominance in the federal Parliament may themselves be factors in making the Liberal party the most broadly supported throughout the various ethnic, religious, occupational, and class groupings in Canadian society. Recent research surveys have confirmed that the Liberals still appeal more evenly than any other party to members of all occupations apart from farmers. As John

Figure 3-5

SUPPORT IN QUEBEC FOR THE FEDERAL LIBERAL PARTY

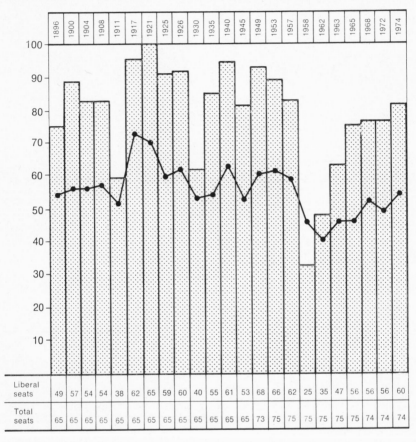

| | Percentage of seats held by Liberals in Quebec

●–● Percentage of votes received by Liberal candidates in Quebec

Source: Thorburn, *Party Politics in Canada; Toronto Globe and Mail*, 2 November 1972 and 10 July 1974.

Meisel says in summing up his analysis of the 1965 and 1968 federal election data:

> In Canada as a whole, the Liberals continued to receive above average support from Catholics, people with high-

Figure 3-6

SUPPORT IN ONTARIO FOR THE FEDERAL LIBERAL PARTY

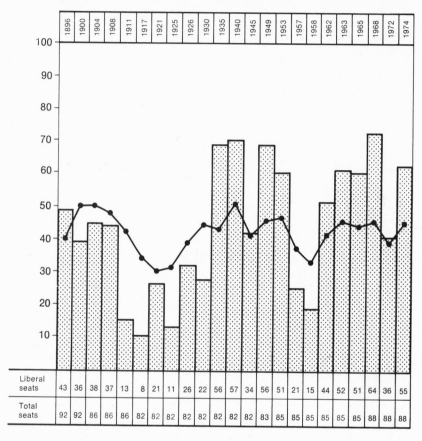

	1896	1900	1904	1908	1911	1917	1921	1925	1926	1930	1935	1940	1945	1949	1953	1957	1958	1962	1963	1965	1968	1972	1974
Liberal seats	43	36	38	37	13	8	21	11	26	22	56	57	34	56	51	21	15	44	52	51	64	36	55
Total seats	92	92	86	86	86	82	82	82	82	82	82	82	82	83	85	85	85	85	85	85	88	88	88

Percentage of seats held by Liberals in Ontario

Percentage of votes received by Liberal candidates in Ontario

Source: Thorburn, *Party Politics in Canada; Toronto Globe and Mail*, 2 November 1972 and 10 July 1974.

ranking occupations, a higher class self-image and more years of formal schooling. They also drew a somewhat disproportionately large number of new Canadians, particularly those who arrived since the end of the Second World War, and they continue to be strongly favoured by

French-speaking Canadians, by younger rather than older voters, by the most urbanized segments of the population and, ever so slightly, by men.[9]

Meisel's attitudinal analysis of the Liberal electorate indicated that

> Liberal voters, despite the fact that a sizeable portion of them lives in Quebec, showed themselves to be the most progressive, liberal, secular and politically interested, and to feel politically effective. . . . the support for Mr. Trudeau's party varied directly with religiosity, moral liberalism, interest in foreign affairs, greater importance being attached to the central government, interest in the election, a sense of efficacy, general optimism about the future and economic expectations; it varied inversely with authoritarianism, respect for law and order . . . and cynicism. . . .[10]

> In short, Liberal voters, more than those of the other parties, included what might be termed the most industrialized, urbanized, technocratic and managerial Canadians. In terms of its supporters, therefore, the Liberal party can be thought of as being most progressive or "modern", in the sense of appealing most to those elements in society which feel at home in the so-called "advanced", urbanized and highly technological world usually associated with urban North America.[11]

Given the advantage which the Liberal party enjoys in the distribution of its geographical and social support, its history of electoral success, and the clear dominance it has exerted over the government of the Canadian federation, an outsider might well expect that its organization would be highly developed, with a broadly based, active membership, a sophisticated structural framework, and a deeply entrenched political culture. In reality the opposite is true. Although no analysis has provided satisfactory statistical confirmation, experience and observation would indicate that the nature of party membership varies considerably not only from region to region, but even from month to month. In more traditional political cultures such as that of the maritime provinces where society is not as highly urbanized as in central Canada, the actual paid-up membership of the party organization is low, while the extent of party identification by citizens is extremely high—to the point where a

---

[9] John Meisel, *Working Papers on Canadian Politics*, enlarged edition (Montreal: McGill-Queen's University Press, 1973), p. 13.

[10] Ibid., p. 25.

[11] Ibid., p. 38.

taxi driver in Charlottetown, Prince Edward Island, can indicate to the tourist the political affiliation of virtually every household on any street. In urbanized areas like Toronto, riding-association membership can fluctuate enormously. When a nomination race is stiffly contested, hundreds, and in some cases even thousands, of new members may be recruited by competitors for the party's nomination, who sign up citizens to support them at the nomination meeting.[12] Once the nomination effort ends, however, the active membership may drop to a few hundred of the basic riding core, along with the winning candidate's immediate supporters.

Since national parties in Canada are federal organizations based on provincial components, and since the different regions of the country are often in very basic opposition to each other (industrial areas historically want high tariffs and other government protection, rural provinces press for free trade; poor provinces favor a strong federal government able to redistribute national income in their direction, rich areas demand local autonomy and less redistribution), the internal workings of national parties are often characterized more by dissension than solidarity. Prime Minister Pearson, for instance, was barely on speaking terms with Ross Thatcher, the Liberal premier of Saskatchewan, who opposed the welfare-state direction in which the federal party was moving. At the same time, Pearson was being urged by Joey Smallwood, premier of poverty-stricken Newfoundland, to increase federal spending on social services, while, from a third side, he was under extreme pressure from Jean Lesage, Liberal premier of Quebec, to abandon whole areas of federal jurisdiction to Quebec and the other provinces. In fact, party disunity was one of the reasons for Mackenzie King's reluctance to move quickly in the direction of social reform. Since he felt the party to be a necessary vehicle for achieving popular consent, King made enormous concessions to preserve its unity, considering it short-sighted to put through a reform if the price were paralyzing conflicts within the party.[13] At the 1973 national meeting of the party rank and file one could hear western delegates attacking their federal Liberal government's policy of keeping down oil prices to favor the maritimes as well as hear deputations from the maritimes inveighing against the excessive nationalism of their central Canadian confrères, who wished to slow down the influx of foreign capital.

---

[12] In the riding of Davenport in 1968 the four candidates for the nomination recruited 5,400 people as party members.

[13] R. MacGregor Dawson, "Mackenzie King as Leader," in Thorburn, *Party Politics in Canada*, 2nd edition, p. 122.

71

More surprising to the outside observer than the ideological and geographical divisions within Canadian parties is their organizational underdevelopment. Originally spontaneous operations set up just at election time to coordinate campaign activity, Canadian parties have been characterized by organizational impermanence. It was as late as 1932 that a central office was first established for the Liberal party. Since it was closed down from 1940 to 1943, the Liberal party's permanent central office with professional staff and a continuing organizational presence is just over thirty years old.[14] None of the Canadian parties has approached the British political parties in the size and sophistication of its permanent office and professional staff. That the Liberal party under Lester Pearson was already thought to be the best organized, most rationalized, and efficient party organization—"Canada's most American party"[15]—in its use of public opinion polls and full-time staff, should be taken more as a comment on the underdeveloped state of the other parties than a measure of its institutional maturity.

Even now that the Liberal party headquarters in Ottawa occupies a whole floor of an office building with a large staff and a considerable communications capacity, the party organization is far from monolithic. Diffusion of power centers and confusion of lines of authority characterize the party, not centralization and simple chains of command. Far from following a rational, bureaucratic model, the party is more like a "stratarchy,"[16] a collection of power centers, often overlapping, sometimes even conflicting with each other. In Ottawa, for instance, the party office by no means rules supreme: it must compete with the well-staffed office of the prime minister, the government staffs of cabinet ministers' departments, and the caucus—the Liberal members of Parliament who are not cabinet ministers but still command a staff of researchers with a government-provided budget of some $250,000. Outside Ottawa the centers of power multiply in geometric progression: each province has its own party organization, with regional and district suborganizations enjoying varying degrees of autonomy. Lowest in the hierarchy come the 264 individual riding associations. Small though their capacity may be to influence and control the actions of the federal party, they are often

14 Joseph Wearing, "Mutations in a Political Party: The Liberal Party of Canada in the Fifties and Sixties," paper presented to the 1975 annual meeting of the Canadian Political Science Association, pp. 5-7.
15 John Meisel, "Recent Changes in Canadian Parties," in Thorburn, *Party Politics in Canada*, 2nd edition, p. 54.
16 Samuel J. Eldersveld, *Political Parties: A Behavioral Analysis* (Chicago: Rand, McNally & Co., 1964), Chapter 1.

jealous of their autonomy when it comes to exercising their major critical function, nominating candidates at election time. Since the overwhelming bulk of the personnel staffing the party power centers in the provinces, regions, districts, and ridings are unpaid volunteers, their turnover is frequent, thus further decreasing continuity, cohesion, and influence. This problem increases in areas where the party is not electorally successful and so offers little prospect of patronage or advancement.

The kaleidoscopic nature of the Liberal party's internal organization is a manifestation of the party's failure to evolve from its simple beginnings as an electoral alliance into a "modern," British-type mass structure. This is not to say that efforts have not been made to democratize the party and expand its mass base. Already during the Pearson period Liberal activists centered in Toronto successfully worked to have considerable power removed from the hands of the leader and placed under the control of the party executive elected at the party's biennial convention. The party constitution was amended to make the leader answerable to the regular party convention and "accountable" to the delegates' secret ballot vote on whether a new leadership convention should be called.

Formal changes in the constitution concerning the party leader were one thing. A new leadership convention necessitated by the retirement of Lester Pearson in 1968 was quite another. It was a moment of truth when the future direction of the party would be decisively shaped through the choice of its new leader. As is normal for parties that have enjoyed long years in office, there was no lack of serious candidates. Most senior was Paul Martin, long-time cabinet workhorse, then holding the portfolio for external affairs that both Lester Pearson and Louis St. Laurent had used as their springboard to the political summit. Most powerful in his corporate backing was Robert Winters, who had been minister for trade and commerce and was then a major figure among the captains of industry. Not to be discounted as serious contenders for the premiership were Paul Hellyer, who had made his national mark as defense minister by integrating the three armed forces under a single uniform; Mitchell Sharp, the articulate minister of finance, who had succeeded two years earlier in rallying the conservative elements of the party to defeat the "economic nationalists" supporting Walter Gordon; handsome, ambitious, but younger John Turner, who would certainly try for the leadership a second time if he failed to win on his first effort; and idealist, intellectual, and nationalist Eric Keirans, who alone injected some discussion of policy issues into the leadership campaign.

That all of these substantial Liberal figures were outdistanced by a political neophyte who had been first elected in 1965 and had but a year's experience in the cabinet indicates how successfully Pierre Elliott Trudeau had appealed to the desire for political renewal beating in the hearts of the party delegates. When Trudeau repeated his success at the ballot box by calling a general election in June 1968 on the themes of "participatory democracy" and a "just society" and gained the party's first clear majority in a decade, the Liberals made a serious attempt to shift policy-making power into the hands of the party rank and file. The ambitious plan for three-phase policy development through thinkers' conferences, riding discussions, regional meetings, and a final policy meeting was tried in 1969 and 1970, but failed when party activists, in their programmatic enthusiasm, came up against their leader's conservatism and the cabinet ministers' pragmatism. When, on the eve of the convention, Trudeau was asked a question about the guaranteed annual income, he rejected it out of hand, even though, the next day, the party was to approve several resolutions supporting such a policy. When the cabinet refused in 1971 to grant the party policy people any role in determining the party's 1972 election positions, it became clear that, formal changes in the party constitution notwithstanding, real power lodged, as ever, behind the closed doors of the cabinet. Given the extremely high socioeconomic status and educational level of party activists,[17] the failure of the leadership to deliver on its much proclaimed breakthrough to participatory democracy led to a severe fall in rank and file morale. When surveyed in December 1972, the most active members of the Liberal party in Ontario showed a striking level of unhappiness with their political involvement. When asked the simple question, "Are you satisfied with your activity in the Liberal party?" 46 percent responded, "Dissatisfied." These dissatisfied Liberals were not, however, opting out: 41 percent of the "dissatisfied" indicated that they had increased their party activity in the past three years, and of these, two-thirds considered themselves "very active." When checked against other data, the level of dissatisfaction appeared to be evenly distributed through the various age, geographical, and status groupings of party members. The only factor which correlated significantly with the high dissatisfaction level was an expressed

---

[17] In a survey of 1,000 of the most active Liberal party members in the central province of Ontario carried out in 1972, 78 percent were found to have post-secondary education, 54 percent indicated an annual family income of over $20,000, 51 percent were businessmen or lawyers. Stephen Clarkson, *Feedback from Active Liberals: Survey of 1,000 Most Prominent Members of the Liberal Party in Ontario*, Toronto, Liberal Party in Ontario, July 1973, pp. 4-6.

inability to be effective in the political system through influencing government policy, members of Parliament, or ministers. As one respondent wrote, the "Party has no influence upon the parliamentary wing. In my opinion democracy within the Party has increased in the last 4 years but the Party's influence upon the parliamentary wing (Cabinet and PMO)—the true centre of power—has decreased sharply." Other comments were more succinct: "It hardly seems to matter. Is anyone listening anymore?" "I don't think the Parliamentary wing of the Government gives a damn about the Party or what it thinks." [18] From the euphoric activity of 1968, when Trudeau was elected party leader and then won a dramatic majority at the polls, active party members had sunk into a listless apathy by 1972, when their leader called another general election. Asked about campaign problems in their individual ridings, 55 percent of the same Ontario Liberal activists responded that campaign workers' morale was worse than it had been in the 1968 election campaign. Sixty-seven percent reported that it was harder to recruit volunteers in 1972 than in 1968.[19] This lack of enthusiasm in the cores of the party's riding associations was clearly a factor in the electoral setback suffered by Trudeau in 1972.

Trudeau's Discovery of the Liberal Party

The Liberals' near defeat in 1972 cannot be understood without recognizing the manic-depressive impact of Trudeau on the party rank and file. In the wake of the "Trudeaumania" of 1968, the prime minister as party leader had espoused a somewhat utopian view of what the party could be: "We are like the pilots of a supersonic aeroplane," Prime Minister Trudeau told the Liberal Party Thinkers' Conference in November 1969. "By the time an airport comes into the pilot's field of vision, it is too late to begin the landing procedure. Such planes must be navigated by radar. A political party, in formulating policy, can act as a society's radar." [20] An excessive stimulant one year, Trudeau was a depressant the next, cutting the party off when it disagreed with him at its policy convention of November 1970 in so sensitive an area as how to handle civil liberties during

---

[18] Clarkson, *Feedback*, p. 29.

[19] Ibid., p. 24.

[20] Thomas A. Hockin, ed., "Pierre Trudeau on the Prime Minister and the Participant Party," in his *The Prime Minister and Political Leadership in Canada* (Toronto: Prentice-Hall, 1971), p. 98.

the F.L.Q. crisis.[21] Trudeau seemed unaware of the impact on party morale of his rebuff to the activists he had been encouraging just a year earlier. He had come into politics from outside the Liberal party and had had no experience with the internal dynamic of such a motley, changeable group of volunteers. But if the 1972 election results were a warning that Trudeau did not know his own party, the 1974 election campaign was to show that this political amateur was able to learn new skills.

That Trudeau became a seasoned "professional" in the 1974 election is due, paradoxically enough, to the amateur and anarchic nature of the party. For this conversion was largely the work of a small group of prominent party activists in Toronto who set themselves up in the wake of the 1972 reversal to advise their leader, just as a similar group had acted in the late 1950s as Lester Pearson's brain trust. Meeting without any formal mandate in lawyer Jerry Grafstein's office, held together by a sense of loyalty to the party, concerned about its policy drift, its lack of leadership, and its shaken will to govern, worried about Trudeau's remoteness from the heart of the Liberal party, the group quickly came to the conclusion that there was no chance of reversing the fortunes of the party in the next election unless a capable campaign chairman were appointed soon enough to mobilize party energies and orchestrate the Liberals' effort. In a meeting at the prime minister's residence, this group put the issue to their leader. "You cannot be both horse and jockey," one Toronto lawyer told the prime minister.[22] The message was strong and clear: a satisfactory chairman was needed to be the jockey. Who that person should be was another question. The Toronto group had canvassed the possibilities and made up its mind: it should be Keith Davey. As a senator he had the time needed for what might be a year's intensive preparatory work; as a perennial optimist he had the enthusiasm and energy needed at this dark period in the party's fortunes. Sentiment throughout the party did not, however, share the Toronto Liberals' confidence in the controversial and flamboyant senator. As campaign director for the elections of 1962, 1963, and 1965, he was associated in the eyes of many party people with the Liberals' failure to achieve a clear majority in the House of

---

[21] In October 1970, when the *Front de Libération du Québec* kidnapped a British diplomat and a Quebec cabinet minister, the government virtually abrogated civil liberties by declaring a state of "apprehended insurrection" under the War Measures Act. Hundreds of Quebeckers were arrested, most without any reason, causing dismay among liberally minded Canadians.

[22] Interview with Jerry Grafstein, 18 October 1974.

76

Commons for Pearson. Dubbed "the rainmaker" for his apparent capacity to fumble great opportunities, Davey provoked as much alarm as enthusiasm among caucus members when they heard his name suggested as next campaign chairman. Reluctant to appear too anxious for another election, Trudeau asked party president Richard Stanbury to canvas the opinion of the party's influentials. Weeks dragged into months, but finally a consensus emerged: Davey was the only man available who had the seniority, the connections, the authority, and even the charisma to establish a game plan and make it stick. As a result of the prime minister's willingness to put this jockey in the saddle and run flat out under his direction, the 1974 Liberal campaign is a study in contrast with the previous election. Rather than reestablishing the bicephalous campaign committee of 1972 that had been doomed to frustration because the two cochairmen, Robert Andras and Jean Marchand, ministers of manpower and regional expansion respectively, were themselves seeking reelection, the campaign organization for English-speaking Canada was to be run by a single full-time, politically experienced organizer, while the Quebec Liberals were left alone to run their own unique political show.

Background to the 1974 Campaign

Those who expected the 1974 campaign to be a rerun of 1972 did not appreciate the changes that had taken place in Trudeau and his government between the euphoric years of their majority government (1968–1972) and the less comfortable times of minority rule (1973–1974). In his first legislature Trudeau had flown high at the beginning, only to crash at the end. The political *Wunderkind*, the apostle of rationalism in politics who had come to power declaring the need to reassess and review all areas of policy before launching in new directions, had, in fact, accomplished remarkably little during his four years of unchallenged power. Foreign policy, fiscal policy, social policy—each area of government was reexamined, with the end result that little change was made from previous patterns. Undramatic results, however, were not electorally important, since only the intellectual community was disappointed by the lack of significant change. Far more damaging politically was Trudeau's personal feat of offending almost every major group in the population outside Quebec. Whether it was church people and reformers whose efforts on behalf of the Ibos' struggle for self-determination in Nigeria he had dismissed with contempt ("Where's Biafra?"), or the large Slav communities in Canada whom he had outraged by equating Ukrainian nationalism with Quebec separatism, whether it was the more staid whom he shocked by mouthing an obscenity in Parliament or the vicarious swingers whom he disillusioned by getting married, it seemed that he could not have done worse by a deliberate program to alienate every important group in the country. But having come within a hair's breath of losing office in 1972, the Trudeau cabinet performed in a decisively different way during their year and a half as a minority government. Crisis management was the order of the day: at any moment they could have been defeated by the New Democratic party switching its voting power from the governing Liberals to the opposition Conservatives. Despite the many difficulties of running the government in these circumstances, government output was more impressive in this period than it had been in the preceding phase of majority rule. Important legislation was brought in and passed in a number of areas, including innovative measures on foreign investment control and election reform. More important in electoral terms, the successful recovery of the 1972 fumble had an important impact on the morale of the party leader, his cabinet, the parliamentary caucus, and even the rank and file at the grassroots. Having weathered the first hours, days, and then weeks of their minority position, Liberals regained their old self-confidence. The months turned into a year. Election planning went on quietly behind the scenes, as the government continued to keep the initiative in its own hands and away from the frustrated Conservatives, who had come within a few votes of taking over.

Even though the Liberals' success in holding off the Tory assault was the crucial factor during this minority period, the political situation on the eve of the election campaign looked bleak for the party. Despite the favorable trends in Gallup poll results (see Table 3-1), Trudeau was the underdog in the estimation of the media, who had tasted blood and were generally supporting Robert Stanfield and the Conservative party on their editorial pages.

The Conservatives, for their part, were spoiling for a fight. Their eagerness was understandable. They were getting good candidates whom they placed in important ridings. The fact that Duff Roblin, former premier of Manitoba, Ron Collister, senior news reporter for the Canadian Broadcasting Corporation, or Ronald Ritchie, former vice-president of the giant Exxon subsidary, Imperial Oil, were anxious to run for the Progressive Conservative party was an indication of the confidence and eagerness in the Conservative camp. Conservatives could also legitimately be gratified by the opinion poll

Table 3–1
GALLUP POLL MEASURES OF PARTY POPULARITY, 1974
(in percents)

Party	Before Campaign		During Campaign			Votes[a]
	6 Feb.	10 April	5 June	22 June	6 July	8 July
Liberals	42	39	40	42	43	43.2
Conservatives	31	34	33	34	35	35.5
New Democrats	21	18	21	18	16.5	15.5
Other	6	9	6	6	5.5	6

[a] Valid votes cast.
Source: Canadian Institute of Public Opinion.

findings that confirmed both that inflation was the number-one issue in the public mind and that wage and price controls (already official Conservative policy during the 1972 election campaign) was the accepted solution.[23] Given this context, the tale of the 1974 federal election can either be told as the Liberal story of victory snatched from the jaws of defeat or the Conservative story of defeat snatched from the jaws of victory.

Victory from the Jaws of Defeat: The Expert Amateurs

Seen in retrospect, the 1974 Liberal campaign was a model operation, run by a group of experienced but nonprofessional men and women who rallied, as usual, to the election call. It was the record of a political leader and his party who were able to learn from their past mistakes.

Strategy. Rather than revive the vague and unsuccessful strategy of the 1972 campaign, which Prime Minister Trudeau had announced as an intellectual "conversation with Canadians," the Liberals were to articulate a clear strategy on the basis of a careful analysis of survey research, the opposition's weaknesses, and their own strengths. The Liberals' latest survey, carried out in the spring of 1974, had again shown the intense public concern about inflation. This was a serious problem for Davey, since there was clear public support for the Conservatives' proposed solution of wage and price control.

---

[23] See Lawrence LeDuc, "The Measurement of Public Opinion," in this volume, pp. 220-223.

As bad as the situation appeared, the Liberal command group knew what the Conservatives' major liability was: Robert Stanfield. Even before the campaign started, the polls were indicating greater public confidence in the Liberal than in the Conservative leader (see Table 3-2). Trudeau outpolled Stanfield by 41 percentage points as best leader, 8 percentage points as most believable, 39 percentage points as most capable of running Canada, 64 percentage points as best speaker, 20 percentage points as most concerned with Canada's future, 22 percentage points as most capable of creating jobs, 43 percentage points as best for the under twenty-five voters, 33 percentage points as best able to handle an energy crisis, 36 percentage points as best for Canadian unity, and 54 percentage points as best representative in foreign affairs.

Given this enormous margin in favor of their leader, the Liberals' strategy was to turn the issue from inflation to leadership. This was to be done by exploiting Trudeau's dynamism, taking the

Table 3–2
PUBLIC ATTITUDES TOWARD THREE MAJOR PARTY LEADERS BEFORE 1974 ELECTION
(in percents)

Opinion	Trudeau (Liberal)	Stanfield (Conservative)	Lewis (New Democrat)
Liked least	19.4	39.7	27.0
Most intelligent	63.8	11.0	7.2
Best leader	55.9	14.7	16.4
Most believable	33.2	25.7	17.6
Most likely to win	69.0	16.6	4.7
Most capable of running Canada	54.6	15.7	11.7
Speaks best	67.6	3.7	21.3
Most concerned with Canada's future	37.3	17.8	15.4
Most capable of creating jobs	34.6	12.9	19.9
Best for the under-25 voters	49.3	6.4	24.8
Best to handle energy crisis	45.3	12.6	14.2
Best for Canadian unity	54.1	18.0	12.7
Best representative in foreign affairs	67.7	13.8	5.7

Source: Boyd Upper, speech to Ontario Liberal Candidates' College, 18 May 1974, York University.

offensive in attacking the Conservatives, taking the initiative in presenting new policy issues to the public and, very simply, running hard and trying to make no errors. The objective was to force the Conservatives to fight on the Liberal issue of leadership and back down from their issue of inflation.

Once the game plan had been worked out, Keith Davey's role as campaign chairman was to captain the team, refusing to allow his players to budge from the plan, monitoring the work of his regional campaign committees and, in particular, telling the prime minister—now ready to listen—what to do every day.

The Leader's Campaign. The basic message that the prime minister gave his candidates at party meetings across the country in the early days of the campaign was a call to take the offensive:

> Last time, Pierre Trudeau told the Ontario candidates assembled for a campaign college at York University on May 18th, the campaign was a conversation with Canadians. Well, we are still going to talk to the Canadian people . . . but there is not going to be any backing up and apologizing and bowing our head. We are going to be on the attack and we are going to show the Canadian people that Liberalism is the way for Canada now.[24]

This time there were no dull written speeches from the party leader and no aimless intellectual chats with anonymous callers on open-line shows. The party leader that Liberal workers saw on their television screens or heard at public meetings was a fighting politician giving an ad lib speech that repeated over and over again a powerful attack on the Conservatives and a strong case for the Liberals:

> This is the art of politics. It's to put forth a team which is united, and if the other team can't even control its own members in an election, how do you believe it's going to control the whole economy? . . . [and] put price and wage controls on the Canadian people, when it can't even control its own supporters? (Kamloops, B.C., 13 June 1974)[25]

Trudeau defended his record, but defended aggressively:

> This budget . . . was cutting taxes, income taxes, . . . was ensuring lower prices for your clothing and your shoes

---

[24] *National Campaign Headquarters Candidates' Update*, Ottawa, Liberal Party of Canada, 24 May 1974.

[25] Blair Williams, "Note to Newspaper Editors," Ottawa, Liberal Party of Canada, 25 June 1974, p. 2.

because we were cutting the 12 percent federal sales tax on those items. This is the budget that the Tories and the NDP preferred to defeat. (Toronto, 17 June 1974) [26]

If [the opposition] talk to you about great profits of great corporations ask them why they voted against a budget which was increasing corporate taxes by 25 percent over last year's, which was increasing corporate taxes by $800,000,000 in order that the government would have $800,000,000 to redistribute to those in our society which need it most. (Montague, P.E.I., 20 May 1974) [27]

As for the Tories' policy of wage and price control, Trudeau attacked with his rhetoric in high gear.

How is price control going to keep down the price of petroleum? Is it going to stop the war in the Middle East? Is it going to make Arabs bring their petroleum down three-fold? Have they got a better solution than ours, which is giving Canadians 40 percent cheaper petroleum than the world? They don't. Wage and price controls is not an answer. Is wage and price controls an answer to the high cost of food which you are paying here? What is price control going to do about food that we import from other countries? Either from the U.S. or from less developed nations, like our coffee or our sugar or our cocoa or our tea? You can't put wage and price controls on what's being produced elsewhere. (Winnipeg, 14 June 1974) [28]

The message was repeated tirelessly.

You'll be stuck with a policy you have seen in operation in the United States, if you've seen on your television or heard on your radio, about farmers gassing their chickens and slaughtering their cattle . . . even if we freeze prices and wages, we can't freeze the price of the farm machinery coming in from the United States, they won't accept our freeze. And . . . we can't freeze the pesticides, which come from out of Canada. So the cost to the farmer goes up . . . he can increase the price of his product but nobody will buy it because they can't resell it at higher prices. (North Battleford, 23 May 1974) [29]

---

[26] Ibid., p. 4.
[27] Ibid., p. 7.
[28] Ibid., p. 5.
[29] Ibid.

The leader's campaign could be called neotraditional, a cunning mixture of old-fashioned politics with modern media management. For four days the prime minister was sequestered on a train, doing a whistle stop tour of the maritime provinces. But it was Jim Coutts, Keith Davey's immediate lieutenant on the prime minister's tour, who was in control of the media on the tour. When the prime minister's regular press officer Pierre O'Neill wanted to allow the journalists covering the tour interviews with Trudeau, Coutts overruled him; they were to be kept at a distance. This way, readers of the *Globe and Mail* of 27 May found on the front page a nostalgic photograph of crowds gathered around the rear platform of a small passenger train and read a long article describing Trudeau's campaigning and warm crowd response with no follow-up critique of Trudeau's policy thinking. When the paths of the prime minister and the leader of the opposition crossed one day in Winnipeg, Trudeau upstaged his challenger by issuing a government announcement that Air Canada would move repair facilities to that prairie city and thereby create 800 new jobs. The next day it was the prime minister who dominated the headlines on the front page of the press, national as well as local.[30]

Policies for the Left. In 1972, party faithful and public alike had waited in vain for the prime minister to present the policies that he intended to implement if reelected—despite the 1970 policy convention that had created more party policy than could comfortably be effected in ten years. In 1974 there were no recent party-policy resolutions to worry about, but the prime minister did announce a large number of policies designed to grab the front pages of the newspapers across the country, dominate radio and television news reporting, and so appeal to the floating vote that campaign strategists guessed was hovering to the left of the Liberals. An ad hoc committee had been created by Keith Davey to prepare policy positions for the campaign, have them approved by the cabinet, and released periodically during the campaign for maximum impact through the media.

Trudeau used ten of these positions for major policy statements between 5 June and 28 June. The policy priorities were determined by the party's survey research.[31] First came three sets of announcements on housing (low-down-payment mortgages for moderately priced homes, expansion of the assisted home ownership program,

---

[30] *Toronto Globe and Mail,* 24 May 1974, p. 1.
[31] Interview with Keith Davey, 13 October 1974.

doubling the interest reduction grants and allowing these over a wider income range, and $500 cash grants for first-home buyers).[32] Transportation policies were also spun over three detailed separate proposals. The first, announced in Edmonton, Alberta, promised fair freight rates; the second, released in Toronto, promised federal aid for urban transit; and the third, released in Cornwall, Ontario, focused on improving intercity bus and train travel. A large agricultural policy designed to stabilize and guarantee farm incomes was unveiled in Humboldt, Saskatchewan. A social security platform, broadening the guaranteed annual income for pensioners and unemployables was announced in Trois Rivières, Quebec. In Ottawa a consumer affairs platform was announced and, finally, on 28 June a nationalist industrial development strategy was unveiled.

Media Management. Whistle stopping and campaign promises restored an air of traditional political reality to Trudeau the campaigner, but the men in charge of the 1974 campaign made very modern decisions about how to relate to the press. Trudeau was kept off the hot-line shows on which he had spent so much time in 1972. By one stroke of campaign policy, the quick-tempered politician capable of annoying countless voters at the turn of a phrase, was frozen for the duration of the campaign. Whether it was Finance Minister Turner whom the private television network wished to have debate with the chief opposition finance critic or the national campaign chairman who was asked for interviews by the press, the same rule applied: no appearance except under controlled and favorable circumstances. The prime minister gave one interview to the media magnate John Bassett on his Toronto station, CFTO-TV, and another on the public television network to his old friend Robert Mackenzie and former supporter Patrick Watson. But except on these occasions, Trudeau campaigned directly before the public, letting the press follow on his heels. His speeches announcing new government programs or promising new measures were timed so as to force the media to report these initiatives while forestalling intensive grilling of either the party leader or his staff. The tactic was eminently successful. Of the ten major policy announcements made by Trudeau himself, seven were reported on the front page of the *Globe and Mail*.[33] During the campaign the *Globe and Mail* carried nineteen news items bearing on the Liberal campaign on its front page, only four of which were negative, as well as eleven policy statements and

---

[32] *Candidates' Update*, nos. 8 to 15.
[33] *Toronto Globe and Mail*, 5, 6, 7, 12, 14, 17, and 18 June 1974, p. 1.

four government announcements. In all, from 4 May to 8 July the prime minister was on the front page of the *Globe* twenty-one times, compared to nine times for Stanfield.

Less successful at sweeping the front pages but probably far more important to the campaign was the Liberals' most powerful secret weapon, the prime minister's wife. Introducing the prime minister to a political meeting in West Vancouver on 4 June, she said, "I want to speak of him as a person, as a loving human being who has taught me, in the three years we have been married and in the few years before that, a lot about loving." By talking about her husband in this romantic vein, Margaret Trudeau apparently opened the heart of many a politically indifferent voter. She was the rookie star of the campaign, a fresh face to be photographed, a new theme on which to play journalistic variations in an otherwise fairly dull reporting scene. Having been kept out of bounds to the press since their marriage, she was a novelty, and the news business gobbles up anything new.

More than a Leader. A government has more than one general. Ministers' tours were organized to get the maximum media mileage out of the better known personalities in the government circle. Rough spoken Agriculture Minister Eugene Whelan, for example, was in demand as a speaker across the country. The finance minister, John Turner, and the secretary of state for external affairs, Mitchell Sharp, traveled widely in addition to running campaigns in their ridings, where each was under heavy fire from a strong Conservative candidate. Whatever the temptations, internecine bickering was absent among the Liberals—in striking contrast to the Conservative camp. Again, there was payoff in the coverage. The *Globe and Mail* had twelve front-page stories dealing with Liberal cabinet ministers; of the twelve, only two were negative, reporting Labor Minister John Munro's implication in a patronage scandal. By contrast, Conservative personalities other than Stanfield only made the front page of the *Globe and Mail* five times, twice in connection with the politically embarrassing Conservative mayor of Moncton, New Brunswick, who had defied Stanfield's leadership on the issue of bilingualism.

Below the leadership and ministerial level, the Liberal campaign was managed nationally, regionally, and at the constituency level. From the national office material was sent out in the form of telexed "candidates' updates" aimed at maintaining consistency in the message delivered by Liberal candidates at the grassroots level and at supplying necessary information on the prime minister's announcements. The "updates" also supplied such "ad lib" ammunition for candidates' speeches as this remark made by John Turner, minister of finance: "Don't compare him [Trudeau] to the Almighty, compare him to the alternative."[34]

Far more important than the national office were the provincial campaign operations. In a class by itself was the Quebec campaign, run as usual as if it were the private preserve of the party's Quebec leader, still Jean Marchand, now the federal minister of transport. In what was the most crucial province for the Liberal party, Ontario, a woman with long campaign experience was made regional chairman. Tempering her own knowledge of experienced party members with the advice of her colleagues, Dorothy Petrie put together a campaign committee that was, in the words of Gordon Dryden, party financial controller, "the best campaign committee that Ontario had ever seen." Of the sixteen members of this committee, only two required some financial reimbursement. The others, as is usual at election time, put in some forty hours of volunteer time per week in addition to their own jobs, two people doing policy research, two running the prime minister's tour in Ontario, two organizing the other ministers' tours, two more organizing special events such as the mass rally at Varsity Stadium, one raising funds, and another administering surveys in critical ridings. The national chairman, Keith Davey, attended the Ontario committee's weekly meetings, as did Jerry Grafstein, coordinator of the federal publicity campaign. It was a group of experienced campaigners, most of whom had already worked together several times in Liberal campaigns. Decentralization was the organizing principle of this instant campaign operation, two dozen campaign coordinators being responsible for finding candidates and supervising the campaigns in the four or five ridings under their charge. The cumulative experience of these middle-level leaders was impressive. While their job was performed almost without a serious error, it retained the amateur quality that characterizes the nonelected wing of the Liberal party.

Although amateur in its staffing, it was modern in its techniques: a telex linked the provincial with the federal office for instant communication; a monitor team recorded news broadcasts so that, when the Canadian Broadcasting Corporation's television news made an apparently exaggerated estimate of the costs of the Liberal campaign promises, the policy research staff was able to respond vigorously

---

[34] *Candidates' Update*, 24 May 1974, p. 3.

and demand a correction from the news service. The two-person policy research staff took pride in trying to outdo the federal party office in research documentation produced for Liberal candidates. Bulletins were prepared and circulated to candidates on issues such as wage and price controls, inflation, budgetary deficits, energy, and growth in the federal civil service. A fighting speech was prepared by the Ontario party policy chairman, Boyd Upper, to provide any Ontario candidates who were inexperienced speakers with a basic line in best platform style:

> Remember 1970? The issue was national unity. What leadership did Mr. Stanfield offer? His leadership was Two Nations. When Diefenbaker got done with him the Tories almost had two parties.

> What did Prime Minister Trudeau offer? One Canada and no appeasement of separatists.

> Remember 1971 and 1972? The issue was unemployment. In the past 3 years new job formation in Canada has exceeded 880,000. That is more new jobs than have been created in the whole of Western Europe in the same period. I'm not saying that unemployment has disappeared. What I'm saying is that unemployment today is not the number one issue in Ontario. It is not number two (energy) or number three (housing) or number four (welfare abuse). It is fifth.

> What is number one issue now? It is inflation and the cost of living.

> What does Mr. Stanfield offer? His answer to inflation is "wage and price control"; a 90-day freeze followed by something he hasn't defined and that no one else can guess. . . .

> Wage and price controls aren't new. They aren't innovative. They aren't magic. They have been tried and tried and always found wanting. Wage and price controls do not work. The distortions they create, the shortages they develop and the pent up pressure for wages unleash more serious problems than those the controls set out to solve.

> What Mr. Stanfield's position amounts to is this. Prices aren't right. Wages aren't right. But, by gosh, the freeze is right.

> In a world of dramatic and dynamic change Mr. Stanfield's response is: "Stop the world, I want to get off—for a 90-day freeze."

> It is a dumb position that even Tories can't defend with much enthusiasm. Stanfield's 90-day wage and price freeze

is not just simplistic—it is simple minded. It is a snow job and Mr. Stanfield is the Abominable Snowman.[35]

Publicity. In the 1972 campaign, Liberal public relations was run without coordination or coherence. The slogan "The Land Is Strong" had been worked out by an ad agency representative without clear input from the campaign committee. It had provoked general dismay among party workers, especially in rural areas where farmers retorted with such blunt jibes as, "It's horseshit, not the Liberals, that makes my land strong." By contrast, the advertising effort in 1974 was run in close coordination with the campaign strategy. Rather than employ one ad agency, the party set up its own, Red Leaf Communications, Ltd., a consortium of ad men from different agencies coming under the command of lawyer Jerry Grafstein, an experienced party campaigner and close political colleague of Keith Davey and Dorothy Petrie. This time the advertising message reiterated and reinforced the basic strategy and message of the campaign. Instead of creating a campaign themselves, the ad men highlighted the effort being made by the leader on his tour. In a full-page print ad that ran in the Saturday newspapers across the country on 29 June, the headline read, "Issues Change from Year to Year. The Ability to Lead Does Not." Leaning on the same survey research and strategic judgment that underlay the prime minister's campaign, it went on: "The leadership of Canada is the ultimate issue in this campaign. Who can do the best job for Canada in the years ahead? For every thinking Canadian there can be only one answer: Pierre Trudeau and the Liberal Party." Tying in with the Ontario candidates' speech it went on,

> Remember 1971? The issue that year was unemployment. You don't hear much from Mr. Stanfield about a job crisis today. Could that possibly be because from 1971 through 1973 880,000 new jobs have been created in Canada? Could it possibly be because that rate of job formation was the highest in the history of this country? Could it possibly be because the number of jobs created in Canada was greater than the number created in all the Common Market countries combined? That's the record the Liberal party is building on.[36]

The impact of all these efforts could be measured on 6 July, just two days before the election, when Peter Regenstrief reported

---

[35] Boyd Upper, speech to Ontario Liberal Candidates' College, 18 May 1974, York University.

[36] *Toronto Star*, 29 June 1974, p. B-8.

his poll in the *Toronto Star*.[37] The Liberals had increased their level of popular support from 40 percent in May to 43 percent. For the first time in twenty years and eight federal elections, the Liberals had maintained their voter support right through the last week of the campaign. The momentum had been kept up. Almost no mistakes had been made. The best index of the Liberal campaign's success was that inflation had dipped significantly as the issue of greatest importance, while the issue of leadership had surfaced in the public mind.[38] The sweetest news of all came from the CTV poll in mid-June. Already by 16 June Complan Research Associates reported for CTV that 49 percent considered the Liberals had the best policy to control inflation, compared to 24 percent for the Conservatives.[39] The Conservatives' major anti-Liberal issue of the campaign had been made to work to the Liberals' own advantage.

Old Generals for New Wars: Defeat from the Jaws of Victory

While the Liberals were fighting hard to win, their two major opponents managed to help them. The New Democratic party, which had precipitated the election by voting against the government's budget, failed to generate a single attention-grabbing issue as powerful as their 1972 attack on "corporate welfare bums." Their leader, David Lewis, had lost his impact. Appreciated by some for his influential role during the last year and a half of minority government ("the best policy chairman the Liberals ever had"), and reviled by others for collaborating with the Liberals in return for marginal improvements in legislation, he was generally resented for having precipitated an expensive and unnecessary election. The resentment of the voters was dramatically demonstrated on election night when Lewis lost his own seat to a neophyte Liberal. While his own policy speeches were reported, they seemed to make little impression. Only two news stories and one policy story on the NDP made the front page of the *Globe and Mail* during the whole election.

The greatest impact of the left-wing party was in adding weight to the Liberal attack on the Conservatives' wage-and-price-freeze policy. Early in the campaign David Lewis used his keynote speech to the annual convention of the Canadian Labour Congress to attack wage and price controls, and labor leaders followed suit throughout

---

[37] *Toronto Star*, 6 July 1974, p. 1.
[38] LeDuc, "The Measurement of Public Opinion," p. 238.
[39] Ibid., p. 224.

the campaign by speaking out against the Conservative position. Regional factors such as the midterm unpopularity of the NDP government in British Columbia helped undermine the NDP's appeal. But it was the campaign policy designed and implemented by its own leadership that deprived the NDP of its toehold in the center, failed to win new support from the inaudible left, and at the same time helped to neutralize the political right.

The Progressive Conservatives were caught even more hopelessly in skeins of their own spinning. Like generals preparing to fight the battles of the last war, they had mapped out plans and built their organization months in advance. Knowing that the major concern of the public was inflation and knowing that wage and price control was considered to be a good solution, they went into battle rigidly overprepared. The highly reputed, professionally staffed "big blue machine," the political brain trust of Ontario Premier William Davis, wrote Robert Stanfield's speeches in Toronto, a procedure that prevented the Conservative leader from responding quickly to issues as they developed. A series of policy announcements, also prepared by the Ontario machine with a view to attracting media attention, was not used in order to focus entirely on the wage and price control solution to the inflation issue. But inflation is an abstract problem and wage and price controls are a concrete solution that conveys a direct message to everyone, especially the majority of voters whose wages would be frozen. As the campaign progressed, the credibility of the simple, tough control policy was undermined by the Conservatives themselves. First, the leader kept adding qualifications to his initially strong policy: union contracts with built-in escalation clauses would still be valid; the prices of farm produce would not be frozen; stock prices and interest rates would be exempted, and so on. Candidates' reservations were voiced with increasing volume as the concern about wage freezes rose. And vendettas against Robert Stanfield left over from the previous leadership convention led to further questioning of the wage and price control idea by the old guard of the party. Urged to go on tour for the Conservatives, former Prime Minister Diefenbaker managed in one sentence in a speech in Prince Edward Island to add to the policy debacle: wages should not be frozen, he told his audience, until they had caught up with price increases. Subsequent explanation by aides could not undo the damage that the Conservatives were inflicting on their own policy, or the opportunities they were offering the Liberals. These Trudeau was quick to seize. How, he asked an audience of 13,000 in the University of Toronto's Varsity Arena, can Stanfield control inflation if he cannot even control his own party? The Trudeau attack, repeated on platform after platform across the country and again on videotape before millions of television-news watchers at night, was hammered home at candidates' meetings in ridings throughout Canada and on doorsteps when canvassers knocked on behalf of the Liberal party.

Though the wage-and-price-freeze policy patently never worked to the advantage of the party, the Tory campaign clung to it, doggedly pursuing the preelection plan. Furthermore, just as the NDP was to lose votes because of feeling against the provincial NDP government in British Columbia, so the Progressive Conservatives would suffer from opposition to the Conservative government of the province of Ontario. Ontario's Conservative premier William Davis, who did some campaigning with the federal opposition leader in his province, was sometimes booed when introducing Stanfield—not the most welcoming of fanfares for a candidate whose lack of forcefulness was already a serious liability.

The Results: Predictably Surprising. The almost universal surprise which greeted the Liberals' decisive victory on election night appears less surprising in retrospect. Even though the Liberals had fought an incomparably better campaign than in 1972, the 1974 election was still generally perceived in 1972 terms by reporters. Not only did the Conservatives replay their 1972 strategy, the media reported the news as if the events of 1972 were repeating themselves. Although public opinion polls taken by newspapers, television stations, and the parties themselves showed the Liberals and Trudeau consistently ahead of the Conservatives and Stanfield, reporters kept discounting the figures by remarking that in 1972 the Liberals had also had a lead, which had narrowed considerably in the last weeks of the campaign. What was not given credence by the interpreters of the poll results was the clear desire for political stability: 72 percent of the respondents to CTV's last poll expressed a strong preference for majority over minority governments.[40] What news pundits also failed to assess was how badly the Conservatives were faring in the news-making of the campaign, not so much in terms of quantity as of quality. Of fourteen news items related to the Conservatives on the front page of the *Globe and Mail* during the campaign, five were negative: Stanfield's discipline problems when a New Brunswick riding association nominated an unacceptably anti-French candidate,

---

[40] Ibid., p. 233.

the objections in the local press to the "parachuting" of Duff Roblin into Peterborough, Ontario, and the photographs showing Stanfield fumbling a football, wearing his trousers incorrectly inside cowboy boots, and bearing a Liberal sticker on his back.[41] The Conservatives were never on top of their news making. Thus, while editorialists and columnists were generally hostile to Trudeau (all three Toronto papers supported the Conservatives), the opinion columns appear to have had less effect than the news copy, which consistently showed the Liberals in a better light than the Conservatives: more united, more positive, more decisive, more authoritative.

Forty-three percent of the popular vote (compared to 35 percent for the Conservatives, 16 percent for the NDP and 5 percent for Social Credit) was the payoff for the Liberals' superiority in leadership and campaign management. Their victory was not a landslide; only marginal gains were made in the maritime provinces and Quebec, while the West remained nearly as Tory as before, except in British Columbia where the Liberals doubled their seats from four to eight. It was, nevertheless, a major victory, since Ontario fell to the Liberal attack, nineteen new seats being added to the thirty-six which they had held there before. Ontario constituted a feather in the Liberals' cap for another reason: they had attracted an overwhelming 70 percent of the new voters in the eighteen-to-twenty age bracket. (In the country as a whole the Liberals had received 45 percent of the newly eligible votes, compared to but 17 and 10 percent going to the Conservatives and New Democrats respectively.)[42]

In one sense, the meaning of the election was clear. First and foremost, it was a personal triumph and vindication for Pierre Trudeau who had shown himself to be a seasoned leader to the core, lasting through the honeymoon with the media of 1968, but also weathering its hostility of 1972. He had proved that his appeal was solid in Ontario and the maritimes and significant in the West. By the end of this term in office he will have been prime minister for ten years, the longest prime ministerial tenure since Mackenzie King's.

For the Liberal party, though, the meaning of the victory is unclear. When a cabinet is firmly installed in government, it generally ignores its own party. There is no indication that the traditionally quiescent role of the party between elections will be altered. The election campaign created such a bond between Pierre Trudeau and

---

41 *Toronto Globe and Mail*, 31 May, 3 June and 12 June 1974, p. 1.

42 Jon Pammett, Lawrence LeDuc, Jane Jenson and Harold Clarke, "The 1974 Federal Election: A Preliminary Report," paper presented to the 1975 annual meeting of the Canadian Political Science Association, pp. 10, 12.

Keith Davey that the senator comes close to being the prime minister's Anglophone lieutenant—a position Trudeau has never filled until now. As for the party organization, there is no reason to think that it will develop any new inter-election role, although the "Daveymobile," as the party machine has now been dubbed, has received far better attention from the prime minister in the twelve months following the 1974 victory than it did under his first period of majority government.[43]

The loss of the NDP's balancing role in Parliament will probably facilitate a return to more conservative government, especially in a situation where inflation must be dealt with, even if this means postponing or tabling the more expensive of the Liberals' election promises. Given the complete control which the cabinet exerts over the civil service in a parliamentary system, the return of the "Grits" to the governing benches indicates that no change in policy is likely to come from the federal bureaucracy, although a generational change now shifting senior personnel in the Ottawa ministries may produce some new thinking at the top.

The election results were sufficiently favorable to make the Liberal party optimistic about its future. At the same time as the Liberals managed to expand their position in Quebec, their complete sweep of all Montreal seats confirmed the party's appeal to the non-French elements in that province. The success in Ontario, where the Liberals won fifty-five of eighty-eight of the federal seats, appeared to be the key to the party's future fortunes. All eleven cabinet ministers from Ontario were reelected—even Labour Minister John Munro, despite the adverse publicity he had received. Agriculture Minister Eugene Whelan was credited with swinging five rural ridings in southwest Ontario from the Tories. Looking at the Ontario results under various hypothetical swings of the electorate suggests that the NDP is not a major factor in Liberal fortunes. Even a pro-NDP swing of 5 percent at the expense of the Liberals would only deprive the Liberals of six seats. A pro-NDP swing at the expense of the Conservatives would yield five seats for the Liberals. But a 5 percent swing in favor of the Conservatives at the expense of the Liberals would mean the loss of seventeen seats, as can be seen from Tables 3-3 and 3-4.

As for party morale, there seems little doubt that, at the top at least, it is excellent. As one strong Liberal put it, the party's mission in Canada is to reconfederate the nation at each generation. Trudeau

---

[43] Christina Newman, "That Big Red Machine Is the Daveymobile," *Toronto Globe and Mail*, 7 July 1975, p. 7.

Table 3-3

MARGIN OF VICTORY/DEFEAT OF ONTARIO LIBERAL CANDIDATES, 1974, 1972, 1968

	Candidates Winning by Margins of:					Candidates Losing by Margins of:				
	20%	15–19.9%	10–14.9%	5–9.9%	0–4.9%	0–4.9%	5–9.9%	10–14.9%	15–19.9%	20% +
1974	25	3	9	14	4	8	9	8	5	3
Over/to PC	15	3	8	12	3	6	8	5	4	2
Over/to NDP	10	0	1	2	1	2	1	3	1	1
1972	7	4	6	6	13	11	10	6	12	12
Over/to PC	3	4	5	3	12	8	9	3	10	10
Over/to NDP	4	0	1	3	1	3	1	3	2	2
1968	22	10	8	17	7	9	8	5	1	0
Over/to PC	13	5	5	9	7	3	8	5	1	0
Over/to NDP	9	5	3	8	0	6	0	0	0	0

Source: Office of the Prime Minister, *1974/1972/1968 Ontario Election Results*, Ottawa, 1974, Appendix 4.

Table 3-4

HYPOTHETICAL ELECTION RESULTS IN ONTARIO, ASSUMING NINE VARIATIONS OF THE 1974 VOTE

	Toronto			Rest of Ontario			Total		
	Liberal	PC	NDP	Liberal	PC	NDP	Liberal	PC	NDP
5% Liberal increase from:									
PC	24	1	1	49	9	5	73	9	6
NDP	24	2	0	41	16	5	65	18	5
Both	24	2	0	44	13	5	68	15	5
5% PC increase from:									
Liberal	11	13	2	27	29	6	38	42	8
NDP	19	6	1	34	23	5	53	29	6
Both	15	10	1	30	26	6	45	36	7
5% NDP increase from:									
Liberal	16	5	5	33	23	6	49	28	11
PC	20	2	4	40	16	6	60	18	10
Both	18	3	5	34	22	6	52	25	11
1974 results	21	2	2	34	23	6	55	25	8

Source: Office of the Prime Minister, *1974/1972/1968 Ontario Election Results*, Ottawa, 1974, Appendixes 7-10.

reestablished the Quebec-Central Canada confederation in his first term. He regained Ontario in his second term. Now he faces the challenge of bringing the prairie provinces back into the federation through the Liberal party.[44] Whether the flexible Liberal party that, even under an antinationalist leader, could take on nationalist hues in the 1974 election campaign, can manage to bring the western provinces back into the Liberal fold is uncertain. Whether Trudeau can pull off a third political coup remains to be seen. But, as one observer put it in answering a hot-line caller after the election, "Lady, when a man like Trudeau has both his sons born on Christmas Day, he has something special going for him up There."

---

[44] Interview with Jerry Grafstein, 18 October 1974.

4
THE PROGRESSIVE CONSERVATIVE PARTY IN THE ELECTION OF 1974

George Perlin

Background

From Dominant to Minority Status. In the first three decades of confederation the Progressive Conservative party (then called the Liberal-Conservative party) won six out of seven federal elections.[1] Since 1891, however, the party has won only six out of twenty-four federal elections. This transformation from dominant to minority party status is largely due to the party's failure to compete effectively among the French Catholic community, which constitutes four-fifths of the population of Quebec.

The Conservatives' alienation of Quebec has deep historical roots. Conflict between French Catholics in Quebec and English Protestants in Ontario had immobilized government in Canada before confederation. The federal constitution established by confederation, of which Sir John A. Macdonald, the Conservative leader, had been a principal architect, attempted to deal with this problem by delegating to the provinces the authority to legislate on matters of language and religion. For a time this mechanism worked and Macdonald was able to build a Conservative majority which cut across the traditional cleavages. But linguistic and religious issues could not be kept out of federal politics. In 1885 Macdonald refused to commute the death sentence imposed on Louis Riel, a French-speaking métis who had led an armed rebellion against the civil authority in western Canada. Riel's hanging, which was bitterly opposed by French-Canadians,

---

[1] The party has changed its name several times. The current name, Progressive Conservative, is frequently abbreviated in one of three forms: "PC," "P.C.," or simply "Conservative."

inflamed opinion against the Conservative party in Quebec, with the result that the Conservative majority in Quebec was overturned.

Defeat in Quebec became self-perpetuating. Left in the control of an English Protestant majority, which remained persistently insensitive to French-Canadian opinion, the party continued to make decisions that offended French-Canadian voters and permitted Quebec to become a Liberal party stronghold. Only once since 1887 has the Conservative party been able to win a majority in Quebec. Its normal share of Quebec's seats has been less than 20 percent. Thus the party has been excluded from significant support in a province which elects more than one-quarter of the members of the federal Parliament.

At one time the Conservatives could count upon a countervailing majority in Ontario. In the fourteen elections from 1878 to 1930 they won a majority in Ontario twelve times and secured one plurality and one tie. But as Ontario developed a predominantly industrial-urban character, the concern of its English-speaking Protestants with the issues of language and religion, which had bound them to the Conservative party, gave way to new concerns, and the Conservative majority was broken. In the thirteen federal elections since 1935, the Liberals have won Ontario nine times. Today the Conservatives have no secure base with which to offset the Liberal advantage in Quebec.[2]

The Conservative party has survived as the only serious rival to Liberal power for two reasons. First, provincial Conservative parties have continued to compete at the level of government or official opposition in all but three provinces. Provincial leaders, responding to their own needs and to the pressures of intergovernmental relations in a federal system, have frequently limited their support to the national party, but the existence of competitive provincial parties is of symbolic value to the national party and assures it of access to some minimal level of financial and organizational assistance. In the five provinces—Prince Edward Island, Nova Scotia, New Brunswick, Ontario, and Manitoba—in which the Conservatives have been most successful provincially, they have consistently had a larger than average share of the popular vote in federal elections. The provinces

---

2 There is a popular belief that the three prairie provinces—Manitoba, Saskatchewan, and Alberta—have constituted a solid Conservative base since the 1958 election. In fact, the Conservatives have only done consistently well in one of these provinces, Alberta. On the other hand, the Liberal party has had very little success in the prairie region since 1958. In this sense it may be argued that the prairies, with forty-five seats, constitute, on a somewhat smaller scale, the same kind of problem for the Liberals that Quebec constitutes for the Conservatives.

Table 4-1

CRITICAL STAGES IN THE ELECTORAL HISTORY
OF THE FEDERAL CONSERVATIVE PARTY

Period	Number of Elections	Elections with Conservative Majority or Plurality	Conservative Popular Vote		
			Highest	Lowest	Mean
1867–1891 [a]	6	5	53%	46%	51%
1896–1917 [b]	6	2	51 [c]	47	49
1921–1930 [d]	4	2	49	30	43
1935–1974	13	3	54	27	34

[a] The assignment of party votes in the first three elections after confederation is rather arbitrary since a number of candidates ran as independents, although later voting with one of the parties.

[b] In 1917 the Conservatives campaigned in coalition with conscriptionist Liberals.

[c] The 1917 election was not included in this calculation.

[d] In the 1925 election the Conservatives elected 116 members and the Liberals 99, but the Conservatives did not form a ministry because the Liberals chose to meet Parliament. In 1926 they briefly formed the government and then were defeated in a new election.

Sources: Data compiled from J. Murray Beck, *Pendulum of Power, Canada's Federal Elections*, Toronto, 1968, and Reports of the Chief Electoral Officer, Ottawa.

in which the party has remained a major competitor at the provincial level include these five, plus Alberta and Newfoundland.[3]

Second, in the Anglophone provinces, the Conservative party, in contrast to the smaller parties, the New Democratic party on the left and Social Credit on the right, has been able to adapt its appeal to the conditions of a country which is divided by cultural and economic characteristics into distinctive regional societies. Regionalism in the form of a strong attachment to regional and provincial political identities has persistently blunted the effect of appeals to interests cutting across regional boundaries. The Conservative party, which seeks to accommodate a broad range of socioeconomic interests and which has adapted itself to this characteristic of the Canadian political culture, has been better able than the smaller parties to mobilize interregional support.

---

[3] It should be noted that, although the party has been weaker historically in Alberta and Newfoundland, both provinces now have PC provincial governments.

Social Structure of the Party. Data presented elsewhere in this volume show that, despite its aggregative strategy, the Conservative party does not draw its support in the same proportion from all groups in Canadian society.[4] Reflecting these patterns, members of the Conservative party's parliamentary caucus are predominantly English-speaking, Protestant, and from small towns and rural communities. Their socioeconomic status, as might be expected, differs significantly from that of the party's voters in that most members of Parliament come from high status and/or high-paying occupations. This is also true of people active in leading roles in the extra-parliamentary party. But in other respects members of the extra-parliamentary elite are much more representative of Canadian society as a whole.[5] This has created a special problem for the party because it has meant that on many issues of both public policy and political strategy the extra-parliamentary party and the parliamentary party have had different perspectives.

Party Policy. It has been argued that in ideological temperament and tradition the Progressive Conservative party is quite similar to the Conservative party of Britain. According to this view, the model of a conservative as a laissez-faire economic liberal—the image usually evoked to describe American conservatives—does not fit the mainstream of opinion in the Canadian party.

Robert Stanfield, current leader of the Progressive Conservative party, says the fundamental principle of Canadian conservatism is a belief in the achievement of freedom through the recognition and maintenance of social order.[6] This implies more than just "law and order." It implies a conception of the community as an integrated whole, respect for the mutual responsibility of all members of society toward one another, and a belief that the public interest transcends

---

[4] See John Meisel, "The Party System and the 1974 Election," Chapter 1 of this volume.

[5] This is because the formal structures of the extra-parliamentary party have been organized in a manner which ensures that all regions and all constituencies are fully represented. Data on the characteristics of members of the extra-parliamentary elite have been gathered in two studies, one by the author in collaboration with Professors H. G. Thorburn and J. K. Lele of Queen's University, and the other by the author. The joint study embraces surveys of delegates to the national leadership conventions of the Progressive Conservative party in 1967, the Liberal party in 1968, and the New Democratic party in 1971. The other study consists of a survey of delegates to the biennial meeting of the Progressive Conservative Association of Canada in 1971.

[6] This account of Stanfield's position is taken from the text of a memorandum he circulated on 14 November 1974 to members of the Progressive Conservative parliamentary caucus.

any particular private interest. The history of the party demonstrates that while Canadian Conservatives believe in private enterprise, they have been willing to use the power of the state to intervene in the economy to protect the interests of weaker members of society or to pursue purposes deemed to be in the broader collective interest. As Stanfield puts it, the philosophical tradition to which the Progressive Conservative party belongs holds that "self-reliance and enterprise should be encouraged, but [it] does not place private enterprise in a central position around which everything else revolves." [7]

Extensive interviews with a sample of the current party elite suggest, however, that Canadian Conservatives are less willing to use state power than Canadian Liberals. Members of the sample commonly opposed what they called "Liberal statism," that is, what they believe to be the Liberal party's conception of state action as a sufficient and desirable instrument for dealing with any social problem. This distinction between the two parties is confirmed by data from surveys of delegates to the Conservative and Liberal national leadership conventions of 1967 and 1968.[8] Substantially larger numbers of Conservative delegates agreed that "government interferes too much with business," "too much money is spent on welfare," and "social security benefits, such as old age pensions and family allowances, should only be paid to those who need them."

While the Conservative party as a whole opposes the Liberals on this question, there are invariably disagreements among Conservatives themselves about the scope and need for government action with respect to specific issues. This has given rise to a view, frequently asserted in the press, that the party is deeply divided between "progressive" and "conservative" wings. Analysis of data from the 1967 convention survey and from a separate study of delegates to the 1971 biennial meeting of the National Association [9] suggests that this ideological divergence has been exaggerated. Relatively few members of the two samples take consistently opposed views on all issues, or to put it another way, most members of the two samples

[7] Ibid., p. 12.

[8] These are the surveys to which reference is made in note 5 above.

[9] National Association is the term most often used to refer to the Progressive Conservative Association of Canada, the integrating structure which embraces all elements of the extra-parliamentary party and the parliamentary caucus. The main continuing responsibilities of the National Association are vaguely defined, but it has one specific formal power of considerable importance: its constitution authorizes it to convene party leadership conventions. In addition to this role in leadership selection, the association usually debates and adopts policy resolutions at its biennial meeting. Its policy decisions have no formal authority, however, and are not in any sense binding on the party.

take positions from issue to issue which diverge in a variety of patterns. The only issues on which there is any significant linking of opinion are those of a regional and cultural nature. For example, substantial minorities among both samples opposed both special language rights for French-speaking Canadians and proposals to grant a special constitutional status to the province of Quebec.

The Leader. Ultimately, party policy at any given time is what the party leader declares it to be. This authoritative role of the leader is partly inherent in the nature of parliamentary government. The only members of the party who have the capacity to give public effect to party policy are the leader and his colleagues in Parliament. They alone have the power to create public policy. In principle this is a shared power, but the leader is recognized to have the continuing and untrammeled right to make overriding pronouncements on behalf of the parliamentary caucus or to designate others to make such pronouncements. This right can be ascribed both to the leader's broadly based legitimacy—he is the only figure in Parliament who is chosen by a body representative of all elements of the party (a national convention)—and to the practical consideration that only the leader can embody the collective will of the caucus when the caucus is not assembled. It can also be ascribed to the emphasis placed on leadership in the party's internal system of values—an emphasis incorporated from the British conservative tradition. In addition, because of the party's efforts to embrace the full range of regional interests that comprise Canadian society, the leader has had a special role in giving symbolic expression to the party, of giving it both coherence and cohesion. It is not surprising, therefore, that the party has found a symbol for its failures in its leaders. Since the death of Macdonald in 1891, except during the tenure of Sir Robert Borden from 1901 to 1921, there has been recurring conflict over the party leadership. No leader has long remained unchallenged and no leader since Borden has left office without some conflict, usually ill-concealed.

Each conflict over the leadership has left the party scarred. The Conservative party's fractiousness and reputation for fractiousness have had two serious consequences. First, in any parliamentary system party cohesion is essential to effective government. It is all the more important in a country in which national unity remains a vital political issue. Thus the party's appearance of disunity casts doubt upon its competence to govern. Second, to the extent that any party is absorbed in internal conflict, its efficiency in the performance of its organizational tasks is impaired. In this sense the party may be said to be caught in a minority party syndrome. Because it is unsuccessful it is internally unstable, and because it is internally unstable it is unsuccessful.

Stanfield's Leadership. Robert Stanfield's assumption of the Conservative leadership in 1967 was the climax of the most extended and debilitating leadership conflict in the history of the party. The convention which chose Stanfield as leader was called only after a three-year struggle by Stanfield's predecessor, John Diefenbaker, to retain the leadership. Diefenbaker had been prime minister from 1957 to 1963, leader of the first Conservative government since 1935. Divisions within his cabinet, focusing on his leadership, had been an important factor in the defeat of his government. In 1964 and 1965 dissatisfaction with his leadership spread through sections of the extra-parliamentary party, but, supported by a majority of his colleagues in the parliamentary caucus, he successfully resisted attempts to submit his leadership to review.

Constitutionally his opponents had no means to test Diefenbaker's leadership because the rules of the National Association, which has the constitutional authority to call leadership conventions for the party, contained no provision to limit the tenure of the leader. As a result, the anti-Diefenbaker groups were compelled to wage a public campaign to persuade the association to adopt a special resolution providing for leadership review. This resolution was adopted by the biennial meeting of the association in November 1966, and a leadership convention was called for September 1967.

The conflict over Diefenbaker's leadership created factional divisions within the party which have troubled it ever since. Stanfield's leadership was never wholly accepted because he was closely identified with Dalton Camp who, as president of the National Association, had led the campaign for leadership review. In the caucus a small but vocal group of members who had been loyal to Diefenbaker publicly expressed their criticism of Stanfield at every opportunity.

A second legacy of the Diefenbaker conflict was a seriously weakened party organization. Organization has always been a problem for the party. It is particularly weak at the constituency level for several reasons: the party does not have sufficient resources to employ paid constituency staff; since there is no partisan involvement in municipal politics in Canada, there is no continuing focus for local party activity; and the party's minority status deprives it of access to patronage resources with which to induce participation. The Diefenbaker conflict aggravated this problem. One effect was to drive some local members out of active party politics. Eventually the factional divisions among the party elite infected the constituency associations, so that, when Stanfield assumed the leadership, the local organization of the party was in a condition of minimal effectiveness.

The national organization had been similarly weakened. National headquarters, which is the main administrative arm of the party, had been caught between its responsibility to serve the interests of the party as a whole and its responsibility to carry out the will of the leader. Since the national director, the party's chief administrative officer, owes his appointment to the leader, national headquarters, in effect, had organized the resistance to the review of Diefenbaker's leadership. Quite apart from this, its main administrative efforts had been directed first toward the biennial meeting of 1966, and then toward the leadership convention of 1967; its responsibilities for election organization had been completely neglected.

The Progressive Conservative party, therefore, was totally unprepared for the general election called in 1968. Its difficulties were compounded by the fact that Stanfield's leadership was ineffective in mobilizing popular support. A cautious and hesitant speaker, he presented a dull and uninspiring image in contrast with the dynamism, strength, and excitement generated by the new Liberal leader, Pierre Trudeau. The outcome was the election of a Liberal majority government, the first majority government the country had had since Diefenbaker's landslide victory in 1958.

Following the 1968 election, Stanfield's main objectives were to restore party unity, to rebuild the party organization, and to create a more favorable public image for the party. One part of his strategy for achieving these objectives consisted in engaging the party in an extended series of policy discussions leading to the formulation of a new and comprehensive statement of Conservative policy. He hoped by this means not only to improve the party's image, but also to recruit candidates and party workers and to find a consensus through which to unite the party behind his leadership. Another part of his strategy was to reconstruct the national party organization. This involved both administrative reforms in national headquarters and the creation of new organizational structures. These efforts had little effect on the traditional weaknesses in constituency organization, but they produced important innovations in national campaign structures. The most important of these was the establishment of a national campaign planning committee in the fall of 1971. This committee undertook to establish and direct campaign organization for the election expected in 1972, adopting the new techniques of professional campaign management which had been developed in the United States during the 1960s.

Despite Stanfield's efforts to achieve party unity, the party's defeat in 1968 had further weakened his leadership and encouraged his opponents in the caucus to take actions designed to embarrass him. While the anti-Stanfield group was not strong enough to force his resignation, it remained a constant irritant and a reminder of Stanfield's failure to impose his authority on the party. This, in turn, reinforced his image of incompetence in contrast with Trudeau. The persistence of this image in the popular consciousness was a serious handicap to the party in the 1972 election campaign. The Trudeau administration's popular support had declined sharply, but up until the very last stages of the campaign party and public polls showed that voters were reluctant to accept the Conservatives as an alternative. The stalemate that was the outcome of the 1972 election reflected popular ambivalence toward the Conservative party as much as it demonstrated the failure of Trudeau's leadership.

Conservative strategy in the new Parliament, which met in January 1973, was predicated on the assumption that the shift toward the party in the 1972 election would gather momentum and propel it to certain victory in a new election. As a result, the party's main objective was to force a new election as quickly as possible. To do this it would need the support of the New Democratic party, but the NDP, having made a similar assumption about the likely outcome of an early election and fearing that it would be caught in a reaction against minority government, was determined to keep the Liberals in office as long as it could. It was soon apparent that the Conservative strategy was in considerable trouble. If there was any prospect of securing cooperation from the NDP, it was diminished by inflammatory attacks on the NDP by some members of the Conservative caucus. In addition, in its aggressive efforts to bring the government down, the party exposed itself to the criticism that it was more interested in achieving office than in producing solutions to national problems. As the session wore on, the Conservative position in the House of Commons, and in the country, grew weaker.[10]

Adding to the party's difficulties was the Liberal response to the 1972 election. The government initiated several changes in policy

---

[10] In a Canadian Institute of Public Opinion national survey in November 1972, 29 percent of the sample expressed a preference for the Conservatives and 28 percent for the Liberals. In another CIPO survey in April 1973, 23 percent preferred the Conservatives and 30 percent for the Liberals. The party's own survey in September 1973 reported a somewhat smaller spread between the two parties (five points) but the Liberals were still ahead. The variations among the three surveys are partly accounted for by shifts in the proportions of voters who expressed a preference for the New Democratic party and the proportions who expressed no preference.

with a view to reducing the effect of the criticism that it was remote, insensitive, and unresponsive to popular concerns. As a result, some of the more effective points in the Conservative case against the government were blunted. Particularly damaging was the fact that some of the government's policy changes had been adopted from the Conservatives, which left the opposition with little basis for criticizing the government program. Stanfield expressed the frustration of his party during a debate in 1973: "We have a lame duck Liberal government, bargaining with the New Democratic Party to keep it in office so that it may attempt to implement some Progressive Conservative policy." [11]

Other events also contributed to the deterioration of the Conservative party's position. The most important of these occurred in June when the government introduced a resolution asking Parliament to affirm its support for the principles of the policy of official bilingualism. Stanfield was anxious to ensure full Conservative support for this resolution, both because he was convinced of the intrinsic merit of the policy and because he wanted to strengthen the party's position in Quebec where it had won only two seats in 1972. However, sixteen members of the Conservative caucus voted against the resolution. The effect was threefold: the party was cast once again in an anti-French posture, even though most of its members had supported the resolution; Stanfield's personal image of weakness was reinforced; and the party's reputation for internal fractiousness was revived.

The party's vulnerability to internal conflict was exposed yet again at the biennial meeting of the National Association in March 1974, when a fight developed over the election of the national president. The elements of factionalism left over from the old controversy about Diefenbaker's leadership were played up in the press. To the external observer the Progressive Conservative party seemed totally bound up in old feuds which had little relevance to the problems of governing Canada. Just six weeks later the Conservatives and New Democrats joined to defeat the government's budget and precipitate a new election.

In retrospect it is difficult to understand why the Progressive Conservative party ever allowed itself to become involved in this maneuver. The party's survey research firm had been interviewing for a week when the vote was taken in the House; daily tabulation of the results would have shown that it was not a propitious moment

---

11 *House of Commons Debates*, vol. 117, no. 3, p. 47.

for the Conservatives to force an election. When the survey was completed, it revealed that, among voters who had formed voting intentions, the Conservatives had lost all of the gains they had made since the beginning of the 1972 campaign.[12] One source claims that the party's House strategists were never informed of this change in the party's electoral popularity. Another explanation is that, even if they were informed, they were disposed to ignore it because there was not likely to be for some time another opportunity to bring the Liberal government down. Furthermore, the party's electoral strategists may have been inclined to doubt the survey, because there was a substantial discrepancy, overrepresenting the Liberals, between the reported voting behavior of members of the sample in 1972 and the actual 1972 election results. The 1974 sample, too, might have overrepresented Liberal support among the electorate. In any event, it is clear that a very large majority in the parliamentary caucus, and of the party's key election planners, wanted the election.

The Conservative Party in the 1974 Election

Campaign Organization. Following the 1972 election, for the first time in its history the Conservative party established a permanent organization concerned exclusively with campaign planning. A new position (director of campaign planning) with unprecedented powers was created for the head of this organization. The terms of reference were drafted by Malcolm Wickson, a former national director of the party and director of operations for the 1972 campaign, who was appointed to the new position. The terms of reference interposed the director of campaign planning between the party leader and every other staff and support structure in the party, including, for some purposes, the personal staff of the leader and the party's parliamentary research office (a publicly funded body that assists members of Parliament in the execution of their legislative responsibilities). Wickson was made responsible for all campaign-related functions, including the "overall election plan," the appointment of personnel, the preparation and administration of the campaign budget, the direction of "the operations aspect of . . . provincial campaign organizations," and candidate recruitment. He was further empowered to "advise and

---

[12] In the party's survey in May 1974, 21 percent of the sample expressed a preference for the Conservatives and 32 percent for the Liberals. This eleven point spread was larger than that in any other party or published survey since September 1972.

be advised on matters that relate to Policy and Issue Development, Programming and Scheduling, and Speech Content" for the leader.[13]

This comprehensive grant of powers posed serious problems. For one thing, the emphasis on tactical and administrative responsibilities left the principal campaign official, the person responsible for the "overall election plan," with little time for the development of strategy—yet this responsibility was specifically assigned to him. In addition, the highly centralized campaign structure was incompatible with the forces of provincialism and localism in the Canadian political culture and with the decentralized and federative nature of Canadian party structures.

The leading figures in the organization which Wickson created were committed to the principles of the "new politics." Paradoxically, most of them were technocrats, even though one thrust of the Conservative campaign in 1972 had been to attack the technocratic style of the Liberals. They were thoroughly convinced of the efficacy of their organizational skills and the structures they had created [14]—so much so that an obsessive concern with the organization as an end in itself became one of the weaknesses of the Conservative campaign.[15] Associated with this technocratic obsession was an extraordinary secretiveness. For example, some survey information relating to Stanfield's personal image was never shown to him and some senior members of the party with important roles in the campaign complained that they could not get information from the survey which they needed to make decisions about campaign tactics.[16] Another

---

[13] *Terms of Reference for Director of Campaign Planning*, party document, no date.

[14] In an interview, the party's national director, John Laschinger, claimed the improvement in the party's performance in the 1972 election as against 1968 was the result of improvements in campaign structure and of the adoption of new organizational and campaigning techniques.

[15] One illustration was the charge by Wickson early in the campaign that the Liberals had copied, for use in their own manual, sections of the Conservative campaign manual for candidates. The charge was represented as an important issue in the campaign and was accompanied by a warning from the campaign's legal officer that legal action was being considered. The manual contained no confidential information related to the campaign and no information which would not be available from the conventional literature on advertising and campaign techniques.

[16] The author has had extended interviews with more than forty persons who had leading roles in the 1972 and 1974 campaigns, including most of the principal officials of the party and key persons in the campaign organizations in four provinces. To protect sources, most of the information relating to the two campaigns which is reported here is not attributed. No piece of evidence is reported unless it was corroborated by at least two persons other than the original source. In some cases where personal opinions are involved or there is no question of breaking a confidence, specific attributions have been made.

weakness lay in the use of skills available to the campaign organization. While success demanded a high level of expertise in each role, friendship networks were the principal mechanism of recruitment. As a result, many roles were filled by persons with no special competence, while the skills of others were never properly employed.

These weaknesses were reinforced by structural defects, in particular a lack or clarity in role definition and insufficient coordination of tasks among the different parts of the organization. In this situation, the location of part of the organization in Toronto and part in Ottawa, despite its functional logic, aggravated intra-organizational tensions and impaired efficiency. Similar problems had beset the campaign organization in 1972, but perhaps one reason they were not recognized and solved in 1974 was the widespread feeling that, at least in a tactical sense, the 1972 election had been a Conservative victory. People who held that opinion believed that since the Conservatives had begun the 1972 campaign at a serious disadvantage they had done well just to come close to the Liberals. The campaign, therefore, was viewed as a success and it was believed that there was no need to adjust campaign structures and organizational techniques in 1974.

Campaign Strategy. An important assumption behind the Conservative strategy for 1974 was that the swing toward the party which had begun in the second half of the 1972 campaign had retained its momentum. Therefore it was decided that the 1974 campaign should be treated as an extension of the 1972 campaign. This decision contributed to the further decision that Stanfield should be the central focus for the 1974 campaign. The analysis of 1972 explained the party's disadvantage in polls at the beginning of the campaign in terms of the relative strength of the personal images of Stanfield and Trudeau. In this view the main problem had been to alter the public images of the two leaders, and this had been partially accomplished. It was argued that the Conservative attack on the government had cast doubt on Trudeau's leadership qualities, but that there had not been sufficient time to develop a strong positive image for Stanfield as prime minister. The objective in 1974, therefore, would be to convince voters that Stanfield possessed the qualities to be prime minister.

The party's national survey at the beginning of the campaign confirmed that Stanfield was still thought of as considerably less "strong," "competent," and "intelligent" than Trudeau, and most respondents thought these qualities very important for a prime minister. In addition, substantially larger percentages of the sample said Trudeau would be best able to handle problems in eight out of nine areas of public policy. It did not follow, however, that the only strategy open to the Conservatives was to focus on building a more favorable image for Stanfield. Indeed, it could be argued that this was the least promising strategy, since Stanfield's disadvantage had been fixed in the popular consciousness since 1968 and was therefore unlikely to be changed by a six-week campaign. There were at least two alternatives. One was to run a policy-centered campaign built around the comprehensive range of detailed proposals in thirty-one policy papers prepared for discussion at the biennial meeting in March. The second was to concentrate not on Stanfield's personal image as prime minister, but on the collective image of a team of Conservative leaders, the prospective members of Parliament from whom a Conservative cabinet would be chosen.

Neither of these options was seriously considered. It was believed by the key figures in the campaign organization that the personal image of the leader "is what is most important" in determining the voting behavior of Canadians.[17] This, however, was an untested assumption never examined in the party's own survey research and certainly not accepted as established truth in other research on Canadian voting. Why, then, were the campaign planners so thoroughly committed to it? One possible explanation is that they were influenced by the importance of "the leader" in the value system of the party. Another is that, in adopting American ideas about electoral politics and campaign techniques, they had failed to recognize that the emphasis on personal image in the American model is, at least in part, a function of necessity, imposed by the fact that there are separate elections for executive and legislative offices in the United States. The separation of powers in the United States emphasizes individual rather than collective responsibility. Thus, in American campaigns gubernatorial and presidential candidates do not have the option of merging their images with those of candidates for legislative office.

Their survey research provided Conservative strategists with convincing evidence that inflation should be the main issue in their campaign. Nearly 90 percent of a national sample interviewed in May ranked inflation the most important current problem in Canada, and 55 percent disapproved of the Trudeau government's handling of it. But apart from identifying the issue, the survey offered the

---

[17] Norman Atkins, interview with the author. Although Atkins had no publicly specified role, he was a leading figure in guiding the national campaign.

party little encouragement. Only 27 percent of the sample said the election of a Conservative government could improve the handling of inflation, and most of these people identified with the Conservative party to begin with. In addition, 55 percent of the sample believed the election of a Conservative government would have no effect on inflation, and 50 percent said inflation was a world problem which was beyond the control of any Canadian government.

More important, there was a serious flaw in the party's research. The survey contained no question designed to evaluate responses to the Conservative policy of wage and price controls. The only question which dealt with policy was open-ended, asking simply what should be done about inflation. Not surprisingly, 34 percent of the respondents gave the tautological answer, "control prices." But there was a warning to the party: only 13 percent of the sample proposed wage controls. Apparently this warning went unobserved, for wage and price controls became the main plank in the party's platform.

It may be argued that this decision was inescapable, since the party was already committed to a policy of controls. The principle of a compulsory incomes policy had been accepted by the finance committee of the parliamentary caucus as early as January 1973. But the substance of the policy had not been settled, and Stanfield had considerable latitude to define it so as to minimize its adverse political effects. In addition, he had the option of reducing the emphasis on controls, making them not the centerpiece of the party's platform, but just one part of a broader anti-inflationary program. This was a viable option to the extent that the policy papers contained a wide range of proposals which could have been tied to an anti-inflation campaign. It appears to have been rejected for two reasons. First, several of the policy papers had been published during the 1972 campaign, and there was some feeling that if they were used again it might appear that the party had nothing new to say. Second, it was felt that the tough controls policy could be used to cast Stanfield as a strong and decisive leader: policy would be exploited in the campaign merely as an adjunct to the strategy of convincing the electorate that Stanfield had the ability to be prime minister.

Stanfield's first national tour was organized around a series of press conferences in which his mettle could be publicly tested. The result was disastrous. Stanfield was questioned intensively about the details of his prices and incomes policy, and he gave answers which seemed evasive and contradictory. Pressed by the journalists, he conceded that parts of the program had not been worked out and indicated that there would be exemptions from controls for certain groups. Far from demonstrating his competence and strength, Stanfield's performance on the tour reinforced his established image.

Stanfield and his advisors had failed to anticipate either the aggressiveness of the press or the vulnerability of the incomes policy. The journalists, of course, were simply doing their job. Stanfield had not been subject to the same critical scrutiny in 1972 because his tour arrangements in that campaign had prevented close contact with the press. At the same time, the Conservative strategy, the changed competitive position of the party, and the Liberal strategy, all demanded Stanfield be assessed as a potential prime minister. For some members of the circle around Stanfield, the press very quickly became the scapegoat for the faltering Conservative campaign. There may have been some truth in Conservative complaints—every campaign has its share of inaccurate and partisan reporting [18]—but the real problem was with the party, not the press.

Stanfield had only himself to blame for the vulnerability of his policy. The substance of the policy had never been worked out, either in preparation for the campaign or in anticipation of the need to apply it.[19] At a caucus in May, James Gillies, who had first proposed the incomes policy, while urging that it be given "the hard sell," had joined others in warning of its adverse political implications. Stanfield's campaign advisors had argued, however, that he should avoid public discussion of substantive proposals, and their advice was consistent with his own disposition. Stanfield's approach to conflict resolution is to seek consensus. He has always tried to formulate policy statements in general terms that permit the adherence of the largest number of interests. The difficulty was that, in this case, general language provoked maximum concern. The benefits of an incomes policy were cast in doubt by the Liberal argument that inflation is an international problem for which there is no domestic solution; meanwhile, all groups with any leverage to adjust their incomes feared that controls would deprive them of their only defense against inflation.

---

[18] The party was particularly concerned about what it believed to be partisan coverage by the publicly owned Canadian Broadcasting Corporation. The CBC's main telecasts were monitored and data compiled on the relative coverage accorded each party's campaign. As a result complaints were made to the CBC and a meeting was held between representatives of the party and the corporation. Subsequently the CBC announced that it would ensure that all parties had proportionate coverage.

[19] Stanfield had had advice from leading economists about the principle of wage and price controls, but no independent professional advice was ever sought about the details of its application. There was no professional economist on Stanfield's personal staff or among the staff of the parliamentary research office.

This problem was soon apparent to Conservative candidates in the constituencies. The parliamentary research office was receiving "as many as forty or fifty calls a day" from candidates who wanted to know how to answer specific questions about the scope, duration, and administration of controls.[20] Yet for three weeks the directors of the campaign rejected suggestions for the preparation of a comprehensive statement explaining the substance of the policy. Staff from the research office provided answers to the questions asked of Stanfield and the candidates as they arose but there was never any single comprehensive statement of the policy from which they could work. When a substantive statement was finally prepared for distribution in the constituencies, its form—a pamphlet of questions and answers about inflation—reflected the ad hoc evolution of the policy.

Bewildered candidates, left to their own devices, responded to the situation in different ways. Some, like the former leader, John Diefenbaker, virtually renounced the policy. Others tried to make the policy credible by working out their own explanations of its content. Still others focused their explanations on the principle of wage and price control, and assured their audiences of the party's good intentions. There was considerable pressure from some candidates to jettison the controls policy, despite the obvious devastation this would wreak upon the whole campaign. Only Stanfield's firmness in private meetings prevented defections.[21] But this was not sufficient to conceal the dissension within the party from the press—or from the public.

On Stanfield's second national tour, because he was less exposed to direct examination by the press he found himself accused of backing away from the incomes policy. It got to the point where he could never leave the controls policy out of a speech without provoking comment. His own wry observation on the situation was, "If I were to walk on water the press would say it was because I couldn't swim."[22] In effect he had lost the ability to choose his own course. The direction of the campaign had been set and he would have to follow.

The Conservatives were unable to reverse this pattern in their advertising campaign because their media strategy was inflexible. The budget was largely committed to a radio and television spot campaign,

[20] Geoffrey Molyneux, director of the Progressive Conservative parliamentary research office, interview with the author.

[21] The policy was challenged directly by some of the party's candidates at meetings between Stanfield and groups of candidates in Toronto and Montreal.

[22] Bill Grogan, interview with the author. Grogan is Stanfield's principal personal assistant and speech writer.

the content of which had been fixed soon after the election was called. The only substantial print advertisement was a rotogravure newspaper insert that was to be published in the last week of the campaign, but which had to be prepared five weeks before it was to be published. For contractual, budgetary, and technical reasons, the basic advertising plan could not be altered to accommodate the direction that campaign events were taking.[23]

Candidates. Manifest disunity among Conservative candidates contributed to Stanfield's difficulties. The prices and incomes policy was only one source of dissension. Several candidates held views that were inconsistent with those of the leader on a wide range of issues. But Stanfield had had no control over the selection of candidates. Wickson had asked for a mandate to engage in candidate recruitment, but there is no evidence that he ever attempted to do this. In fact, even if he had, it is unlikely that he could have had much success. Progressive Conservative candidates are chosen by the constituency associations at nominating conventions in which any member of the local party can participate. This procedure accords maximum weight to the local organization and to the powerful localist sentiment characteristic of the Canadian political culture. The "parachuting" of candidates from outside a riding has never been a common practice.

To the extent that there was any recruitment of candidates, it was done by provincial campaign committees, but they had to act with considerable care to avoid offending constituency party elites. Quebec was the only province in which there was extensive intervention, and there it was a function of necessity: Conservative constituency organization is so weak in Quebec that recruitment at the provincial level is necessary just to ensure that every riding has a candidate. But, generally speaking, parachuting is only considered acceptable when a local association cannot find a candidate itself. There was very little parachuting in 1974. In most ridings the candidates were local residents chosen without the participation of either the national or the provincial campaign committee.

There were a few notable exceptions to this pattern.[24] In particular when Leonard Jones was nominated as the Conservative candi-

---

[23] Attempts were made to explain the controls policy in two television broadcasts and one national newspaper advertisement. Although the party was in a position to make changes in its television and radio spot commercials, these were too brief to be used effectively for this purpose.

[24] One notable exception was the candidacy of Duff Roblin, a former Conservative premier of Manitoba, in the Ontario riding of Peterborough. Roblin had been living in Montreal since his defeat as a federal candidate in 1968. Although

date in Moncton, New Brunswick, Stanfield refused to accept him. Jones, the mayor of Moncton, had become a national symbol of anti-French prejudice by refusing to permit the use of French in the municipal government of Moncton, where 30 percent of the population is French-speaking, and by challenging the constitutionality of the federal Official Languages Act in the Supreme Court. Stanfield was personally repelled by the views with which Jones was identified and feared that his acceptance of Jones would undermine the party's attempts to build support among French-Canadians. There was no explicit authority in the party constitution for Stanfield's action and it had no precedent, but the Moncton constituency executive complied with his decision and submitted the incumbent member of Parliament, whom Jones had defeated at the nominating convention, as its candidate. As a result, Jones ran as an independent candidate, splitting the local constituency membership and attracting support from sympathizers all across the country.

The Jones candidacy was damaging to the Conservative campaign in three ways. First, while Stanfield's action could be used to demonstrate his commitment to bilingualism, the fact that Jones had succeeded in winning the party's nomination emphasized that there were many Conservatives who opposed bilingualism. This problem was compounded by the fact that it was difficult to explain how Jones was different from several candidates who, as members of Parliament, had voted against bilingualism and whose right to run as Progressive Conservatives had not been challenged. Second, Stanfield's action could be construed as an abrogation of the principles of local autonomy and party democracy. Jones skillfully exploited this theme in the Moncton campaign, playing upon the fact that Stanfield had never discussed his views with him before denying his candidacy. Third, the incident drew attention once again to the divisive tendencies of the Progressive Conservative party. Paradoxically, therefore, although it demonstrated Stanfield's decisiveness and his willingness to be tough, it raised questions about the general competence of the Conservative party to act effectively as a government.

The Campaign in the Constituencies. Because the electorate can only express its preference by voting for a member of Parliament, the outcome of a Canadian federal election depends upon the outcome of the 265 separate constituency elections. Thus, each party's federal

---

the constituency executive apparently invited him to be its candidate (after his interest in running had been made known), his lack of local ties became an important issue in the campaign.

election campaign actually consists of two quite different parts: the national campaign, focused on the election of the party, which is seen collectively as a prospective government, and the constituency campaigns, focused on the election of the party's candidates, who are seen individually as prospective members of Parliament.

The constituency campaign is both a national campaign in miniature and a campaign with distinctive functions, in particular the myriad tasks associated with getting the party's supporters to the polls. It therefore requires elaborate organizational structure, large numbers of workers, and a great diversity of skills. It is difficult to be certain about how many Conservative constituency associations had adequate corps of workers or how many were organized to use them effectively. We have already observed that the quality of the party's local organization varies considerably, and there are no accurate records of party membership. Furthermore, even if a constituency association is relatively active and has a substantial membership, its members may be unwilling to perform the tasks required in the campaign. This author's analysis of two constituency campaigns in Ontario found that, while both riding associations had paid-up memberships of 1.5 percent of the eligible electorates in their ridings, the campaign committees were unable to recruit enough workers to complete more than 60 percent of the household canvasses which are a vital means of soliciting support and provide information for polling day activities.

A second problem revealed by these case studies was the limited expertise available at the constituency level. For example, both committees needed to prepare literature for household distribution, to produce and purchase radio and television commercials, and to design and place newspaper advertisements. The sophisticated skills needed for these purposes are uncommon in constituency associations, and few local campaign committees had the financial resources to employ professional advertising assistance. The committees dealt with this problem very differently. In one of the two cases examined for this paper, the committee had to rely entirely on the help of amateurs. In the other case the committee joined with campaign committees in three adjacent ridings to hire an advertising agency. Neither approach produced very satisfactory results.

The national campaign committee compensated for some of this weakness at the local level by providing constituency associations with a variety of materials and services. A candidate services division distributed to each constituency a campaign manual, a policy manual, supplies of posters and photographs of the leader, pamphlets for household distribution, canvass kits to be used in door-to-door campaigning, and, on request, a variety of other advertising materials, such as bumper stickers and buttons, with a national motif. In addition, in some provinces constituency committees received special briefings on campaign techniques, and all constituency committees were assisted with policy research by the staff of the parliamentary research office.

Although the candidate services division maintained regional desks to link the constituency committees with the national committee, the experience of the sample constituencies in Ontario suggests that some communications problems were not solved. Local officials complained, for example, that they were not informed either of the extent, scheduling, or content of commercials booked by the national committee on local radio and television stations, with the result that they could not properly plan their local advertising campaigns. Another problem for some constituency campaign committees was budgeting. In one of the two sample constituencies there were serious difficulties in campaign planning because financing was uncertain and the committee was unwilling to risk the accumulation of large debts. When it could not secure a definite commitment of support from the national party, it made a substantial cut in the major item of variable cost in its budget: local advertising. Three days before the election it received an unexpected financial supplement from the national campaign committee and wound up the campaign with a surplus. The irony was not appreciated by the committee, whose candidate lost by a relatively narrow margin which might have been reversed by a strong local advertising campaign.

Quite apart from these questions of organizational capabilities, the effectiveness of the party's constituency campaign depended upon the local relevance of national issues, the existence of distinctive local issues, and the personal attractiveness of local candidates. It would require an independent investigation of the campaign and voting behavior in every constituency to evaluate the relative significance of these variables. Their potential importance is illustrated, however, by the Moncton campaign in which a national issue, bilingualism, had special local salience; a local issue was created by Stanfield's intervention in the nominating process; and one of the candidates, Jones, had independent personal appeal because of his record as mayor. The Moncton result provides a striking example of the effect of local variables in the final outcome of the election. Jones won the Moncton seat and the Conservative incumbent ran third. The Conservative share of the vote fell from 51.9 percent to 12.1 percent.

There is good reason to believe that Moncton is not as exceptional as it might at first appear. Comparisons of constituency results, even in areas that are contiguous and socially very much alike, reveal wide variations in swings in party support. In Ontario, for example, while the Conservative vote for the province as a whole dropped by 3.3 percentage points, there were ten constituencies in which it either did not change or increased. Moreover, in the seventy-eight constituencies where it did fall, the extent of the loss varied from 0.6 percentage points to 19.2 percentage points. These figures are not presented in an attempt to dispute the significance of the national campaign, but rather to emphasize the need to take account of the effect of the constituency campaign. The fact is, of course, that the Conservative party did lose support in most Ontario constituencies, and there is reason to believe that its campaign had the effect of shifting votes from the New Democratic party to the Liberal party.[25] Ultimately the Conservative party's electoral failure in 1974 was the result of a failure in its national campaign.

Conclusion

This chapter has looked at the 1974 election in the light of the Progressive Conservative party's effectiveness as a party. Its thesis is that the party's persistent failure at the polls can be related to its internal divisiveness. Conflicts within the party have had two effects: first, to undermine public confidence in the party's competence to govern, and second, to impair the party's ability to execute its organizational tasks. Many of the mistakes that were made by the Conservative organization in the 1974 campaign were personal mistakes for which particular individuals must assume responsibility—and which must be expected in any campaign. But it is also true that weakness is endemic in the party. The national organization always seems to be distracted in some way by internal conflicts; constituency organization remains weak; communication between the national organization and constituency organizations is still problematic; and campaigns are invariably run on an ad hoc basis.

This endemic weakness in the Progressive Conservative party is partly the result of conditions it encounters in its social context, but it is also partly a product of what I have called the minority party

---

[25] Although there is no survey evidence to test the hypothesis that New Democrats voted Liberal to prevent the election of the Conservatives, there is some evidence to support it in returns from canvasses made by the NDP before the election in one of the sample ridings in Ontario.

syndrome. This metaphor is intended to express the idea that the party's minority status is constantly self-regenerating. It will be discussed more fully in a general study of conflict within the party which the author is currently preparing for publication. However, one final point needs to be made about it here. To the extent that the Conservative party has, in fact, become a permanent minority party, the vitality of Canadian democracy is threatened. Even elitist theories of democracy assume as a minimum condition for democracy meaningful competition for political office. Leaders who are secure in office are exposed to temptations which do not confront those who must be constantly mindful that they may be replaced.

Soon the Progressive Conservative party will have to choose a new leader. Robert Stanfield, having been defeated in three elections, has announced his intention to resign. Stanfield has the notable achievement to his credit of having held the party together after it had come dangerously close to permanent schism. In this sense he has given the party an opportunity to try once again to end its minority party status. Whether it succeeds is not just a question of importance for Conservatives. It has implications for everyone concerned with the future of democratic government in Canada.

5

PURISTS AND PRAGMATISTS: CANADIAN DEMOCRATIC SOCIALISM AT THE CROSSROADS

Jo Surich

The time between the foundation of the New Democratic party (NDP) in 1961 and the 1974 general election was a period of fairly steady if unspectacular growth for the democratic socialist movement in Canada. The party's share of the popular vote at general elections rose to about 18 percent and the number of seats it held in the House of Commons grew to thirty-one in the 1972 elections. After 1968 the advance of the party at the provincial level was much more rapid. NDP governments were formed in Manitoba (1969, 1973), Saskatchewan (1971, 1975), and British Columbia (1972). A series of spectacular by-election victories throughout the 1960s gave credence to the idea that one day the NDP might form a national government in Canada.

However, the 1974 federal election changed all that. The party's popular vote declined to 16 percent and the number of seats it held in the Commons was nearly halved, to sixteen. Its greatest reversals occurred in traditional strongholds. Ridings like Vancouver Kingsway, which had been held by the NDP's predecessor, the Cooperative Commonwealth Federation (CCF), since the 1930s, and Vancouver East were lost in the tide. In British Columbia majorities that had been as high as 15,000 votes in the 1972 election were cut down to 2,000. Having gone into the election with eleven seats in British Columbia, the party came out with two, while the popular vote dropped by twelve percentage points. In York South, David Lewis, the leader of the NDP, was defeated by an unknown Liberal. From an atmosphere of optimism and a conviction that it might one day achieve power in Canada, the movement descended into a state of bewilderment in two short months. Something had apparently gone wrong.

121

The Historical Background

While the beginnings of Canadian democratic socialism are to be found in the early labor movement in Canada and in the plethora of labor and socialist parties which formed and disappeared prior to the 1930s, its formal beginnings were in the depths of the Great Depression of the 1930s. Trade unionists, farmers, and members of small socialist parties met in Calgary, Alberta, in 1932 to form the Cooperative Commonwealth Federation (CCF). They met again in Regina, Saskatchewan, in 1933. Here they were joined by a group of academics from the League for Social Reconstruction (a Canadian version of the British Fabians) who wrote a document which came to be known as the Regina Manifesto. The manifesto was probably the first systematic Canadian attempt to detail the measures by which Canada could move to socialism democratically. The last sentence of the manifesto read: "No C.C.F. Government will rest content until it has eradicated capitalism and put into operation the full programme of socialized planning which will lead to the establishment in Canada of the Co-operative Commonwealth." Inspired by such ringing phraseology, a new political movement and party were formed, bringing together farmers, unionists, and intellectuals.

Almost from the beginning the CCF received a large vote in all of the provinces west of Ontario. These were times in which vast proportions of the population in that part of the country were unemployed and on welfare. The West has also had a greater tradition of labor militancy than the rest of Canada. James Shaver Woodsworth, the first leader of the new party had been arrested for conspiracy during the Winnipeg General Strike in 1919. Other leaders of the new movement had been active in a large number of labor struggles, particularly in British Columbia.

Almost from the beginning also, the CCF displayed the signs of the factionalism which was to cause difficulties throughout its history. Much like social-democratic parties in Europe, the Canadian movement was beset by pressure from the left for truly radical political action and by opposing pressure from those who realized that the Canadian people were not ready to vote for a "total" socialist program of the kind which envisaged the total eradication of capitalism. There was also great dissension within the movement over the relationship which the CCF ought to have with the other left-wing political groupings, particularly the disciplined and well-organized Canadian Communist party. The leadership of the CCF always adamantly opposed any suggestion of cooperation with the Communists, while labor members of the movement, particularly in Ontario, wanted to throw their lot in with a Communist-inspired united front. Tensions within the Ontario party ultimately led Woodsworth to dissolve its Provincial Council. The farmers also found that they could not live with the high level of government involvement which the Regina Manifesto implied, and the United Farmers of Ontario quickly withdrew.

The zenith of CCF support occurred during the war years. In 1943 the Gallup poll showed the party with a greater level of support than either the Conservatives or the Liberals. The CCF regularly won by-elections, including one in 1943 in Toronto-York South in which the new leader of the Conservative party was beaten. In 1943 also, the party came within four seats of forming a government in Ontario. A year later the first socialist government in North America was elected under the leadership of T. C. (Tommy) Douglas in Saskatchewan. The Canadian trade-union movement under the leadership of some of the CIO-founded unions in the Canadian Congress of Labour (CCL) made efforts to develop links with the CCF, although usually over the violent objection of the large Communist faction in the CCL.

With the beginnings of the cold war, however, support for the CCF began to wane. Canada was moving into an era of great prosperity; the standard of living of the Canadian people rose; and people saw Communists under every bed. Despite the efforts of the CCF leadership to distinguish the party from the Communists, Canadians were generally suspicious of any group that advocated the eradication of capitalism and the implementation of a wide range of social welfare measures. The CCF had strongly promoted measures like unemployment insurance, government hospital insurance and ultimately government health insurance, and it had implemented such programs in Saskatchewan. But the Liberals were generally able to co-opt such programs and to put them into effect. The CCF had become redundant as a force for reform at the same time that it was being viewed with suspicion and hostility by most of the population.

In 1956 efforts were made to adapt the CCF program to modern times and to tone down the strident nature of the Regina Manifesto. No longer was it thought necessary to eliminate capitalism entirely. Instead, many in the CCF, led by David Lewis, followed the doctrines of G.D.H. Cole in Britain and decided that it might be necessary only to nationalize the "commanding heights" of industry, while allowing small capitalist enterprises to flourish. These efforts led to the Winnipeg Declaration of Principles. But it was too late. By 1958 the rising tide of populism which Conservative John Diefenbaker embodied swept them out of even their stronghold in Saskatchewan. The federal party became moribund. It looked like the end for Canadian democratic socialism.

The party had been able to break into the growing urban areas of Canada only occasionally and tended to win most of its seats in rural areas. Only the very militant labor areas in the east end of Vancouver, the north end of Winnipeg, and Cape Breton Island continued to give the CCF support.

After the virtual decimation of the CCF in the Diefenbaker Conservative sweep of 1958, efforts were made by elements within the CCF and the newly formed Canadian Labour Congress (CLC) to found a new political party as the vehicle for a coalition of farmer groups, unions, and progressive individuals. The process of negotiation ultimately led to the formation of the NDP in 1961 and to talk of a "marriage" between labor and the CCF. New funding arrangements were created which eliminated some of the financial insecurity that had always plagued the CCF. A system of direct grants from unions, especially during elections, and of affiliation arrangements between local unions and the NDP both provided substantial sums of money. The affiliation fee, which was set at five cents per affiliated member per month, and which was revised upwards to ten cents in 1973, provided not only for the financial participation of the trade-union movement in the NDP, but also created a system of representation for the union movement in all the decision-making bodies of the party. A very direct link, therefore, exists between the NDP and the Canadian labor movement. Some union meetings even passed resolutions calling the NDP the "political arm of labor."

Not all was, of course, quiet and agreeable between the party and the trade-union movement, even at the beginning of their close relationship. Significant elements in the CCF opposed the marriage of the movement with labor, and their champion, Hazen Argue, who had been parliamentary leader after the defeat of M. J. Coldwell, left the party shortly after having been defeated in a bid for the leadership of the new movement. (He ultimately ran as a Liberal candidate and wound up in the Canadian Senate.) Argue left because he felt that the labor movement had been given excessive power within the NDP, despite major efforts to devise a system of representation that would not normally give the labor movement a majority in party councils.

The beginnings of the new party were mixed. While a seat had been won in the House of Commons by a "new party" candidate even prior to the founding convention, the 1962 election proved less successful than had been hoped. Indeed, even the new leader of the party, Tommy Douglas, who had been premier of Saskatchewan at the head of a CCF government, was unable to win a seat and was only brought into the House of Commons after a by-election had been forced by the resignation of a member who held a "safe" seat. Nevertheless, in the elections that followed the NDP vote continued to climb, so that after the 1965 election an apparently solid base had been established.

The 1968 federal election brought some reverses. Both the Progressive Conservative and Liberal parties had elected new leaders (Robert Stanfield and Pierre Elliott Trudeau respectively) and the sudden emergence of Trudeau led to an extensive Liberal sweep, particularly in the urban areas of Canada. Five years of minority government from 1962 to 1967 had given the NDP a significance beyond its numbers. The election of 1968, however, proved difficult. Tommy Douglas again lost his own constituency, but was able to reenter the House of Commons when one of the older members, Colin Cameron from British Columbia, died, leaving another "safe" seat open.

The Waffle Crisis. The prelude to the 1974 election can perhaps most logically be said to have started with the 1969 convention of the federal NDP in Winnipeg. That convention brought with it the first serious questioning of NDP policies and approaches in some years. A movement within the party, which came to be known as the Waffle,[1] drafted and circulated a proposal which expressed serious concern about the great extent of foreign (read American) ownership of Canadian industries and resources. The new manifesto had been signed by some 100 prominent party members and led to a great deal of debate and friction at the Winnipeg convention.

Ultimately a substitute resolution, which toned down the language of the document substantially, was passed at the convention. Essentially the Waffle manifesto, which came to the floor of the Winnipeg convention as Resolution 133, sought to achieve two objectives. It called first of all for a radicalization of the New Democratic party, arguing that the NDP "must be seen as the parliamentary

---

[1] The origins of the name "Waffle" are obscure, but Desmond Morton argues that it was invented by Ed Broadbent, currently the NDP parliamentary leader. Morton suggests that when Broadbent helped write the manifesto he said that it would reject "concessions to consensus radicalism: if it waffled, it would 'waffle to the left.'" Desmond Morton, *NDP: The Dream of Power* (Toronto: Hakkert, 1974), p. 92.

Table 5-1

NEW DEMOCRATIC PARTY FEDERAL ELECTION RESULTS, VOTES RECEIVED AND SEATS WON, BY PROVINCE, 1935–1974

Election Year	Total Canada Votes (V)	Seats (S)	Yukon & N.W. Territories (V)	(S)	British Columbia (V)	(S)	Alberta (V)	(S)	Saskatchewan (V)	(S)	Manitoba (V)	(S)
1935	9%	3	a		34%	19	13%	0	20%	10	19%	12
1940	8	3	a		28	6	13	0	29	24	19	6
1945	16	11	28%	0	29	25	18	0	44	86	32	29
1949	13	5	17	0	32	17	9	0	41	25	26	19
1953	11	9	a		27	32	7	0	44	65	24	21
1957	11	9	a		22	32	6	0	36	59	24	36
1958	10	3	a		25	18	4	0	28	6	20	0
1962	14	7	a		31	46	8	0	22	0	20	14
1963	13	6	a		30	41	7	0	18	0	17	14
1965	18	8	3	0	33	41	8	0	26	0	24	21
1968	17	8	10	0	33	30	9	0	36	46	25	23
1972	18	12	29	50	35	47	13	0	36	38	26	23
1974	16	6	32	50	23	9	9	0	32	15	25	15

a No candidates.
b Less than 1 percent.

wing of a movement dedicated to fundamental social change. It must be radicalized from within and it must be radicalized from without." [2] The party was to return to its root commitment to the building of a "socialist" society in a more strident and radical way. The main issue was foreign ownership of the Canadian economic system since "American corporate capitalism [was] . . . the dominant factor shaping Canadian society." [3]

Melville Watkins, a University of Toronto economist, had worked for the Liberal government preparing the Watkins Report on Foreign Ownership. Having discovered that the Liberal party was, in fact, unwilling to deal with the problem in a forthright way, he had moved to the NDP. He was joined in the initial stages by a number of people, most of them academics. The Toronto Daily Star described them this way: "With union researcher Giles Endicott, Toronto education professor Gerry Caplan, who was expelled from

[2] Dave Godfrey and Mel Watkins, Gordon to Watkins to You (Toronto: New Press, 1970), p. 103.

[3] Ibid., p. 103.

Ontario		Quebec		New Brunswick		Nova Scotia		Prince Edward Island		New-foundland	
(V)	(S)	(V)	(S)	(V)	(S)	(V)	(S)	(V)	(S)	(V)	(S)
8%	0	1%	0	a		a		a			
4	0	1	0	b	0	6%	8	a			
14	0	2	0	8%	0	17	8	4%	0		
15	1	1	0	4	0	10	8	2	0	b	0
11	1	2	0	3	0	7	8	1	0	1%	0
12	4	2	0	1	0	4	0	1	0	b	0
11	4	2	0	2	0	5	0	b	0	b	0
17	7	4	0	5	0	9	8	5	0	5	0
16	7	7	0	4	0	6	0	2	0	4	0
22	11	12	0	9	0	9	0	2	0	1	0
21	7	8	0	5	0	7	0	3	0	4	0
21	12	6	0	6	0	12	0	7	0	5	0
19	9	7	0	8	0	10	9	5	0	9	0

Sources: 1935-65: J. Murray Beck, *Pendulum of Power: Canada's Federal Elections* (Scarborough, Ontario: Prentice-Hall, 1968); 1968-72: Canada, *Report of the Chief Electoral Officer* (Ottawa: Queen's Printer, 1969, 1973); 1974: *Toronto Star*, 9 July 1974.

Rhodesia in 1966, and graduate student Jim Laxer, Watkins has issued a nationalistic manifesto."[4]

While no extensive organizational base had been laid within the party, the manifesto spread rapidly through the riding associations, many of which had endorsed it and had elected delegates who would support it at the Winnipeg convention. Indeed, so much support for the document had developed in the party that a counter-document had been drafted in an attempt to present ideas similar to those contained in the Waffle manifesto while removing the strident language and blunting the demand for extensive nationalization by calling for "public control of investment and other priorities and democratic social planning to use our resources for the enrichment of the human condition."[5] With the drafting of the counter-manifesto, which came to the convention as Resolution C-17, the battle between the ideological purists and the pragmatists was joined. Despite changes and upheavals of various kinds, this would continue to be

[4] Steven Langdon, *Toronto Daily Star*, 11 August 1969.
[5] Godfrey and Watkins, *Gordon to Watkins*, p. 110.

the main problem confronting the NDP right through the period of minority government and up to the 1974 general election.

The manifesto and the organization of the Waffle movement led to tremendous turmoil within the New Democratic party, particularly in the provinces of Ontario and Saskatchewan. The new tendency attracted into the party large numbers of fringe leftists of all types, who focused on the Waffle and thereby attempted to gain a secure foothold within the party. Very rapidly, all through the years following the 1969 convention, an extensive internal rift developed of the kind which has always bedeviled social-democratic movements. Conventions of the Ontario and Saskatchewan parties fought over the origin of resolutions and individuals rather than about their merits. Splits, acrimony, and name-calling became the order of the day.

Within the federal party, the question came to a head at the 1971 convention. Tommy Douglas had resigned as leader, which confronted the party with the question of leadership for the first time since its founding. Five people sought the leadership—David Lewis, Frank Howard, Ed Broadbent, John Harney, and James Laxer. Of the candidates, David Lewis had perhaps the longest standing connection with the party. He had been the first permanent secretary of the CCF in the 1930s and had been a significant and powerful influence within the Canadian social-democratic movement almost since its inception. Frank Howard had been the member of Parliament for Skeena in British Columbia since 1957, and Ed Broadbent had been elected to the House of Commons for Oshawa-Whitby in Ontario in 1968. John Harney was also from Ontario, and while he did not hold a seat, he had been full-time secretary of the Ontario section of the party for four years. James Laxer was one of the leaders of the Waffle movement.

The 1971 federal convention is significant for two reasons. First, by electing David Lewis leader it significantly broke with a tradition of "saintly" leaders,[6] and second, it starkly drew the lines between the Waffle and the mainstream of the party. After Howard, Broadbent, and Harney had been eliminated on the first three ballots, the final ballot presented delegates with a choice between David Lewis, clearly the establishment candidate, and James Laxer, very clearly the antiestablishment candidate. While David Lewis won on

---

[6] J. S. Woodsworth and M. J. Coldwell, the two CCF leaders, and Tommy Douglas all had reputations at least of being people who stood above the day-to-day struggles of political life. On Woodsworth see, for example, Kenneth McNaught, *A Prophet in Politics* (Toronto: University of Toronto Press, 1959, 1967).

the final ballot, the very substantial vote which Laxer received revealed to the world a deeply divided party. The divisions and tensions which had been developing within the NDP since the founding of the Waffle intensified and led ultimately to a confrontation within the Ontario section that effectively eliminated the Waffle as a movement within the NDP. Indeed, the main battleground was the seriously weakened section of the party in Ontario, where the 1971 provincial elections had returned a Progressive Conservative government with an overwhelming majority.

The Waffle movement had become an increasingly autonomous group within the Ontario section and split the party neatly into at least two factions. When the Waffle shifted its attention from the problems of foreign ownership and the suggested remedies (extensive nationalization, particularly in the resource sector), to the problems of foreign-dominated trade unions, the conflict broke into the open more clearly than ever before. More than any other section of the NDP, the Ontario section enjoys the support of about 85 percent of the total affiliated Canadian union membership. The largest of the affiliated unions are the United Steelworkers of America (USWA) and the United Auto Workers (UAW), and both enjoy a very high level of representation at meetings of the Ontario section.

The Waffle attempted to develop extensive organization within certain local unions, ostensibly on the basis of a radical program, but in fact on the basis of an appeal to nationalism and "national" unions. Since the dissidents in most Canadian unions tend to be nationalists, the Waffle organizers managed to gather together most of the antiestablishment elements in various local unions on the basis of their nationalist appeal. The leadership of the union movement reacted quite naturally and began to demand that the party place restrictions on the Waffle and its ability to affect the policy and leadership of the "political arm of labor."

The Waffle crisis within the Ontario section of the NDP deepened throughout 1971. The first indirect attack by the party leadership on the activities of the Waffle occurred in the spring of 1971 at a provincial council meeting in Waterloo. During the 1971 Ontario election, on several occasions members of the Waffle leadership issued well-reported statements which directly contradicted official statements on policy made by the party leadership. Tensions within the Ontario section continued to mount with the Waffle now issuing its own newspaper and having a de facto membership. One of the methods the NDP has always used to purge fringe leftists is to argue that they are members of another political organization. The Ontario

NDP membership application asks individuals to declare that they are "not a member nor supporter of any other political party." Thus the fact that the Waffle maintained membership lists and solicited individual donations became the cornerstone of legalistic arguments against the organization.

Finally, in March 1972, Stephen Lewis, leader of the Ontario section, made a speech at a party provincial council meeting in Oshawa in which he joined battle directly with the Waffle and its leadership and attacked its pressures on party policy. A three-man committee to investigate the role of the Waffle in the party was formed, composed of Gerry Caplan (one of the erstwhile founders of the movement, but by then a close supporter and one-time executive assistant to Stephen Lewis), John Brewin, the Ontario treasurer, and Gordon Vichert, the party president.

The committee reported to an executive meeting on 6 May 1972 and recommended essentially that the Waffle be dissolved, since it had taken on the character of a party within the party. A period of furious intraparty warfare followed, leading up to the next provincial council meeting in Orillia in June. The party split into three ideological groupings, a left which supported the Waffle and opposed the executive recommendation that the Waffle be dissolved, a right which supported the leadership and the executive recommendation, and a center which sought to find a compromise between the two extreme positions.

It is in the nature of democratic-socialist movements like the NDP that massive changes in party policy occur as a result of pressure from the left, while the resistance to such changes usually comes from the right, which includes a large proportion of trade union delegates. The center of the party supports one side or the other depending on the issue under discussion. At Orillia, however, the center of the party assumed a dominant role, presenting the resolution which was to be carried. Essentially, the center called for the Waffle to cease existing as a separate organization with a distinct name and recommended that only the "official" organs of the party, such as the parliamentary leadership, the executive and councils of the party, and the riding associations be allowed to issue public statements of any kind. Groups and caucuses would be allowed to continue to exist and be active *within* the party organization.

The compromise resolution won support at the Orillia meeting, and the Waffle, having been given time to decide whether it would dissolve or withdraw from the party intact, met later that summer in London and decided to form an essentially independent political movement called the Waffle Movement for an Independent Socialist Canada. This group in time split, forming a Waffle party which ran some candidates in the 1974 election, and a "Left Caucus" which continued for some time to operate within the NDP. Four federal candidates who had been nominated to contest the 1972 election, including Melville Watkins and Jim Laxer, resigned as NDP candidates.

In a sense, the story of the Waffle within the NDP ends here. In Saskatchewan one member of the NDP caucus, John Richards, resigned from the caucus and sat as an independent member in support of the new political party. However, the crisis left a legacy of distrust and bad feeling within the party, which bubbled to the surface occasionally, particularly at conventions. It also left the Ontario section in a state of advanced disarray just as the 1972 election was about to be called. Some of the tension and cynicism which were to exist during the period of minority government may be said to be a direct result of the tensions generated by the Waffle crisis.

The 1972 Federal Election. The NDP entered the 1972 election a deeply divided party. Yet political conditions were excellent. The Trudeau Liberal government had gained a reputation of being arrogant and uncaring; unemployment was high; there was great dissatisfaction with the bilingualism programs which were then being established in the civil service; the NDP had just elected a government in British Columbia; and the Progressive Conservative party did not appear to be particularly strong. David Lewis fought an intensive and intelligent campaign, which for the first time gained serious media coverage and recognition for an NDP leader.

The campaign was based initially on the theme of "corporate welfare bums" [7] and launched a major investigation of tax write-offs, tax credits and deferred taxes, showing that most of Canada's major corporations were able to escape many corporate taxes. Week after week David Lewis added to his honor roll of corporate organizations which were able to avoid the payment of any taxes or at least of what he considered to be reasonable taxes. In terms of media coverage the campaign was an immense success, although the final result, the percentage of the popular vote gained at the polls, does not reflect this. However, the election did see NDP representation

---

[7] See David Lewis, *Louder Voices: The Corporate Welfare Bums* (Toronto: James Lewis and Samuel, 1972).

in the House of Commons rise to thirty-one seats, the largest social-democratic contingent ever in the House. Furthermore, a precarious minority government emerged, leaving the Liberals with just two more seats than the Conservatives and placing the balance of power in Parliament in the hands of the New Democrats.

Walter Young, in his epic study of the CCF, suggested that one of the primary problems facing political parties like the CCF and the NDP lies in the struggle between the ideological demands of a political movement and the organizational and directly political demands of a political party.[8] Faced with an environment not always conducive to electoral victory, particularly at the national level, any political party of the democratic left must from time to time compromise some of its principles. The NDP is no exception, and the so-called Waffle crisis is a symptom of the problems parties of this kind always face.

Canadian democratic socialism has always been confronted with the co-optation of its programs, especially by the Liberal party, and there has always been some movement of CCF-NDP politicians—of whom Hazen Argue is only one example—to the Liberals. Faced with a minority Parliament in which the NDP caucus would be able to play the role of balance of power, the party needed to make a number of decisions which would affect not only its political position, but also its internal cohesion. Deep though the distrust of Liberal politics was, many New Democrats remembered vividly the effects of the 1957 Conservative minority Parliament, which was followed in short order by a general election in which the Conservatives secured an overwhelming majority, 208 out of 265 seats. The smaller parties, notably the CCF and the Social Credit party, had been almost obliterated in that sweep. In the period after the 1972 election the national Conservative party again appeared to be on the rise and might have been expected to form a government if an election were to occur soon. Therefore, the NDP caucus determined to support the Liberals on a day-to-day basis. However, based on the fear of a quick election in which the Progressive Conservatives might be expected to do well, the NDP's support for the Liberal party emerged as a de facto coalition without any of the privileges or responsibilities, such as cabinet membership for a few key people, which are normally attached to such an arrangement.

---

8 Walter Young, *The Anatomy of a Party: The National CCF, 1932-1961* (Toronto: University of Toronto Press, 1969). See also Peter Gay, *The Dilemma of Democratic Socialism* (New York: Collier Books, 1962).

There is no need to describe the course of the 1972–1974 minority Parliament here except as it profoundly affected the NDP and its membership. Large parts of the membership failed to understand why it was suddenly necessary to back an apparently discredited government of the traditional political and ideological enemy. As the months of compromise and bargaining dragged on in Parliament, larger and larger sections of the party rank and file became uncomfortable and started to pressure those elements of the leadership to whom they had access to vote against the government. For a socialist movement, purity is one of the greatest assets, and it was quite clear to most members of the NDP that purity was being sold out. As Conservative no-confidence motions continued to be phrased in terms which the NDP would have demanded, and as the NDP parliamentary caucus continued to vote against them and with the government, relations between some parts of the caucus and the party became testier. The small pieces of party policy adopted by the government were overshadowed by the embarrassment of supporting programs to which NDP policy was at least partly opposed. The membership wanted to flex its muscles in the sight of the enemy, but the caucus apparently did not.

As time went on, and as the consumer price index continued to climb, the Conservative policy of so-called temporary but sweeping price and wage controls appeared to gain popularity throughout the country. Politically, it became more and more undesirable to defeat the government, since an almost certain Conservative victory seemed to be in the offing. In a Conservative sweep several members of the NDP caucus could expect to be defeated, particularly those who represented Saskatchewan constituencies. It thus became more difficult to satisfy the ideological needs of the party. On the other hand, the policy of supporting the government would be a political liability on the prairie provinces until the prices of farm commodities such as wheat started to rise. All of the problems of politics in a country as regionalized as Canada began to plague the NDP and came to be reflected in the operations of its caucus.

At the same time, members of the caucus gained satisfaction from the process of consultation and discussion with the government, which the government had to undertake in order to survive. Many felt that for the first time they were having a significant effect on the operation of government in Canada.

At the July 1973 convention, David Lewis's frustration with the minority situation also came to light. In a tough, hard-hitting speech to the convention he suggested that he personally could not much longer bear to participate in propping up a government which, he said, had failed to meet some of the major problems facing Canadians, especially the rapidly rising prices of food, shelter, and clothing. Speculation that the Parliament was about to end heightened, and NDP riding associations started to prepare for an election. Nothing happened, however, and Parliament dragged on, the despair of much of the NDP membership being relieved only by the backing down of the government during the oil crisis. No new exciting legislation came out of the government during the winter of 1974. Finally, the NDP caucus voted against an antiprofiteering bill, which looked much the same as one the party had demanded in policy statements, and then voted against the government on its budget on 8 May 1974.

Where NDP members of the House of Commons might have gained some measure of satisfaction out of their achievements in terms of changes in government policy which resulted from their pressure, very little sense of achievement filtered down to the party membership. This was partly because the press took great delight in detailing the areas in which the NDP had voted with the government in apparent contradiction of NDP policies and principles. In the words of a longtime NDP parliamentarian, Max Saltsman, "After the defeat of the last government . . . Canadians perceived the NDP as one of the old-line parties, as they do the Liberals and the Conservatives."[9] The party membership felt this even more deeply and exerted pressure through letters and meetings of the caucus to defeat the government. There was no guarantee in the spring of 1974 that the NDP might do well in an election, and it might have been politically fruitful to enter into a more formal relationship with the government. Two alternatives at least suggested themselves. Either a formal political coalition might have been established, or the NDP might have entered into a "nonaggression pact" with the Liberals, which would have allowed the government to survive for a certain period of time in return for some concessions to the NDP program. Neither of these two alternatives appeared to be possible because the ideological demands of the movement pulled in the opposite direction, calling for a break with the government and a face-off at the polls. Indeed, when the federal NDP executive voted on the question of whether or not the government was to be defeated prior to the budget vote, it voted overwhelmingly to ask the caucus to defeat it, and several members then started to take bets on the number of seats they could expect to *lose* during the election.

---

[9] *Oshawa Times*, 24 September 1974.

The 1974 Election

Strategies of the National Campaign. National NDP campaigns are characterized by a very high level of decentralization, which is a function of the diversity of the country, the very different levels of support enjoyed by the party from region to region, and the financial position of the party. Campaign expenses are discussed in detail elsewhere in this volume, but it would be fair to say that NDP expenditures are no more than one-tenth as large as those of the other two major political parties. The federal office of the NDP spent approximately $379,000 on the 1974 campaign. Almost half of that amount was spent on organizational and media assistance to areas which presented such low chances of success as to require outside funds to generate any type of activity at all or in constituencies which were deemed to be winnable or which were already held by the party.

Donations were received from the Committee on Political Education (COPE), a political education fund established by the national offices of the major trade unions, and from the provincial sections of the party by way of quotas assessed against them. Almost all such quota payments were made by the provincial parties in British Columbia, Saskatchewan, Manitoba, and Ontario. In turn, these four provinces received most of the funds set aside for "concentration" purposes, since they were the only ones with sitting members and since most of the winnable seats were there.

Control over the campaign rested nominally with a national election planning committee, which had members from all provincial sections. In fact, this group met only infrequently and vested most of its power in the federal secretary, the federal leader, and the various provincial election planning committees. The provincial committees exercised authority over their section of the national campaign, determining within guidelines prepared by the federal committee which ridings would receive concentration help, both in terms of paid organizational staff and mass-media assistance. A typical concentration riding in Ontario would have received $2,400 in media assistance and three full-time paid organizers, most of them donated by the trade union movement, notably the United Steelworkers and the United Auto Workers.

Each of the provincial parties had a budget of its own for the federal election. A portion of this budget was contributed by the federal party for use in media and organizational assistance and the balance was raised through a system of quotas assessed against individual constituency campaigns. In Ontario, for example, these quotas amounted to 20 percent of the amount actually spent by the candidates in each riding. The total quota income for the Ontario section of the NDP was approximately $105,000. Other donations to the provincial sections during federal elections are drawn largely from provincial labor organizations.[10] The pattern and flow of fund raising by the various sections of the NDP are outlined in Figure 5-1. No specific point of national control over an NDP campaign can be identified, since many decisions are made at the local level. For example, the slogan "People Matter More," which was generated by the advertising agency employed by the federal party and adopted for the national campaign was not used in the province of Saskatchewan, where the local election planning committee decided to use "The New Ideas Party" as the provincial slogan.

The national leader's election tour was also only partially controlled from the center. While a schedule was prepared by the national committee, advance work was left up to the provincial sections, many of which executed that part of their work with extreme inefficiency. Occasionally halls were empty when the tour arrived; a salt mine in Saskatchewan, which was to have marked the highlight of a visit to a small town, turned out to be shut for renovations; crowds failed to materialize in many places—indeed, the press reports leave an impression of a level of disorganization not normally tolerated in a national campaign. While much of the failure can be blamed on a lack of funds, a problem which has always plagued parties like the NDP, some of it is probably a direct function of the lack of central control over the whole campaign.

Decentralization of the NDP and its election campaigns was built into the structure of the party at its founding, when the federal party was established as essentially a wing of the provincial sections. Individual memberships which provide the major source of day-to-day operating funds are funneled through the provincial sections, and members are only incidentally members of the national party. Their direct allegiance is to provincial riding associations and to the provincial sections of the party. The major stimulus for this decentralizing tendency lies, of course, in the regionalized nature of the country. Political practices and political cultures appear to vary from one region to another, and there is tremendous variation in the strength of the provincial party sections. Ontario and the provinces to the west have relatively strong organizations with substantial financial bases, while the provinces to the east, except in isolated

---

[10] New Democratic Party, "Preliminary Statement of Revenue and Expenditures," 31 July 1974.

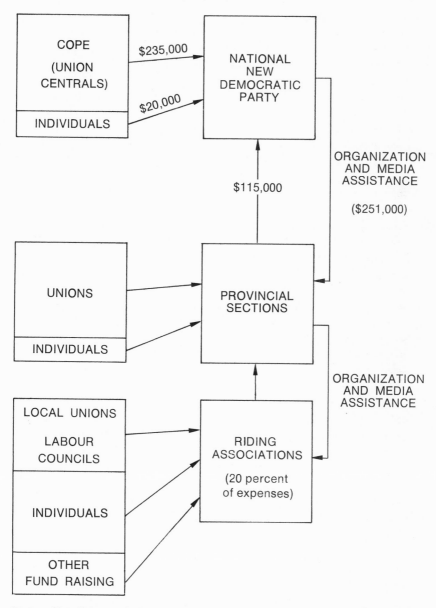

Figure 5-1

FLOW OF FUNDS, 1974 NDP CAMPAIGN

Source: New Democratic Party, "Preliminary Statement of Revenue and Expenditures," 31 July 1974, and discussion with Clifford Scotton, Federal NDP secretary.

pockets, have little or no organization and very low membership, and gain very few votes.

The nature of the country demands that all of the political parties which attempt to operate on a national basis be decentralized, but both the Liberals and the Progressive Conservatives maintain tighter central control, especially over the leaders' tours. Squads of advance men tour the countryside ensuring that the visit by the leader will be good theater and will generate an impression of mass popular support for the benefit of the press. In the 1974 federal election the NDP failed almost entirely to perform this function.

The NDP's national campaign itself, at least insofar as the leader's contacts with the public were concerned, was a much more ambitious affair than had ever been attempted before. Where Tommy Douglas, during campaigns in the 1960s, would climb down from a commercial plane accompanied by perhaps one person to carry his bag, David Lewis, in both 1972 and 1974, chartered an airplane for the latter stages of the campaign. In the initial stages of the election, visits were made to all of the major Canadian media centers by commercial airlines to generate publicity. Later a much more systematic tour of the country was undertaken, with at least one, and usually two, visits to each of the concentration areas. A careful blend of press conferences, visits to places with local color, and mass rallies was staged, usually outside the major centers. On the surface at least, the NDP's campaign was very much like those of all the other parties, though its pace was much slower than those of Trudeau and Stanfield, both of whom used jets, as opposed to Lewis's piston-engined plane.

In strategic terms, the campaign was a disaster. The 1972 election had generated a great deal of controversy and excitement around the issue of corporate taxes and had received a much greater than usual amount of attention from the press. In 1974 a basic spark appeared to be missing. Attempts to create public excitement around the issue of corporate control and power failed, and David Lewis was pushed into an essentially defensive campaign, attacking not the government party but rather the principal opposition party, the Progressive Conservatives. NDP advertising on the electronic media, on which considerable sums of money were spent (about 15-20 percent of the total budget), focused on the cost of living and on the activities of the major food chains, but failed to generate much support. This lack of support may have been caused in part by the complexity of the NDP's proposed solutions to the rise in the cost of living. A suggested two-price system which would charge Canadians less than the world price for basic commodities (such a system was already in effect for oil and wheat) failed to have any positive effect on the electorate. The argument that corporate profits should be curtailed to control rising prices appeared to people to be excessively one-sided and, to the cynics at least, to be motivated by the close ties which exist between the NDP and the trade-union movement.

Policies and programs, then, were not clearly enunciated and believable. In strategic terms, the tough attack on Progressive Conservative wage and price controls apparently had the effect of convincing large sections of the urban working class that the Conservatives had to be defeated and that consequently the Liberals were the logical party to vote for. The NDP's campaign appeared to provide the stimulus for that type of argument, and its record during the period of minority government lent credibility to the notion that the Liberals were much less the enemies of the traditional NDP voter than were the Conservatives. While data are not yet available, this appears to be a plausible explanation for the massive drop in votes in traditional NDP areas. The working classes voted Liberal to keep the Tories out.

It is not the sole explanation for the drop in NDP support, however. First, the sense of malaise which the party had inherited from the Waffle crisis played a role in generating less than the normal high level of commitment from the party rank and file. Second, the period of minority government did not lend itself to the emotional appeals for party solidarity and socialism which can normally be used to mobilize the membership. Third, special local circumstances contributed to the malaise. In British Columbia especially, large segments of the party were dissatisfied with the performance of their newly elected government, particularly with respect to its implementation of party policy. It is an article of faith with the membership of democratic socialist movements that their governments will be tightly held to policies and programs established at party conventions. The British Columbian government had failed in some respects to do this, often for perfectly sensible political reasons. As a consequence, it was apparently difficult to generate enthusiastic support from the membership in British Columbia.

The problems within the NDP, then, which contributed to the lackluster quality of the 1974 campaign, appear to have arisen mainly out of the internal tensions which are built into democratic socialist movements. The sense of mission, the commitment to socialist achievements, the sense of purity and justice coupled with a deep anger at the injustices of a capitalist economic system were blunted and turned aside by the political demands of the time. The Waffle movement had to be disbanded because it was costing votes and public support, and the Liberals had to be supported in the minority Parliament because of electoral realities. The electoral consequences of apparently unstable minority government, of a Conservative policy which seemed both appealing and dangerous, and of some demand for majority government, combined with a profound malaise internal to the movement to bring about the effects of the 1974 election.

Candidates and Candidate Selection. A fairly extensive survey of all candidates in the 1972 election exists,[11] and a preliminary analysis of data for candidates in the 1974 election collected by the authors of the 1972 survey suggests that very little change occurred between the two elections. NDP candidates were found to differ from those contesting the election for other parties in a number of respects. Almost two-thirds of all women candidates were NPD—this was broadly the case in the 1974 election, too—and 72 percent of all candidates who claimed to have no religious affiliation ran for the NDP. On the whole, NDP candidates also tend to be younger than the norm for all candidates. Two occupational groups are more extensively represented in the New Democratic party than they are in the other Canadian political parties: liberal professionals, such as teachers, and manual workers—while far fewer NDP candidates are engaged in the various business occupations. In a real sense, these characteristics reflect the nature of the NDP membership in terms of its trade union connections and its progressive base.

Almost all NDP candidates had been members of either the NDP or the CCF for from two to fifteen years, while the other three parties ran many candidates who had been members for very short periods (especially among Conservatives) or for much longer ones. NDP candidates also tended more often than Liberal or Conservative candidates to have had fairly lengthy records of involvement in the party bureaucracy at all levels. The tendency in the NDP is for riding associations to turn long-time trusted party officials into candidates, rather than to seek out local "stars" or successful local politicians without serious party affiliation.

These generalizations, of course, hide tremendous regional variations and differences. The incidence of contests for party nominations

---

[11] See Joachim E.-C. Surich and Robert J. Williams, "Some Characteristics of Candidates in the 1972 Canadian Federal Election," paper presented to the annual meeting of the *Canadian Political Science Association*, June 1974.

varies with the possibility of success and, in fact, one of the immediate functions of the provincial and national election planning committees is to seek out candidates for constituencies where there is little chance of winning. A special fund of $18,600 was set aside during the 1974 election to provide for the payment of $200 deposits for such candidates. Ninety-two candidates, then, ran in constituencies in which the local organizations were sufficiently moribund to be unable to raise the deposit fee. Many of the large numbers of working class candidates ran in such constituencies, and a large proportion were union officials.

In areas, however, where functioning local organizations exist, the process of candidate selection is largely autonomous. The central party organizations interfere only occasionally, and then usually unsuccessfully. Provincial riding associations normally form federal committees which appoint nominating committees to seek out potential candidates. The preponderance of party officials among NDP candidates is probably at least partly a function of this method—it is easier to ask a friend to run for public office, especially where the chances of victory are not great. NDP candidates are not normally asked to make substantial contributions to their own campaigns, so the financial status of the potential candidates is usually not taken into account.

Once a list of potential candidates or a single potential candidate is found, a nomination meeting to which only paid-up party members are invited is called, and the meeting chooses a candidate by majority vote. Voting members at a nomination meeting must have been members of the party for a period of time, usually fourteen days, or they must be members of affiliated locals living within the boundaries of the constituency and registered with the local party secretary for at least a month. Every effort is made to prevent the "packing" of nomination meetings through the sale of large numbers of party memberships just prior to the meetings, a practice which is fairly common especially among Liberal and Progressive Conservative riding associations. Once a candidate has been chosen by a nomination meeting, his name is forwarded to the provincial council of each provincial section for approval. Only then does the national party organization play a role in the candidate selection process by informing the chief election officer of the identity of the official party candidate. According to Canadian election law, the process is then legitimized when the party label is placed next to the name of the candidate on the ballot.

Effectively the candidate selection process is a local one within the NDP, with few exceptions in ridings which have active party organizations. Only in areas where the local organization is weak does the center help in the selection of candidates. Until Canadian election law was altered in 1970 to provide for placing the party labels on the ballot, the national NDP had no method of approving or rejecting a candidate selected at the local level and approved by the appropriate provincial party.

The Local Campaigns. All political parties in Canada campaign with a heavy local emphasis. In a sense, the sheer size of the country and the diversity of the cultures and peoples demands this. Because of the shortage of funds in the central organization, NDP campaigns tend to be even more localized than those fought by the Liberals and the Progressive Conservatives. Most are run according to one of two or three standard patterns, depending largely on the state of the local organization and its ability to raise money. Two publications produced by the New Democratic party, the *Campaign Guide* and the *Publicity Guide,* provide models for most local campaigns.[12] The techniques outlined in them have been found to be effective, particularly in by-elections, in which money and personnel can be focused on a single constituency. The backbone of a well-fought NDP campaign is the canvass, a technique used in many other political systems. An attempt is made in a well-organized constituency campaign to personally contact each voter three times at his door. A system of markings identifies voters for subsequent canvasses and for the election-day organization.

The advantages of the canvass technique are obvious. There is little doubt that personal contact with the voters by an army of volunteers has the effect of making the candidate well known and of reminding the voter of the fact that an election is coming. Whether or not the technique actually changes any votes is hard to discern, but a study of a by-election in Middlesex South (Ontario) indicates that there is some relationship between votes and the frequency of contact, or at least voter-recollected contact, between voters and party canvassers.[13] In addition, the use of the canvass as the major campaign tool means that NDP campaigns can be run with much less

---

12 Desmond Morton, *Campaign Guide* (Ottawa: New Democratic Party Publications, 1972), and *Publicity Guide* (Ottawa and Toronto: New Democratic Party Publications, 1972).

13 See Joachim E.-C. Surich, *The Nature of Political Change: The Case of Middlesex South* (M.A. diss., University of Waterloo, 1970).

money than is required when, for example, the mass media are used extensively.

The disadvantages are also obvious. Where the morale of the party is low or where the local candidate is unpopular the volunteer workers are very difficult to mobilize. This may in part explain the tendency of the NDP to nominate candidates who have fairly lengthy party histories and who have participated actively within local organizations. Such persons are likely to have contacts among the potential volunteer force which help to induce people to participate actively. Another drawback lies in the likelihood that only a relatively small proportion of potential canvassers will have the communications skills required for contact with the uncommitted voter. The success of the technique in by-elections may well be a result of the fact that highly qualified canvassers can be imported from other areas, as well as of the fact that no national campaign exists to diffuse the effects of repetitive mass canvassing.

Few local NDP campaigns invest heavily in the mass media. The average campaign committee spends perhaps no more than $1,000 on a combination of newspaper and radio advertising (see Table 5-2). Television is only rarely used. Instead, large numbers of lawn signs placed on the properties of NDP supporters are used, usually displaying the name of the local candidate and of the party. Many local campaigns spend a larger proportion of their budget on lawn signs than on the mass media. It is argued that a massive display of the standard orange and black signs will provide a greater indication of the candidate's strength than the small amounts of advertising which the local candidates would be able to afford. The final aspect of most well-organized NDP campaigns is election-day activity, much as it is for all political parties. A major effort is made to take to the polls all of those voters who have been identified as supporters during the canvassing.

The logic of the campaign technique is probably unassailable. Massive and frequent personal contact with the voters, coupled with lawn signs which establish for the world a direct link between a household and a candidate, are followed up by a highly organized election-day machine which brings committed supporters to the polls. The technique is well suited to a political party which is chronically even more short of funds than the other political parties, but which can draw on a fairly large pool of committed members and supporters.

The deep sense of malaise which afflicted the party in several key sections of the country as a result of a combination of factors— internal cleavages, the period of minority government, dissatisfaction

Table 5-2
INCOME SOURCES AND EXPENDITURES IN A TYPICAL WINNING NDP CAMPAIGN (WATERLOO-CAMBRIDGE)

Local Income	
Local union donations	$ 4,000
Individual donations	12,000
Special fund-raising events	3,200
	$19,200
Local Expenses	
Leaflets for three canvasses	$8,000
Lawn signs	1,000
Committee rooms, telephones, supplies	4,000
Newspaper and radio	1,000
Hall rentals, band for leader's visit, bus rental	2,000
	$16,000
Quota payment to Ontario NDP (20 percent)	3,200
	$19,200
Central Assistance	
Radio advertising	$2,400
Organizational assistance	600
United Auto Workers organizer	1,800 [a]
United Steel Workers organizer	1,200 [a]
	$6,000

[a] Estimated value.

Source: Waterloo-Cambridge New Democratic Party Association, *Budget for the 1974 Re-elect Max Saltsman Campaign,* submitted to the Waterloo North and Waterloo South NDP associations for approval, 17 April 1974.

with the performance of the NDP government in British Columbia, fatigue from having had to fight several elections in a short space of time, and so on—all would have had their impact on the capacity of the party to generate enthusiastic volunteer support.

Purists and Pragmatists: Where to from Here?

The failure of the New Democratic party to make gains in the 1974 Canadian election is likely to have a profound effect on future party strategies. Since the NDP victories in Manitoba, Saskatchewan, and British Columbia, the process of decentralization for which the seeds were laid at the founding convention has speeded up. More and more the federal party is becoming a ward of the big provincial parties from Ontario west, while in turn the small provincial parties from Quebec east continue to be wards of the federal party. We have, then, a situation in which a national political party has very little control over party activities in its strong areas and great control in those areas where little electoral strength exists.

The largest sources of day-to-day operating funds for the federal party are the affiliation fees paid directly to it by local unions and the Saskatchewan and Ontario sections. In June 1975 Saskatchewan reelected an existing NDP government, and later in the year the Ontario NDP section will take another stab at unseating the Progressive Conservative party which has been in power in Ontario since 1943. The tendency in Saskatchewan was for the provincial party to concentrate all available financial and personnel resources on the provincial scene, and this will be true also in Ontario. Since the national party does not have any independent existence in these provinces, this will mean effectively that no federal activity will take place beyond the selection of delegates to a national leadership convention.

The federal New Democratic party is in a real sense a victim of its own organizational forms. The major sources of money, power, and control rest with the stronger provincial parties, and the opportunities for electoral success are much greater at the provincial level. Beyond the organizational problems, the party was bedevilled in the last half of 1974 by an apparent move to the left on the part of the Liberal party. The effect of such a move might well be to further chip away at the hard-core working-class support that the NDP has always had.

On the solutions to these problems purists and pragmatists will sharply divide. The ideological purists will argue that the party should move to the left and take solid socialist positions which will clearly differentiate the party from the others in the political system. The party membership would probably feel most comfortable with such a movement, since a return to the basic socialist urges and commitments always stirs the hearts and minds of democratic socialists. Many others will recognize, however, that this course might hopelessly alienate a large section of the potential NDP electorate and would therefore be self-defeating, however good it was for the soul.

Pragmatists will urge several partly opposed strategies. Some will suggest that many of the democratic socialist programs which the NDP has adapted from Western European models are not really applicable in an expanding and essentially optimistic society. Canada has already built medicare and pension schemes which are far superior in terms of the services offered to what is available to people in the United States and which are more comprehensive and democratic than many European schemes. Instead they will argue that Canadian democratic socialism must opt for an approach which is in some senses more "conservative." Programs, it will be argued, must be found to free people from the domination of big interests in general—government, the large multinational corporations, perhaps even the large trade unions. In other words, they will want to opt for an approach which moves the party closer to the Canadian ideological center in the hope that will push the Liberal party to the right.

Furthermore, many will argue that a national party which has virtually no organization in the second largest Canadian province, Quebec, is a national party in name only. Serious attempts will probably be made to form an arrangement with the separatist *Parti Québécois*, because of its essentially social-democratic program. Premier Barrett of British Columbia made some unsuccessful overtures in this direction some time ago. Finally, efforts will be made by some to strengthen the financial and organizational base of the federal party, to centralize NDP support rather than to allow its continuing diffusion among the provincial parties.

The 1974 Canadian election marks a turning point for the national New Democratic party. The optimism of the 1960s has dissipated, and for the first time a national leader who is not identified with the struggles to establish the CCF in the 1930s will emerge. Major new directions and initiatives will appear, but only social scientists or fools would attempt to predict their outcome.

Postscript

As this book goes to press, the New Democratic party is engaged in a leadership contest to replace David Lewis. For the first time since the founding, no "saints, prophets, or messiahs" are seeking to lead the party. Instead, the four main contestants are more or less ordinary people who fit into the categories suggested by the title of this paper, purists and pragmatists. All, of course, pay lip service to the old ideals of the party and the principles embodied in the Regina Manifesto. Indeed, at one meeting of all four candidates in Saskatchewan, all suggested that the party needs to return to the tried ideals of the manifesto.

The real debate, however, is being waged at two levels. Rosemary Brown, a Jamaican-born, black member of the British Columbia Legislature, represents the more militant sections of the feminist movement in the party, placing fairly great emphasis on the need for substantial reforms in the treatment accorded women in Canadian society, from freer access to abortions to improved day-care facilities. In addition, she tends to take the most radical positions on economic matters. The latter in itself does not set her substantially apart from the other candidates. While the debate in the 1971 leadership contest centered on the question of public ownership, particularly of the resource industries, in 1975 the perceived need to nationalize the natural resources sector, particularly oil and natural gas, is almost a truism in the NDP. Nevertheless, Brown would most logically fit into the purist category.

Two of the candidates in the current leadership contest ran in 1971. The apparent front-runner in the campaign is Ed Broadbent, current NDP leader in the House of Commons, while John Harney, who finished a strong third in 1971, is now seen to be lagging badly, apparently unable to generate the kind of enthusiasm which surrounded his candidacy last time. The fourth serious candidate is Lorne Nystrom, a member of Parliament for Yorkton-Melville, in Saskatchewan. On his election in 1968 at the age of twenty-one, Nystrom was the youngest person ever elected to the Canadian House of Commons.

All three fit most neatly into the pragmatist category. They argue about the need for new organizational forms for the federal party, having recognized the problems which are faced by a federal party which is merely a ward of its stronger provincial sections. Broadbent already has a record of opposition to the power of the provincial party sections, particularly on the question of money distribution. The new Canadian Election Expenses Act, which was proclaimed shortly after the 1974 election, provides for tax credits to individuals who give money to registered political parties, making it possible for the NDP to increase the size of the large number of small financial contributions that it receives. With the passage of the act, the provincial sections, particularly Ontario, immediately established procedures which would have funneled into the provincial coffers all of the money generated under the federal act. Broadbent strenuously opposed this move and ultimately succeeded in having the Federal Council of the NDP establish a rule which requires the provincial parties to contribute to the national party 15 percent of their take under the federal act.

All of the candidates for the federal leadership understand the problems the federal party faces with respect to its relationships, particularly its financial relationships, with the provincial sections west of Quebec. In addition, Broadbent and Nystrom argue that the federal party needs to acquire its own organizational forms to establish a federal presence in those constituencies which are winnable in a federal election. Included in these seats are all those areas in which the NDP has placed first or second over the last few federal elections and those in which provincial parties hold seats. The numbers of such constituencies range from 50 to 100 depending on the criteria used.

John Harney has an added fillip. Since he is the only one of the leadership candidates who is fluently bilingual (his mother was French and he was raised in Quebec City), he suggests that only he can establish the ties which are needed to pull the NDP out of the doldrums in Quebec. As the data in Table 5-1 (pp. 126–127) show, the NDP has never won a federal seat in Canada's second largest province, and Harney suggests that the Canadian public will never recognize the party as a serious *national* force unless it can demonstrate a capacity to win seats in Quebec. Furthermore, he suggests that it might be possible to effect an alliance with the *Parti Québécois* which will allow the NDP to use that party's organization in Quebec during federal elections.

Overall, the leadership campaign has been dull. New Democrats have come to expect their leaders to be somehow larger than life, and none of the candidates this time are. However, interest in the convention is great, as most ridings are electing full slates of delegates for the first time this decade. A large and noisy convention can be expected in Winnipeg in July.

6

SOCIAL CREDIT PARTY IN THE CANADIAN GENERAL ELECTION OF 1974

Michael B. Stein

Introduction: The Pundits' View of the Social Credit Campaign

Prior to election day, many experienced observers of Canadian politics predicted that the Canadian general election of July 1974 would mark the elimination of the Social Credit party from federal politics. Since 1935, the party has been generally recognized as one of four distinct elements in what has been described as a two-plus or four-party system, composed of two major parties, the Liberals and Conservatives, and two minor parties, the Cooperative Commonwealth Federation-New Democratic party (CCF-NDP) and Social Credit. Social Credit has had unbroken representation in the Canadian House of Commons from the time the party was founded in 1935, with the exception of a brief interlude between the elections of 1958 and 1962 when all opposition parties succumbed to the Diefenbaker sweep. In the period 1962–1963 Social Credit reached its height of thirty legislative representatives drawn from three provinces (Quebec, Alberta, and British Columbia) and held the balance of power in a minority government situation. But after a split between its western and Quebec wings, it experienced a rapid decline. After the 1968 election, the party was reduced to a regional party, with its parliamentary representatives drawn exclusively from Quebec (see Table 6-1 below). In the period between the elections of 1972 and 1974, the party suffered further serious reverses at the provincial level. Its dynamic grassroots leader from rural Quebec, Réal Caouette, was ailing. Few pundits were willing to allow the party more than six or seven seats in preelection forecasts.

Yet when the ballots were finally counted on 8 July, Social Credit had won eleven seats and was in close contention for a twelfth. Several incumbents had again received overwhelming pluralities from their constituents. The conclusion of most commentators was that the Social Credit party had once again defied all logic and managed to hold its own.

How accurate is this pundits' view of the Social Credit campaign? What role did the campaign itself play in determining the party's fortunes? What are its policies, its financial resources, the quality of its candidates, and its techniques of campaigning? What are its major areas of strength and weakness? What do the results suggest about the long-run prospects of Social Credit in Canada?

In order to answer these questions, we must place our discussion of the Social Credit campaign in historical context. Consequently, this essay will be divided into three parts: the historical background of the Social Credit Party of Canada, the pattern of the 1974 campaign, and an evaluation of Social Credit's performance and prospects.

The Historical Background

Evolution of the Federal Party, 1935–1974. The Social Credit party first emerged as a political force in the provincial elections of Alberta of 1935. In that election campaign, its first at any level of government, it swept into power with fifty-six of the sixty-three seats in the Alberta legislature.

The party had initially established itself in Canada in 1933 as a nonpartisan movement under the leadership of William Aberhart, an Alberta high school principal and fundamentalist preacher. He had grasped the relevance of social credit, a monetary reform doctrine first propagated in England by Major Clifford Hugh Douglas in 1918, to the problems of drought and depression in the prairie provinces of the early 1930s.[1] In two years, he had spread the doctrine to all parts of the province through his Bible radio broadcasts, study groups, and lecture tours.[2] When the election was called in 1935, the combination of severe economic crisis, scandal and mismanagement in the previous administration, and brilliant campaign organization and leadership produced a stunning victory for Social Credit.

Soon after the provincial election, the party entered candidates from Alberta and Saskatchewan in the 1935 federal election campaign,

---

[1] For a brief description of this doctrine, see pp. 165-166 below.

[2] See John A. Irving, *The Social Credit Movement in Alberta* (Toronto: University of Toronto Press, 1959), and C. B. Macpherson, *Democracy in Alberta: The Theory and Practice of a Quasi-Party System* (Toronto: University of Toronto Press, 1953).

seventeen of whom managed to win seats in the Ottawa Parliament. It then concentrated on spreading its doctrine to other provinces and establishing an organization which would be able to compete effectively in both provincial and federal politics. It did not have much success in these efforts, however.[3] It also sought to implement its monetary reform proposals in Alberta, and it clashed directly with the federal authorities on the question of jurisdiction over money and banking matters. When the courts ruled that only the federal government could legislate in such matters and declared the Alberta legislation ultra vires, Social Credit was forced to modify its provincial economic program. It gradually transformed itself from a right-wing populist-type movement into a moderate right-of-center party which prided itself on its economic orthodoxy and its efficient, honest administration. This trend, which began in the early 1940s, accelerated after the death of Aberhart in 1943 and the accession to power of his former lieutenant, Ernest Manning. Manning also moved to transform the federal party (of which several parliamentary representatives had clung to orthodox Social Credit doctrines) into a mirror-image of its Alberta counterpart.[4]

The Social Credit party had failed in its efforts to spread eastward from Alberta into the other prairie provinces and Ontario. However, a stroke of good fortune permitted it to gain an important base in the province to the west, British Columbia. W. A. C. Bennett, a former Conservative member of the provincial legislature, had split from that party and formed a Social Credit party which entered the provincial election of British Columbia in 1952 and emerged a surprising victor.[5] The Bennett administration, which merely paid lip-service to Social Credit doctrine, had, like the Manning government, a moderate right-of-center complexion and held orthodox and conservative economic views.

During the first twenty-three years of the federal party's existence, while it was directed by Solon Low, a former provincial

---

[3] Its efforts to spread into Saskatchewan and Manitoba in 1940 and British Columbia in 1945 were totally stymied. See Table 6-2 below.

[4] His actions brought him into conflict with the then small but rapidly expanding Quebec wing of the party, the *Union des Electeurs*, headed by Louis Even and Gilberte Côté-Mercier. The resulting split in 1948 between the eastern and western branches of Social Credit seriously weakened the party's efforts at national expansion over the next decade. See Michael B. Stein, *The Dynamics of Right-Wing Protest: A Political Analysis of Social Credit in Quebec* (Toronto: University of Toronto Press, 1973), Chapter 2.

[5] Under the alternative vote system established for the election by the coalition of Liberals and Conservatives, the Social Credit party won enough second ballot choices to elect the largest number of parliamentary representatives of any party and form the government.

treasurer of Alberta, all but three of the total number of Social Credit M.P.s came from Alberta and British Columbia.[6] After declining from its original representation of seventeen members, the federal caucus slowly increased from a low of ten members in 1940 to nineteen at dissolution in 1958. That election wiped out the entire Social Credit parliamentary delegation, forced the resignation of Low, and led to efforts at reorganization and reunification of the various branches of the party under the leadership of Robert Thompson, a former chiropractor and teacher from Alberta, and the deputy leadership of Réal Caouette, a car dealer from Rouyn, Quebec. The alliance produced thirty members in the 1962 federal election, of whom no fewer than twenty-six came from Quebec.

The base for Social Credit's federal representation from Quebec had been laid by the entrenched, indigenous Social Credit movement, the *Union des Electeurs*, between 1939 and 1957. The electoral activities of this organization proved largely abortive—it managed to elect only one member—but its propaganda and educational efforts were most successful. Beginning as a small mass movement in the rural and semi-urban areas of Quebec, the union expanded its membership to over 60,000 through the circulation of a bimonthly newspaper, *Vers Demain*, the organization of study groups, and the effective use of symbols such as the white beret, which all members were required to wear. It also maintained interest and enthusiasm by participating in all federal and provincial elections in Quebec between 1940 and 1949, and by organizing marches, demonstrations, and pressure group activities. In doctrinal terms, it boasted adherence to social credit orthodoxy, but it blended with the original English doctrine elements of Roman Catholic theology and strong doses of French-Canadian nationalism. Its views on doctrinal questions and political tactics brought it into frequent conflict with the national party and ultimately led to a complete rupture between the Quebec and federal wings that lasted from 1948 until 1959.[7]

Caouette was a member of the more politically conscious second generation of Quebec *Créditistes*. When he sensed an opportunity to wrest the leadership of the national party away from Thompson in 1963, he issued an ultimatum to the national executive and thereby forced a split between his own wing and the national party. The schism produced two Social Credit delegations in the federal House

---

[6] One exception was Réal Caouette, then a member of the *Union des Electeurs*, who won a by-election in Pontiac in 1946 and sat in the House of Commons until his defeat in the general election of 1949. There were also two M.P.s elected from Saskatchewan in 1935.

[7] See Stein, *Dynamics*, Chapter 2.

of Commons, which continued to operate under the separate leaderships of Caouette and Thompson until the election of 1968. In that election the western contingent was completely wiped out. Caouette, acknowledged by then as the leading federal spokesman for Social Credit, moved immediately to reunite the fragmented national party under his leadership and succeeded three years later. By the election of 1972, the organizational structures of the national party had been reestablished across Canada, and the party competed for the first time under Caouette's national leadership. Although it won no seats outside Quebec, it did manage to increase the number of votes it received over its 1968 total.[8] In Quebec itself it increased its legislative representation from fourteen to fifteen and its popular vote from 16 percent to 24 percent of the provincial total. Much of the increment came from the substantial increase in the Quebec party's support in the east end of Montreal.

The period following the 1972 election, then, was a time of some optimism for the federal party. In Quebec, a split between two factions of the *Ralliement Créditiste du Québec*, the provincial party formed in 1970, had been temporarily healed, and a convention had been called to choose a new provincial leader. But cracks were already beginning to appear in the fragile structure of the reunited party. By the time the election was called in 1974, they had become apparent to most observers.

Bases of Support for the Federal Party, 1935–1972. A brief glance at Table 6-1 reveals clearly how both the legislative representation and the popular vote support for the national Social Credit party increased gradually under the leadership of Solon Low, from a low of ten seats and 3 percent of the popular vote in 1940 to a high of nineteen seats and 7 percent of the popular vote in 1957. The following year, however, the Conservatives amassed a record majority of 208 seats and 54 percent of the popular vote, completely devastating the other parties. Social Credit failed to win a single seat and retained only 2 percent of the popular vote. After the reorganization of the party under Thompson and Caouette, however, the party rose in 1962 to a new high of thirty seats and 12 percent of the popular vote. It retained that proportion of the popular vote the following year— while dropping six seats in Quebec. The split between Thompson and Caouette soon had destructive consequences for the party. The Thompson group won five seats and 4 percent of the popular vote in 1965, whereas the Caouette group won nine seats and 5 percent

---

[8] See Table 6-1 below.

Table 6-1
CANADIAN GENERAL ELECTION RESULTS, 1878–1974

Election Year	Party Forming Federal Gov't.	Total Seats	Conservative Seats	Conservative Votes	Liberal Seats	Liberal Votes	Progressive Seats	Progressive Votes	CCF-NDP Seats	CCF-NDP Votes	Social Credit Seats	Social Credit Votes	Reconstruction Seats	Reconstruction Votes	Other Seats	Other Votes
1878	Conservative	206	140	53%	65	45%									1	2%
1882	Conservative	211	138	53	73	47										
1887	Conservative	215	128	51	87	49										
1891	Conservative	215	122	52	91	46									2	2
1896	Liberal	213	88	46	118	45									7	9
1900	Liberal	213	81	47	132	52									1	1
1904	Liberal	214	75	47	139	52									1	1
1908	Liberal	221	85	47	135	51									1	2
1911	Conservative	221	134	51	87	48									1	1
1917	Conservative [a]	235	153[b]	57	82[c]	40									3	3
1921	Liberal	235	50	30	116	41	65	23%							4	6
1925	Liberal	245	116	46	99	40	24	9							6	5
1926	Liberal	245	91	45	128	46	20	5							6	4
1930	Conservative	245	137	49	91	45	12	3							5	3
1935	Liberal	245	40	30	173	45			7	9%	17	4%	1	9%	7	3
1940	Liberal	245	40	31	181	51			8	8	10	3			6	7
1945	Liberal	245	67	27	125	41			28	16	13	4			12	12
1949	Liberal	262	41	30	193	49			13	13	10	4			5	4

1953	Liberal	265	51	31	171	49	23	11	15	5			5	4
1957	Conservative	265	112	39	105	41	25	11	19	7			4	2
1958	Conservative	265	208	54	49	34	8	9	2					1
1962	Conservative	265	116	37	100	37	19	14	30	12				
1963	Liberal	265	95	33	129	42	17	13	24	12				
1965	Liberal	265	97	32	131	40	21	18	5	4	9[d]	5[e]	2	1
1968	Liberal	264	72	31	155	45	21	17	0	1	14[d]	5[e]	0	1
1972	Liberal	264	107	35	109	38	31	18	15	8			2	1
1974	Liberal	264	95	35	141	43	16	16	11	5			1	1

[a] Wartime coalition
[b] Government
[c] Opposition
[d] *Créditiste* seats
[e] *Créditiste* votes (percent)

Sources: Hugh G. Thorburn, ed., *Party Politics in Canada*, 3rd ed., revised (Scarborough, Ont.: Prentice-Hall of Canada, 1972); *The Montreal Star*, 9 July 1974, p. 1. Figures for 1974 are based on 96 percent of polls.

of the popular vote, giving Social Credit a combined total of only fourteen seats and 9 percent of the popular vote, well down from its performances in 1962 and 1963. In 1968 the western group (no longer headed by Thompson) failed to win a single seat and garnered only 1 percent of the popular vote, whereas the Caouette group increased their representation to fourteen seats and maintained their share of the popular vote at 5 percent, producing a combined Social Credit total of fourteen seats and 6 percent of the popular vote. It is not surprising, then, that Caouette was so easily able to reunite the party after 1968, despite a residue of bitterness in the national party over his 1963 secession. Clearly, the hopes for Social Credit rested on Caouette and the Quebec wing. In 1972, these hopes seemed to have been justified to a degree: under the leadership of Caouette, the reunited party increased its legislative representation to fifteen seats and its popular vote total to 8 percent. It should also be noted that throughout the period 1935–1972 Social Credit was the fourth party in Canada in terms of popular vote. Although its seat representation was occasionally greater than that of the CCF-NDP (in 1935, 1940, 1962, and 1963), its proportion of the popular vote in Canada at no time equaled or exceeded that of the third party.

Furthermore, in addition to being a fourth party, Social Credit was always a highly regionalized party and could never seriously support its pretensions to being a national party. Table 6-2 indicates from where that regional support has been largely drawn. In 1935 Social Credit won fifteen of Alberta's seventeen seats in the House of Commons and 48 percent of that province's vote. Thereafter, it never won as many federal seats or votes in the province. Nevertheless, it did retain between ten and thirteen of Alberta's seventeen seats, and its popular vote was relatively stable, between 35 percent and 41 percent of the provincial total. Even in the Diefenbaker bandwagon of 1958, the party managed to capture 22 percent of the provincial vote. In the period 1962–1968, the party won only two seats in Alberta, but retained between 23 percent and 29 percent of the popular vote. In 1968, however, after Thompson had defected to the Conservatives, it plunged to only 2 percent of the provincial vote, and has failed to recover since. In British Columbia, Social Credit support never was as high. Even after Bennett captured power there in 1952, the party won only four of the province's twenty-two seats in the House of Commons and 26 percent of its popular vote. After 1958 its vote total dwindled to between 10 percent and 17 percent of the provincial total and, after the disaster of 1968, fell to less than 5 percent.

In Quebec, the *Union des Electeurs* failed to win a single seat in any federal general election between 1940 and 1949, but its popular vote reached a high of 5.1 percent in the last federal election in which it competed. The *Ralliement des Créditistes*, the union's successor, won twenty-six seats and 26 percent of the popular vote in the first election which it contested (1962), and thereafter steadily lost ground until its slight resurgence in 1972. But the entire Social Credit representation in the House of Commons, with the exception of two Social Credit seats in Saskatchewan in 1935, was confined to these three provinces. There was a scattering of Social Credit support in Saskatchewan, which reached a high of 10 percent in 1957, after declining drastically from its original total of 16 percent in 1935. After 1958, popular vote support dropped to below 5 percent. A similar pattern can be discerned in Manitoba. In New Brunswick, Social Credit support attained a high of 9 percent in 1963, then dropped below 5 percent again. In no other province did the party manage to win even 5 percent of the vote in any federal general election. The chief hopes for the party in 1974, then, apart from Quebec, were Alberta and British Columbia, where there was some prospect of rebuilding an earlier base.

Social Credit's Campaign in 1974

The Events. The 1974 campaign began on 9 May 1974, when Prime Minister Trudeau called on Governor General Jules Léger to dissolve Parliament and proclaim an election for 8 July. The governing Liberals had been defeated on a nonconfidence motion on the budget initiated by the New Democratic party and supported by the Progressive Conservatives. The Social Credit party had voted with the Liberals against the motion.

The want-of-confidence motion caught the Social Credit party by surprise.[9] The fate of the minority Liberal government had always hung on the support of the NDP, which held the balance of power in the House of Commons. Its leader, David Lewis, had expressed his strong dissatisfaction with the budgetary proposals outlined by Finance Minister John Turner, Liberal measures which he considered inadequate to fight inflation. Nevertheless, in numerous want-of-confidence motions put forward by the Conservative party since the 1972 election, the NDP had rescued the Liberals from defeat. It was

---

[9] In Caouette's more colorful phrase, the party was caught "with our pants down" (*avec nos culottes baissées*). *Le Devoir*, 20 June 1974, p. 12.

Table 6-2

SOCIAL CREDIT FEDERAL GENERAL ELECTION RESULTS BY PROVINCE AND TERRITORIES, 1935–1974

Provinces [a]

Election Year	Party Forming Gov't.	British Columbia			Alberta			Saskatchewan			Manitoba			Ontario		
		Total seats	SC seats	SC votes	Total seats	SC seats	SC votes	Total seats	SC seats	SC votes	Total seats	SC seats	SC votes	Total seats	SC seats	SC votes
1935	Liberal	16	—	—	17	15	48%	21	2	16%	17	—	—	82	—	—
1940	Liberal	16	—	—	17	10	35	21	—	3	17	—	2%	82	—	—
1945	Liberal	16	—	2%	17	13	37	21	—	3	17	—	3	82	—	—
1949	Liberal	18	—	1	17	10	37	20	—	1	16	—	—	83	—	—
1953	Liberal	22	4	26	17	11	41	17	—	5	14	—	6	85	—	—
1957	Conservative	22	6	24	17	13	38	17	—	11	14	—	13	85	—	2%
1958	Conservative	22	—	10	17	—	22	17	—	—	14	—	2	85	—	—
1962	Conservative	22	2	14	17	2	29	17	—	—	14	—	7	85	—	—
1963	Liberal	22	2	13	17	2	26	17	—	4	14	—	7	85	—	2
1965	Liberal	22	3	17	17	2	23	17	—	2	14	—	4	85	—	—
1968	Liberal	23	—	5	17	—	2	13	—	—	13	—	2	88	—	—
1972	Liberal	23	—	3	17	—	5	13	—	2	13	—	1	88	—	—
1974	Liberal	23	—	1	17	—	3	13	—	—	13	—	1	88	—	—

Table 6-2 (continued)

Election Year	Party Forming Gov't.	Provinces [a]												Total		
		Quebec			New Brunswick			Newfoundland			Territories					
		Total seats	SC seats	SC votes	Total seats	SC seats	SC votes	Total seats	SC seats	SC votes	Total seats	SC seats	SC votes	Total seats	SC seats	SC votes
1935	Liberal	65	—	—	10	—	—	—	—	—	1	—	—	—	17	—
1940	Liberal	65	—	1%	10	—	—	—	—	—	1	—	—	245	10	3%
1945	Liberal	65	—	5	10	—	1%	—	—	—	1	—	—	245	13	4
1949	Liberal	73	—	5	10	—	—	7	—	—	2	—	—	262	10	4
1953	Liberal	75	—	—	10	—	—	7	—	—	2	—	14%	265	15	5
1957	Conservative	75	—	—	10	—	1	7	—	—	2	—	—	265	19	7
1958	Conservative	75	—	1	10	—	1	7	—	—	2	—	—	265	—	3
1962	Conservative	75	26	26	10	—	5	7	—	—	2	—	7	265	30	12
1963	Liberal	75	20	27	10	—	9	7	—	—	2	—	4	265	24	12
1965	Liberal	75	9	18	10	—	—	7	—	2%	2	—	—	265	14	9
1968	Liberal	74	14	16	10	—	1	7	—	—	2	—	—	264	14	6
1972	Liberal	74	15	24	10	—	6	7	—	—	2	—	—	264	15	8
1974	Liberal	74	11	17	10	—	3	7	—	—	2	—	—	264	11	5

[a] The Social Credit vote has never exceeded 1% in Nova Scotia or Prince Edward Island. Total federal Parliament seats from Nova Scotia were twelve in 1935, 1940, 1949-1965; thirteen in 1945; and eleven, 1968-1974. Prince Edward Island has had four seats in the federal Parliament during the entire period covered by this table.

Sources: Howard A. Scarrow, *Canada Votes, A Handbook of Federal and Provincial Election Data* (New Orleans: Hauser Press, 1962); Thorburn, *Party Politics in Canada; The Gazette*, 3 July 1974, p. 9; and *The Montreal Star*, 13 July 1974. The 1974 results are unofficial and include only 98.8 percent of total polls in Canada.

known that a number of the thirty-one members of the NDP caucus were opposed to an early election, fearing that the NDP would suffer a defeat due to popular sentiment in favor of majority government. At the very least, some Social Crediters speculated that the NDP caucus would split on the question, thus allowing Social Credit to determine the fate of the Liberal government.[10]

The Social Crediters were ill prepared for the election. Caouette had been absent from the House of Commons from January until April, recovering from a snowmobile accident which had hospitalized him twice and had damaged his vocal chords. In the interim there were rumors that several Social Credit incumbents, afraid of losing their seats, had explored the possibility of defecting to the Conservatives.[11] Enthusiasm for the cause was also at a low ebb among the party's old-time supporters, who had opposed the intervention of Caouette in provincial politics on behalf of one candidate (Yvon Dupuis) for the leadership of the Quebec Social Credit party the previous year. Dupuis was elected provincial party leader, and subsequently led the party to a disastrous defeat in the 1973 provincial election.

The Social Credit campaign was marked by several false starts. Whereas the other party leaders held their first press conference in Ottawa on 11 May, Caouette delayed his until 17 May. He announced at that time that he had met with the provincial presidents of the party, who were in the process of putting together a list of all the candidates that the party would field, of whom there would be about 200.[12] Caouette officially launched his campaign on 25 May at a small rally in Sainte-Germaine-de-Bellechasse. But he canceled a planned reception that night in Montmagny and a scheduled press conference the following day in Mont Joli, Rimouski, and returned to his home town of Rouyn. He was subsequently hospitalized for three days for what was termed a "routine" examination of his diabetic condition. Several observers noted, however, that he had looked extremely fatigued at his first public meeting of the campaign.

Although Caouette denied that ill health has disrupted his campaign—referring to those who spread such rumors as *maudits cochons* ("damn pigs")—he did allude to a leadership convention in the fall, and promised to resign if his doctors instructed him to do so. He

---

10 *La Presse*, 7 May 1974.
11 *Le Devoir*, 10 April 1974, p. 1.
12 This was to include at least one candidate in every province and a candidate in all seventy-four constituencies in Quebec. *La Presse*, 17 May 1974. As we shall see below, the number of candidates actually nominated fell far short of that mark.

mentioned René Matte of Champlain, deputy Social Credit leader in parliamentary matters, André Fortin (Lotbinière), the former House leader for Social Credit, and his son Gilles (Charlevoix), recently named to succeed Fortin as possible candidates for the leadership of the party. When interviewed by reporters, Fortin declared that he would wait until the fall to declare his candidacy, but opined that a leadership convention would be desirable "to rewarm the cold hearts" of *Créditistes* disaffected over the Dupuis affair. Matte asserted that he was ready to replace Caouette and would contest the leadership at the October congress. He also pointed out that he had been named "assistant leader" in April 1973 to coordinate the parliamentary work of Social Credit and assume the leadership if the eventuality should arise. Both incumbents indicated that they were not at all surprised to learn of Caouette's illness.[13]

Caouette issued an immediate and angry retort. He pointed out that the prerogative of calling a leadership convention rests entirely with the national executive, and that the plans that then existed were to hold a National Council meeting in the fall. No leadership convention was likely until 1975 or 1976. He cast aspersions on Matte's and Fortin's leadership capabilities, pointing out that they could not speak English. He mentioned, along with his son Gilles, James Roland Chabot, a native Quebecker transplanted to British Columbia who had served as minister of education in the Bennett administration, as another possible candidate.[14]

This open challenge to Caouette by several of the Social Credit incumbents in the midst of a campaign could only damage Social Credit by further weakening confidence in its leadership. Nevertheless, having received a clean bill of health from his doctor, Caouette left on 4 June for a whirlwind tour of the western provinces. Caouette's first stop, on 4 June, was Vancouver, where he conducted a press conference, appeared on two radio call-in shows, and attended an evening rally for local party supporters. He addressed his audiences with vigor and won plaudits for his spirited criticism of the New Democratic provincial government. However, the hoped-for support from the British Columbia Social Credit party was not forthcoming. The following day Caouette flew to Red Deer, Alberta, where he held a press conference, taped a half-hour television broadcast, and attended a banquet and political rally for Social Credit party workers. He concentrated his attack on the Conservative candidate's proposal

---

[13] *La Presse*, 28 May 1974, p. A-8.
[14] *La Presse*, 1 June 1974, p. A-1.

of a wage and price freeze. This time his efforts seemed to bear fruit; he received an endorsement from the Alberta Social Credit League President Francis Porter. On 6 June Caouette flew to Saskatoon, Saskatchewan, where he attended a local party rally and a dinner meeting, and participated in a radio call-in show. He assailed his opponents for "stealing Social Credit clothes"—in particular, its program of a universally guaranteed annual income, and its proposal for an old-age pension of $200 a month for all people over sixty years of age. The last stop in the western leg of the tour was Winnipeg, with another press conference, a radio show, two television interviews, and an evening rally for a small group of party supporters. Caouette issued a challenge to the three other party leaders to join him in a television debate. He also denounced Liberal failures in housing and home mortgages.

Caouette's style of campaigning had changed markedly from that of earlier elections. Instead of speaking before large public meetings, he confined himself almost entirely to the electronic media, particularly radio call-in shows. His speeches were shorter and were delivered in a much more subdued manner than in the past, when he had often treated his audience to long harangues. According to Caouette, these changes permitted him to reach large numbers of people at far less expense. Moreover, he wished to play the role of elder statesman, in keeping with his newly acquired national stature. But there were clearly other motivations for the altered format, including the need to preserve his fragile health. Moreover, the potential size of audiences for public meetings was much smaller than in the 1960s, when Social Credit could still pose as a national party.

Upon his return to Quebec, Caouette toured *Créditiste* strongholds in the Eastern Townships and the region southeast of Quebec City. He concentrated his attacks on the Conservative program of a wage-price freeze, which he envisaged as leading to a black market. He promised to use the balance-of-power position, if it were accorded to him, to force the Conservatives to abandon the policy. In Montreal, on 13 June, he exhorted *Parti Québécois* leaders to disobey their leaders' call for annulment of their ballots or abstention and to support Social Credit as "the least evil." He boasted of his party's penetration into metropolitan Montreal for the first time in 1972. He attacked the socialists for their naive belief in universal equality, and he offered as an alternative his own party's program of a guaranteed minimum income, an old-age pension for all individuals over sixty, a discount of 25 percent for consumers on all retail prices, and interest-free loans (paid through the Bank of Canada) to governments, municipalities, and school boards.[15]

On 17-18 June Caouette undertook a quick junket to the maritime provinces. At Moncton, heart of the New Brunswick Acadian community, he refused to denounce ex-Mayor Leonard Jones, the opponent of official bilingualism. Jones had been rejected as a candidate by Conservative leader Stanfield and had subsequently decided to run as an independent. Caouette surprised the local press by announcing that he would accept the former mayor into his own party, which supported bilingualism, if he endorsed Social Credit economic doctrine. In Halifax he warned of the socialist menace posed by Trudeau and the New Democratic party and pointed his finger at the oil executives for artificially creating the impression of an oil shortage the previous winter. Caouette's visit to this part of Canada seemed largely designed to bolster his image as a genuinely national leader and to catalyze local organizers who had been slow to launch their campaigns.[16]

Disarray in the *Créditiste* organization became even more apparent after nomination lists were closed on 18 June. Social Credit had nominated only 154 candidates, well short of Caouette's publicly stated objective of 200. Moreover, no candidates had been presented in Richelieu and Lévis, both areas of considerable *Créditiste* strength in the past. And in Labelle, another area with substantial earlier Social Credit support, two candidates were mistakenly accredited by the party.[17] Embarrassed, the Social Credit leader promised to investigate these "administrative oversights" and expose any possible political subterfuge by the opposition parties in such matters.[18]

On his return to Quebec, Caouette made a brief stop in Chicoutimi, in the Saguenay-Lac Saint Jean region. Aware of the *Parti Québécois's* strength in the region, he again attacked the call by that party for annulment of ballots and defended his position on ex-Mayor Jones. He stressed his party's conception of a decentralized federalism, and its advocacy of every province's right of self-determination and peaceful secession from Confederation. He also mocked the Liberals for floating "electoral balloons," such as the program to nationalize rail passenger service.[19]

---

[15] *The Gazette*, 14 June 1974, p. 8.

[16] *La Presse*, 18 June 1974, p. A-15.

[17] For an elaboration of this anomalous situation, see pp. 164 and 169-170 below.

[18] *The Gazette*, 19 June 1974, p. 51.

[19] *The Montreal Star*, 20 June 1974, p. A-10, and *La Presse*, 20 June 1974, p. A-11.

On 21 June Caouette returned to his home riding of Témiscamingue, ostensibly to participate in formal ceremonies of a non-political nature on the opening of the Tembec paper mill. But Caouette did not miss the opportunity to point out that he had played a key role in bringing the local citizens together with Regional Expansion Minister Don Jamieson, thereby paving the way for a $4.8 million federal grant for the project. For Caouette, Tembec could serve as a model of the kind of partnership of government, private capital, and local populations envisaged in Social Credit philosophy.[20] In reality, Tembec reflected the defensive quality of *Créditiste* campaigning, since the party incumbents were frequently forced to apologize for their failure to obtain fat government contracts or capital projects for their ridings.

The following day, in Quebec City, Caouette met his first overtly hostile reception on an open-line radio show. Residents of Lévis, in the metropolitan area of Quebec, angrily inquired about the absence of a Social Credit candidate in the riding, and one woman accused Caouette of personal negligence in the affair. Caouette promised to continue his inquiry into the matter. In Beauce, the Social Credit leader met a somewhat indifferent audience of party supporters who gave *Créditiste* provincial House leader Fabien Roy a much warmer ovation. The *Beaucerons*, generally the most avid of Quebec political participants, had been angered by Caouette's support of Yvon Dupuis the previous year. At Montmagny, in the Quebec City region, Caouette was somewhat overshadowed by the popular local candidate, Adrien Lambert.[21] But the determined leader counterattacked, blaming local *Créditiste* organizers in Lévis for internal squabbling and poor organization. The same day he received an enthusiastic reception from the supporters of René Matte in Saint-Tite, a village in the Champlain riding.

Recriminations continued, however. Wilfrid Marin, one of the two official Social Credit candidates in Labelle, alleged that Caouette and national party organizer Gilbert Rondeau had been responsible for the mishap in Labelle. He claimed that Rondeau had asked him to withdraw his candidacy in order to uphold the terms of an agreement worked out with the Conservatives to nominate weak candidates in ridings where the other party was strong. Marcel Masse, the former *Union Nationale* cabinet minister and a leading Conservative candidate, concurred in these details, but accused Marin of

[20] *Le Devoir*, 21 June 1974, p. 2.
[21] *Le Devoir*, 22 June 1974; *La Presse*, 24-25 June 1974.

asking for $10,000 from him in payment for the Social Crediter's withdrawal.

Caouette shrugged off these charges, and pursued his gruelling campaign, crisscrossing eastern, southern, central, and northwest Quebec. At times the pace seemed to take its toll. In La Pocatière, in the Bas du Fleuve, he blurted out to one open-line radio participant who was criticizing his positions on a deep-water port for the Bas du Fleuve and on day-care centers (Caouette opposed both): "Vote Communist, socialist, or syphilis, and leave us in peace." His tendency to dwell occasionally on inappropriate themes—for example, the environment while in the Bas du Fleuve and rural issues in urban Montreal—was seen to reflect an insensitivity to his political surroundings uncharacteristic of the Caouette of old. However, in the last week of the campaign he returned to his home territory in northwest Quebec and seemed to recover some of his old-time zest and campaign skills. He held five public assemblies in the three constituencies of the region, drawing some of his largest audiences of the campaign. In the last days prior to polling he confidently predicted that Social Credit would hold the balance of power in Ottawa and would win seats not only in Quebec, but also in the West and New Brunswick. No one took these comments seriously. When the polls closed on 8 July, the general consensus among political observers was that the Caouette strategy of an impersonal electronic campaign had failed, and that the Social Credit organization in Quebec was about to collapse.[22]

Platform, Ideology and Appeal. The Social Credit platform in the 1974 campaign was a vague general statement of the party's goals in most spheres, without precise definition of the policies intended to implement them. In broad terms, these policy goals were derived from general principles drawn from the doctrine of Major Douglas, Social Credit's British founder and ideological mentor.

The central tenets of social-credit doctrine are distillations of ideas first presented in Douglas's early writings in the 1920s and 1930s. In the social-philosophic sphere Douglas stressed the primacy of the individual as against the collectivity. In the economic sphere he emphasized the value of free enterprise and rejected both state socialism and monopoly capitalism. He also offered an explanation for economic crises embodied in what was known as the "A + B theorem." The theorem attributed such crises to a deficiency of purchasing power in the hands of consumers. The gap was to be made

---

[22] See, for example, *The Montreal Star*, 6 July 1974, p. A-7.

up by distributing an annual dividend to all citizens, providing a rebate to sellers to enable them to lower prices, and instituting other similar monetary reform measures. Finally, in the political sphere Douglas opposed centralized bureaucratic decision making and supported forms of plebiscitarian democratic rule.[23]

The fundamental principles of social credit were described in the party's 1974 platform as follows: (1) The individual is the most important factor in organized society. As a divinely created being, he has inalienable rights respecting his spiritual and physical potential and needs. (2) The major function of an elected and responsible government is to secure for the people the results they want from the management of their public affairs. (3) The individual must enjoy both political and economic freedom and security, which are essential for his full development. (4) Whatever is physically possible and desirable can and should be made financially possible.[24] Central to the realization of these principles is the idea of monetary reform, that is, the restoration to the Canadian people through their Parliament of the right to issue all money and credit.[25] These principles are intended to guide Social Credit thinking in each of the major policy spheres: individual and civil rights, financial policy, fiscal policy, foreign affairs, domestic policies, the administration of justice, and parliamentary reform. The right-wing component of the movement was reflected in the party's advocacy of such conservative measures as the establishment of special courts to rule on labor-management disputes when the bargaining process breaks down, the granting of de facto recognition to all democratically elected governments and opposition to all forms of totalitarianism, fostering the system of private, competitive enterprise, buttressing the maintenance of public order, and opposition to abortion and to the abolition of capital punishment. There were also a number of unorthodox economic measures, reflecting the anti-establishment and monetary-reform orientation of the party. For example, the party proposed the establishment of a national credit board to regulate the money supply and to ensure that the aggregate purchasing power at the disposal of consumers is equivalent to the aggregate prices of available consumer goods. These objectives were to be achieved by means of retail price discounts and income security programs. The former involve paying subsidies to retailers on condition that they discount their prices by

---

[23] See Stein, *Dynamics*, Chapter 2, and Macpherson, *Democracy*.

[24] *The Social Credit Party Proposes* . . . , platform of the Social Credit Party, special edition *Regards* (n.d.), p. 3.

[25] Ibid., p. 3.

equivalent amounts in order to eliminate inflation. The latter involve the phasing out of all existing income maintenance programs and their replacement by a guaranteed annual income payment of $1,500 to $6,000, depending on age, marital status, number of children, disability, and so on. (This is a modern version of the national dividend.) Income tax exemptions would be increased to $3,000 per year for single persons and $6,000 per year for married couples. Social Credit also promised to amend the Bank of Canada Act to grant interest-free loans to provinces and municipalities.[26]

The platform for Social Credit campaigns is generally formulated by the party's National Council, a body which is supposed to be comprised of local party members from each constituency in the country (in reality many constituencies are unrepresented), and which meets at least every two years. It is then revised and touched up by the National Executive, made up of the leading organizers from each province. Because the 1974 election was unexpected, the party was unable to call a National Council meeting; the platform in 1974 was essentially the same as that used in the 1972 campaign, with a few minor revisions incorporated at the National Council meeting in Winnipeg in the fall of 1973.

Since the main issue of the campaign was inflation and the general state of the economy, Caouette and the other candidates emphasized the economic aspects of the Social Credit program. In particular, they stressed the idea of a guaranteed minimum income, interest-free loans by the Bank of Canada to provinces and municipalities, pensions for all Canadians over sixty, and a compensatory rebate of 25 percent on the purchase of goods by consumers. There was also strong opposition to the wage-price freeze proposed by the Conservatives, on the grounds that the imposition of controls would greatly centralize power over the economy in the central government, a situation inimical to basic Social Credit principles of decentralized economic and political power. Social Crediters also believed that the controls would be impossible to enforce and would inevitably lead to black market operations.

Caouette adopted a very pragmatic attitude on policy questions which he considered to be ancillary to the main principles of social credit. This explains his refusal to attack Mayor Jones's stance against official bilingualism, despite the party's commitment to this policy in its platform. Similarly, among Social Credit candidates in Quebec were both strong opponents and strong supporters of Bill 22, the

---

[26] Ibid., pp. 7-11.

provincial Liberal government's effort to make French the only official language of the province. Moreover, despite the party's firm commitment to a decentralized federalism within confederation, Caouette accepted separatist *Parti Québécois* militants as candidates and organizers for his party federally, provided they agreed to uphold Social Credit economic principles.[27]

Unlike past Social Credit campaigns, in which Social Credit ideas had been projected in part through use of the electronic media and in part by effective door-to-door campaigning, small-town walking tours, and large public meetings conducted by the national leader, Caouette's campaign relied almost exclusively on the electronic media. This placed a great premium on Caouette's own ability to transmit the party's ideas to both English and French Canadians on short (about fifteen minutes) radio and television broadcasts and on call-in radio shows running about one-half hour each. Caouette's image and charisma were, therefore, important ingredients in the Social Credit message. In the past Caouette's energetic and folksy personality had played a major part in attracting a large following in rural and semi-urban Quebec, though he had never succeeded in winning much support in the large metropolitan centers of Quebec and had almost no appeal to non-Francophone Canadians. By 1974, however, after many years in the federal Parliament, Caouette had become a familiar face to most Canadians. His newly acquired national stature undoubtedly earned him tolerant and even sympathetic audiences among Francophones and Anglophones in all parts of Canada. It is doubtful, however, that this sympathy was translated into many votes for his party. Caouette's personality tended to reinforce the widespread public conception of Social Credit as an ideology of the rural lower-middle class and the working class, with only limited applicability to the complex problems of a large, primarily urbanized and industrialized society. And in his traditional strongholds, Caouette's wan appearance and lack of missionary fervor must have detracted from his message.

Candidate Selection. Because Social Credit has always conceived of itself as a decentralized, grassroots movement, the Constitution and formal structures of the organization provide for the democratic selection of candidates by means of constituency conventions comprised of local party members. In practice, however, centralized control over the selection of candidates has always been maintained through the exercise of a veto by the party leader. This has been true

---

[27] See *Le Devoir*, 22 June 1974, p. 2.

of Social Credit parties at both the national and provincial levels. Indeed, it has been convincingly argued that centralized control of party and governmental decision making is a necessary concomitant of the plebiscitarian democratic ideology to which the party subscribes.[28]

In 1974 the process of candidate selection within the party was subjected to severe criticism in several quarters and even became an issue in the campaign, as we have already observed. From the time he first founded the Quebec branch of the party, the *Ralliement des Créditistes*, Caouette had always maintained a tight control over the selection of candidates running under his leadership. Caouette's attitudes on this question had probably been shaped by his earlier experiences in the *Union des Electeurs* in the 1940s and 1950s. Gilberte Côté-Mercier, one of the co-founders of the union, in Caouette's view, had undermined *Créditiste* election efforts through her high-handed method of selecting only those candidates nominated by local associations whom she considered to be "true believers" in the movement and its doctrine. In that way, she had prevented the selection of "prestige" candidates who could transform the narrow-based, sectarian image of the *Créditiste* movement. Caouette continued Gilberte's practice of handpicking candidates, but he used it to a different end. He retained the option of selecting candidates who might not be the choice of local militants of the movement, but might bring nonpartisan support to Social Credit from outside.

An example of this type of practice occurred in Sherbrooke, Quebec, where Caouette disregarded the local militants and selected André Breton, a well-known local television personality, as the Social Credit candidate. Breton admitted that he had only a fleeting acquaintance with Social Credit ideas. Caouette's action caused much consternation among local *Créditistes*, and several refused to work for Breton. As a result, the organization in Sherbrooke was severely weakened, and the Social Credit vote was far below that of earlier campaigns in the riding. A similar effort on Caouette's part to recruit artist Serge Laprade in Richelieu led to a split in the local organization and, ultimately, to the failure to find any candidate for the riding.

Another rationale for centralized control over candidate selection was the need to maintain freedom of action in order to negotiate electoral bargains with candidates and organizers of other parties. An example of this was the alleged secret understanding with the Conservatives in Quebec over running weak candidates in constituencies

---

[28] See Macpherson, *Democracy*.

where the candidates of the other party were strong. If the account by Marin (corroborated by Masse) is to be believed, Caouette and party organizer Rondeau deliberately tried to set aside the more popular local choice in Labelle and replace him by a virtual unknown in order to ensure Masse's election. But an administrative oversight permitted two form letters over Caouette's signature to be posted, causing the names of both Social Credit candidates to appear on the ballot. When his plan was exposed, Caouette reverted to endorsing Marin, the original local choice. These tactics helped to destroy whatever organization had existed in Labelle and aroused much criticism in party circles. A charge of similar collusion between Social Credit and Liberals in St. Hyacinthe and Brome-Missisquoi was leveled at Social Credit by the Conservative incumbents in those ridings.

Despite this centralized control (or perhaps because of it), the process of candidate selection was poorly administered and led to several glaring examples of mismanagement. As we noted above, in Lévis, a riding with substantial Social Credit support, internal squabbles among party militants could not be resolved by the provincial or national leadership, and no candidate was nominated. In Rivière du Loup, Bernard Dumont, a former member of both the federal and provincial legislatures, was rejected by the party leadership and ran as an independent Social Crediter, thereby splitting the Social Credit vote in the constituency. In Montmorency, another former *Créditiste* stronghold, the party organizers rejected all candidates proposed by the central leadership and threw their support behind the Conservative candidate.

The party organization faced severe problems in attempting to recruit candidates in weak Social Credit districts. In Hull, for example, the failure of the official candidate either to campaign or to answer his phone was attributed by his agent to his "timidity." In Montreal, as well, many Social Credit candidates openly refused to campaign. Poll watchers could not be found in several metropolitan ridings where Social Credit had placed second in 1972.

This problem was exacerbated in other provinces. Outside Quebec, selection and approval of candidates was left to local organizers and provincial executives. Initially, Caouette had predicted that over 200 candidates would be nominated across the country, and his visits to certain areas (Halifax, for instance) were made with the express purpose of rousing the local organizations to action. Yet only 154 candidates were nominated. In British Columbia, where the provincial organization is still strong, only five candidates were nominated out of a possible total of twenty-three. In the Acadian district of Restigouche, New Brunswick, where the party had received over 10,000 votes in 1972, the Social Credit candidate was chosen after the man who had run in past elections defected to the Conservatives, taking with him most of the local Social Credit militants. The Social Credit candidate was left with a unilingual Anglophone octogenarian as his chief organizer.[29]

It is not surprising, therefore, that despite Caouette's desire for "prestige" candidates, the overall quality of Social Credit candidates was very poor both inside and outside Quebec. In Quebec, three of the incumbents, Roland Godin of Portneuf, Henri Latulippe (Compton), and Lionel Beaudoin (Richmond) did not initially wish to run, but agreed to do so reluctantly when suitable replacements could not be found. All three were defeated. The only serious new candidate with any local prestige, Thérèse Mercier, a store supervisor in Frontenac, was also defeated.

These problems were attributed by one leading party organizer to insufficient funds in the party coffers to induce candidates of quality to run: "Social Credit candidates are forced to pay their own expenses, and these may run to $5,000 or $10,000. There are many people who would be ready to become candidates but fail to do so because they don't have the money."[30] However, it seems to this writer that the absence of funds merely exacerbated a problem of candidate selection inherent in the ideological and organizational weakness of the party itself.

Party Finance. Since Social Credit views itself as a grassroots movement, it has traditionally prided itself on its grassroots methods of finance. In fact, the original ideology of the movement rejected the corporate donations accepted by the old-line parties as inherently corrupting. In the orthodox Douglas view, corporate donations were the means by which monopoly capitalism and banking institutions made the traditional parties their handmaidens and ensured that the evils of the existing system would survive.

In practice, however, the national Social Credit party has resorted to a variety of methods of finance, including those which contravene the spirit of its ideology. It is a decentralized organization which has lived a hand-to-mouth existence, relying principally on subscriptions and small donations from local supporters to its constituency associations across Canada. However, in the early days under Solon Low,

---

[29] *La Presse*, 29 June 1974, p. A-11.
[30] Interview with Gérard Croteau, provincial president, Quebec, *Le Parti Crédit Social*, Ottawa, 20 August 1974 (author's translation).

the Alberta provincial Social Credit League, which was generally well funded by corporate donations and oil revenues, contributed a substantial proportion of the national party funds. After 1953, the British Columbia Social Credit party also contributed disproportionately to the national party coffers.[31]

The Quebec branch of the federal party, like the other important provincial wings, has always maintained complete financial autonomy. The *Ralliement des Créditistes* took as its model the methods of self-finance developed by the *Union des Electeurs*. These included annual membership subscriptions solicited in the party newspaper, passing of the hat at party meetings, and revenues from lotteries, bingo games, and similar gambling devices. Parliamentary representatives and more affluent members made somewhat larger contributions. There was also some canvassing of small local businesses. The revenues from these activities, which amounted to between $50,000 and $75,000 for a given election campaign, were used in part to pay the high costs of television broadcasts.[32]

In 1974 the reported revenues available to the national party for its campaign were between $65,000 and $75,000. This amount was slightly higher than the estimated figure for 1972 of $58,000. It compares to an estimated $6 million available to the Liberals and $4.2 million available to the Conservatives. The major portion of these revenues came from a $5 membership fee, $2 of which goes to the newspaper *Regards*, $2 of which is returned to the local organization of the member, and only $1 of which is retained by the national organization for federal campaign purposes. Some money also came from small donations from corporations recently approached by Caouette. A substantial part of the available revenues, about $50,000, was used to pay for two series of eight fifteen-minute color television broadcasts.[33]

Social Credit national party officials seemed uninformed or reluctant to talk about the party's financial situation. According to one official, "The financial situation is so largely decentralized that Ottawa doesn't have much of an effect on the dispensation of funds during the campaign. Each constituency is responsible for accumulating funds of its own. There was a fund arranged for the Province of

---

[31] See Report of the Committee on Election Expenses (Ottawa: Queen's Printer, 1966), pp. 267-271. See also K. Z. Paltiel, *Political Party Financing in Canada* (Toronto: McGraw Hill, 1970), pp. 66-70.

[32] See Michael B. Stein, "The Structure and Function of the Finances of the Ralliement des Créditistes," in Committee on Election Expenses, *Studies in Canadian Party Finance* (Ottawa: Queen's Printer, 1966).

[33] *Le Devoir*, 11 June 1974, p. 6.

Quebec and other provinces had their own fund-raisings as well. They do as well as they can accumulating some money for the provincial level, but the majority of money is collected at the local level."[34] The same official estimated that the total expenditures by Social Credit candidates on the campaign, including those costs borne by the candidates themselves at the local level, amounted to about $200,000. A recent change in party policy has provided that during a campaign the revenues from the sale of memberships remain in the constituencies where the memberships are sold. The purpose of this decision was to increase the amount of money available at the local level. Very little money flows from the national level to the provincial or constituency organizations.[35] Another party executive from Quebec compared the expenditures of the successful Social Credit candidate in Villeneuve, Armand Caouette, with those of the Liberal candidate in the same riding in 1972. Whereas Caouette's campaign had cost him about $4,000, the Liberals had spent between $48,000 and $53,000 in their losing fight.[36]

In summary, it is clear that, in comparison to the major parties, the Social Credit party managed its campaign on a shoestring. It capitalized where it could on free radio and television time, and it occasionally scraped up enough money from local organizers to bear the cost of a Caouette radio and television speech. Even if Caouette's health had been better, it is doubtful that the party could have financed a more active or energetic campaign.

Campaign Strategy: Use of the Electronic Media. From its very beginning in Canada, the Social Credit party has been aware of the revolutionary potential of the electronic media in political campaigns. William Aberhart, the founder of the Alberta party and the original Social Credit premier, was the first Canadian to use radio effectively to produce an electoral success. His Sunday morning Bible broadcasts became the principal medium for transmitting the Social Credit message into Alberta homes in 1935. His successor, Ernest Manning, continued these Bible broadcasts, and they undoubtedly helped to sustain his long tenure of office (1943 to 1968). In Quebec, Réal Caouette was one of the first to rely heavily on television for his election. His fifteen-minute broadcasts, first beamed out of Rouyn-Noranda in 1958 and later extended to Jonquière, Quebec City, and

---

[34] Interview with Robert Klinck, director of research, Social Credit Party of Canada, Ottawa, 20 August 1974.

[35] Ibid.

[36] Interview with Gérard Croteau, 20 August 1974.

Sherbrooke, played a central part in his party's sudden success in sending twenty-six members to the House of Commons in 1962. Later these broadcasts were further extended to Trois Rivières, Montreal, Rivière du Loup, Rimouski, and the Gaspé, contributing to Social Credit penetration into these areas.

After the election was called in 1974, the national executive decided to rely almost exclusively on radio and television in the campaign. In the party's estimation, given the scarcity of funds in relation to the other major parties, the electronic media would ensure that a wide audience would be reached in Quebec and across Canada at comparatively little expense. A second reason for this strategy was that the campaign was held during the summer vacation, when it was likely to be difficult to attract large crowds to public meetings. When Caouette fell ill at the outset of the campaign, the strategy seemed a sensible method of conserving his energy without seriously weakening the Social Credit campaign.[37]

In Caouette's western and maritime tours in early and late June, as we have noted, the party depended almost entirely on free time provided by radio open-line announcers. On the whole, Caouette received a courteous and even warm reception on these broadcasts. If they failed to attract votes, they at least helped to keep the Social Credit party name before the electorate and thereby strengthen the party's claim to being a national rather than merely a Quebec party.

Almost all the party's expenditures on the electronic media, however, were confined to Quebec, and they were designed to ensure that the party's representation in Ottawa remained intact. A major part of these costs, estimated at about 60 percent to 70 percent of the total budget, were subsumed by the pretaped fifteen-minute color television broadcasts featuring the national leader. In addition, during the campaign, there were occasional broadcasts of live speeches by Caouette, the costs of which were borne by local party organizations in regional centers such as Rivière du Loup and Rimouski.[38] The remaining Social Credit programs were covered by the free-time broadcasts provided by the Canadian Broadcasting Corporation. The party's timetable for its television broadcasts during the campaign in Quebec provides clear evidence of the central importance of the electronic media in its electoral strategy. In the period from 17 May to 6 July, the party presented on the French-language private television network no fewer than nine broadcasts in Rimouski, nine in Rivière du Loup, ten in Carleton, eight in Jonquière, ten in Sher-

---

[37] Ibid.

[38] *Le Devoir*, 3 July 1974.

brooke, eight in Quebec City, and nine in Trois Rivières. There were also nine television broadcasts and eleven radio broadcasts (in both French and English) on the public and private networks in Montreal. All but those in Montreal were fifteen minutes in length, and almost all featured Caouette himself.[39]

When asked whether the heavy reliance on the electronic media did not detract from traditional efforts by Social Crediters to establish personal rapport with their electors, one leading provincial organizer expressed party thinking as follows:

> No, on the contrary, even if the campaign is conducted largely at the level of the mass media, that doesn't prevent there being personal contact. If one looks at past practices, the party has always depended enormously on personal contact, but it remains no less, one of the initiators of political television broadcasts. Réal Caouette was one of the principal instigators of that. For years and years now, every autumn, for example, he resumes his television broadcasts. That has never prevented him from remaining close to the people. On the contrary, everything depends on the manner in which one uses it. I think it is an additional method for getting close to the people. It is important, in my opinion, to project a party presence. The mass media become one of the tools one can use for this purpose. Because, for that matter, one does not only use television during an election campaign. In the final analysis, one uses it more *between* elections than *during* elections.[40]

The Results. When the ballots were first totaled on election night, it seemed that the party had succeeded in at least a holding operation. It was originally reported that Social Credit had won twelve seats, thereby retaining its status as a "registered" party. Its popular vote had only slipped slightly. Caouette exulted in what he labeled a "huge victory" for his party, and he mocked the pollsters and media pundits who had predicted that Social Credit would completely collapse. He promised to appoint his son Gilles, who had lost his seat in Charlevoix, the party's national organizer and to groom him for the party leadership.[41] But within a few hours a recount revealed that the Drummond riding had been lost to the Liberal candidate by six votes. The party could no longer qualify as a registered party because it

---

[39] Television election broadcast timetable of the Social Credit party, June 1974.

[40] Interview with Gérard Croteau, 20 August 1974 (author's translation).

[41] *The Montreal Star*, 9 July 1974, p. A-8. Gilles's salary would be paid out of public funds in the form of a research budget.

failed to meet the required minimum of twelve-seat representation. Its right to receive the financial rewards of this status, including the leader's salary and a research budget of $42,000 (enabling it to hire an executive secretary, a press attache, and secretaries), was therefore in jeopardy. Gilles's job and future leadership prospects were also in question. Caouette, in desperation, invited Leonard Jones, who had been elected as an independent in Moncton, to join his caucus, but the ex-mayor turned a deaf ear to his appeal.

The initial exuberance inevitably gave way to a more sober analysis of the party's showing. Table 6-1 (p. 154) shows that the decline in the overall popular vote for Social Credit across Canada—from 8 percent in 1972 to 5 percent in 1974—was greater than that of any other major party. There had also been a drop in seats from fifteen to eleven and the concomitant loss of official party status. Table 6-2 (pp. 158–159) reveals that outside Quebec the party had failed miserably, winning only 3.3 percent of the votes in Alberta, 2.9 percent in New Brunswick, 1.2 percent in British Columbia, and 1.1 percent in Manitoba. In all other provinces, it had failed to garner even 1 percent of the popular vote. This was well below the performance of 1972 in every province except Manitoba, and it revealed the hollowness of the party's organizational efforts outside Quebec. In the French-speaking province itself the proportion of the popular vote had dropped more substantially than had first appeared to be the case, from 24.4 percent to 17.2 percent, placing Social Credit well behind the Conservative party (which earned 21.1 percent of the Quebec vote) in any claim to represent the "official opposition" at the federal level in Quebec. It had lost over 100,000 of the 151,697 votes it had earned in metropolitan Montreal in 1972, which revealed the failure of its vaunted electronic campaign in that area. Even in its rural and semi-urban strongholds, the margin of victory of several successful incumbents had been considerably reduced. Caouette's plurality in Témiscamingue dropped from 8,929 to 7,540; Gilbert Rondeau's plurality in Shefford shrank from 5,875 to 848; Edouard Allard's margin in Rimouski was cut from 2,144 to 1,039.[42] Clearly, Social Credit had been transformed from a party with national aspirations to a marginal regional party with serious opposition even in its provincial bastion of Quebec.

Despite these obvious failures, most Social Credit party officials remained sanguine about the results. The party had performed about

---

[42] *The Montreal Star*, 9 July 1974, p. A-11. These figures are based in some cases on less than 100 percent of polls. Some candidates, such as Gérard Laprise and André Fortin, actually increased their pluralities slightly over 1972.

as well as they had expected, considering its handicaps of insufficient funds and Caouette's uncertain health. One member conceded, however, that the results cast a dark shadow over the party's future. As he said,

> When you get down to it, it's futile to have a party whose strength is localized only in one province, when there's no realistic potential strength outside the province. You'd have to say that that was the case in the [1974] election. . . . My personal opinion is that unless a real effort is made to refurbish the party's organization outside Quebec, then it's inevitable that there will be a diminution of strength in the Province of Quebec, because the [marginal] effect that a regional party could have on policy if it had no prospect of electing a substantial number of members . . . is so evident that people would become discouraged. You know, Social Crediters traditionally have worked out of conviction, but you have to give some indication of positive results flowing from their efforts if you hope they're going to continue to make those efforts.[43]

Social Credit's Performance and Prospects

The results indicate, in this author's view, that the postelectoral analyses of the pundits and of party militants concerning Social Credit's showing in the 1974 election are misguided. The Social Credit party *did* suffer a serious defeat in the 1974 general election, despite its retention of eleven seats. The weakness of the Conservative and NDP parties in Quebec as alternatives to the Liberals, together with the strong personal following of some Social Credit M.P.s, prevented the party from losing even more ground. This was not a mere setback, like those of the Conservative and New Democratic parties, from which the party can hope to recover four years hence under more propitious circumstances. It reflected, rather, a gradual erosion in the party's popular support in all parts of Canada, an erosion that will probably lead to its eventual demise.

The symptoms of this long-term decline were present in every phase of the Social Credit campaign. They manifested themselves first of all in the declining effectiveness of the national leader. Caouette's chronically poor health, due to his diabetic condition, has finally begun to take its toll within the party. His frequent absences from Parliament have deprived the party of leadership and

---

[43] Interview with Robert Klinck, 20 August 1974.

have led to desperate efforts at salvaging Social Credit fortunes by electoral alliances with other parties. They have also invited challenges to his leadership from younger, ambitious elements within the party, which have a debilitating effect on party unity. Finally, as we have observed, illness has reduced Caouette's energy and affected his political judgments on the campaign trail. These problems may not have had a significant direct impact on the 1974 vote, but they have certainly undermined the party's long-term effectiveness.

Second, despite a few remarkable personal successes, the general quality and performance of the party's candidates have deteriorated. Social Credit is no longer able to attract new blood into its ranks, and its stalwarts are aging. It has been unable to divest itself of its rural and lower-class image. Caouette's efforts to attract "prestige" candidates have on the whole been a failure. Considering the importance of the individual Social Credit M.P. in serving as a link between the remote federal government and his constituents,[44] this lowering of the quality of candidates is likely to undermine the confidence of the Quebec rural and semi-urban population over the long term.

Third, the organizational and financial weakness of the party has begun to seriously erode its strength as a grassroots movement. In earlier days it was still possible to conduct a campaign on limited resources and defeat the candidates of the old-line parties, since the party could call upon the loyalty of thousands of unpaid volunteers and converts to the cause. However, over thirty-five years of historical development, with the transformation of Social Credit from a protest movement into a conventional right-of-center party, this élan has gradually dwindled. The electronic media have loomed larger and larger in the modern election campaign, along with public relations experts and polls. These are expensive and generally beyond the means of a small party with such limited resources. The situation is particularly serious in the West, where the organizational structures of past elections have totally collapsed. But it also poses a problem in Quebec, as the style of campaigning begins to change. The use of the electronic media in that province was less effective than in the past because the party lacked the organizational support cadres who might have transformed into votes the message conveyed by the media. In metropolitan Montreal, the support accorded the party in 1972 proved to be largely ephemeral, and it evaporated with the withdrawal of *Parti Québécois* endorsement. Even in the hinterland

---

[44] See Don Murray, "The Ralliement des Créditistes in Parliament," *Journal of Canadian Studies*, May 1973, pp. 13-30. See also Dominique Clift, "How the Créditistes Manage to Survive," *The Montreal Star*, 13 July 1974.

areas where Social Credit is well entrenched, the old magic of the Caouette message seemed to be fading. Local candidates were often accorded better receptions than Caouette himself. But personal popularity is a very fleeting resource and no guarantee of long-term fidelity to the party.

Fourth, the campaign revealed the seriousness of the leadership succession problem. The allegiance of many party voters depends more on their confidence in the leadership than on their attachment to the organization or the ideology. As a national party official put it, "A party has to have a leader, and if you had a leader who was incompetent or negative about social-credit philosophy, the support of convinced Social Crediters which the party relies on in order to maintain its following in the country would erode, and then I think the party would fold." [45] Unfortunately, there does not now appear to be a plausible successor to Caouette who could fill this crucial role. No one has the national stature, the political skills, or the bilingual competence necessary to coordinate the very heterogeneous organizational structures in the different regions of the country.

Fifth, the party's role in Parliament in recent years has been less important than in earlier decades. The party has sought to hold the balance of power, but it has not succeeded since the mid-1960s. In the minority government situation of 1972–1974, it was the NDP and not Social Credit that played the role of balancer. Despite its claims to the contrary, there is little evidence that the party has succeeded in persuading the governing party to adopt any of its major policy planks.

The long-term prospects for Social Credit, then, are rather poor. This does not mean that the party will disintegrate and disappear overnight. It has established deep roots over a long period of time in certain sections of the country, particularly in rural and semi-urban Quebec. Its parliamentary representatives have forged close links with their constituents. They have cultivated their loyalty by acting as effective intermediaries between the average citizen and the vast, impersonal bureaucratic structure. This explains why a campaign which, in many respects, was so ineffective did not cause the party more damage. Many Social Credit faithful continue to support the party despite its recurrent splits, organizational disarray, and disappointing results.

The 1974 election has brought one step closer the absorption of Social Credit in a realignment of opposition forces. After the election

---

[45] Interview with Robert Klink, 20 August 1974.

of 1974 the Social Credit party is a narrowly based regional party which represents the remnants of the right-wing protest movement that emerged almost simultaneously in western Canada and Quebec in the Depression years. As I have indicated elsewhere, the current phase of institutionalization in the movement's development is the natural precursor of a right-of-center alliance of Conservatives and Social Crediters which may well spell the end of the Social Credit phenomenon in Canada.[46]

---

[46] See Michael B. Stein, "Le Crédit Social dans la province du Québec: sommaire et développements," *Revue canadienne de science politique*, vol. 6, no. 4 (December 1973), p. 580.

7

CAMPAIGN FINANCING IN CANADA AND ITS REFORM

Khayyam Z. Paltiel

The Canadian federal general election of 8 July 1974 marks a watershed in the history of political campaign financing in Canada. Less than a month after the election, a new Election Expenses Act was proclaimed which promises to have a far-reaching effect on the fund-raising practices and campaign expenditures of Canadian parties and candidates. The provisions of the new act, which, it is hoped, will make public a great deal of information about future campaigns, are best understood against the background of the history of Canadian party finance. The monetary aspects of the federal general election of 1974 will be used to illustrate the traditional pattern of campaign finance.[1]

The Traditional Pattern

In the twentieth century there have been substantial changes in the fund-raising apparatus of the major and minor parties as well as in the objects of expenditure, but the sources of funds have changed little. Immediately after Confederation in 1867, the raising and allocation of campaign funds were among the normal tasks of the parliamentary party leadership. Today both of these functions are carried out by specialists. The growing sophistication of party organization has permitted the party leadership to disclaim responsibility for the questionable activities of fund-raisers and bagmen. A similar shift

---

[1] For a general review of the history of Canadian party finance and its regulation see Khayyam Z. Paltiel, *Political Party Financing in Canada*, McGraw-Hill series in Canadian politics (Toronto: McGraw-Hill, 1970); see also *Report of the Committee on Election Expenses* (Ottawa: The Queen's Printer, 1966), and Khayyam Z. Paltiel et al., *Studies in Canadian Party Finance*, Committee on Election Expenses (Ottawa: The Queen's Printer, 1966).

has taken place in the object of expenditures away from the mobilization of voters through the once-frequent resort to corruption and alcohol. In the past, too, newspaper support was procured by way of lucrative printing contracts, hidden subventions, or outright ownership, and reliance on the press meant spending considerable sums between elections. The expansion of the electorate and the spread of literacy have put greater emphasis on the print media, but the emergence of radio broadcasting in the 1930s and television in the 1950s has again profoundly altered the style of campaigns. While organization at the polls and constituency levels are certainly not neglected, more and more money is spent on the media during election campaigns as opposed to year-round party activity. Canadian parties lack the large inter-election organizations characteristic of European and British parties and still operate with skeleton staffs on minimal funds.

Raising Campaign Funds: Sources and Methods. The centralized corporations and financial institutions located in Toronto and Montreal provide the bulk of the funds needed by the major parties, the Liberals and the Progressive Conservatives.[2] There are only a handful of these large contributors—hundreds rather than thousands. For the 1972 election half the funds raised in Ontario by the Liberal party were collected personally by the chairman of the party's Treasury Committee from ninety large corporations;[3] and a recent report by a commission appointed by the Progressive Conservative government of Ontario asserts that 90 percent of the funds raised by the Liberals and the Conservatives comes from business donations.[4]

Until now the staffs involved in collecting contributions have been very small. The chief solicitors have not been subject to the formal elected party organizations, nor have the lower-level collectors usually held elective office in their parties. In practice these individuals have usually been co-opted or have simply stepped into the shoes of older members of their families or business and law firms. Although few

---

[2] For details of the financial structures of the major parties see Khayyam Z. Paltiel and Jean Brown Van Loon, "Financing the Liberal Party 1867-1965," in Paltiel et al., *Studies*, no. 3, pp. 147-256; Jack L. Granatstein, "Conservative Party Finance, 1939-1945," in Paltiel et al., *Studies*, no. 4, pp. 257-326; and Paltiel, "The Patterns of Canadian Party Finance," *Report of the Committee on Election Expenses*, study no. 6, pp. 225-278.

[3] Khayyam Z. Paltiel, "Party and Candidate Expenditures in the Canadian General Election of 1972," *Canadian Journal of Political Science*, vol. 7, no. 2 (June 1974), pp. 341-352.

[4] Ontario Commission on the Legislature, *Third Report* (Queen's Park, Toronto, September 1974), p. 6.

of them aspire to elective office, many are rewarded by appointment to the Senate, the Valhalla of Canadian politics. The parties' fundraising machinery has been composed customarily of finance committees in Toronto and Montreal (the Toronto chairman being senior), which are often assisted by similar bodies in other central Canadian cities like Hamilton, London, and Ottawa. In the last decade a shift in the pattern of Canadian party finance has given the party finance chairmen in the western provinces greater prominence.

Once funds have been collected, the parties distribute them somewhat differently. Formerly, the financial structure of the Progressive Conservative party tended to be centralized, monies being pooled and allocated from the national headquarters. Since the Diefenbaker period, however, provincial party organizations seem to have assumed the distribution function. On the other hand, the Liberal party has always been more federalized. The Quebec wing of the federal party retains control of most of the funds raised and spent in that province. However "undemocratic" this highly centralized system of financing the two old Canadian parties might seem, it had important integrative consequences which offset the centrifugal forces in Canadian political life—federalism, a bicultural society, and regional parochialism.[5]

The fragmentation of the two-party system by the emergence of third parties and the growing prominence of the provinces on the political and economic scene have partially undermined the traditional financial pattern. Third parties with provincial bases have leverage in the search for funds. The Quebec-based *Créditiste* wing of the Social Credit movement has successfully maintained itself, relying largely on assistance from members and supporters. The New Democratic party (NDP), like its predecessor, the socialist Cooperative Commonwealth Federation (CCF), relies on its membership for support but is increasingly dependent on donations from the trade union movement. Despite the efforts of the CCF, the New Democrats, and the *Créditistes*, as well as a number of serious experiments by the Liberals and Conservatives, mass fund-raising at the grassroots has not been successful in the past. "Successful fund raising has so far rested on a stable group base: such as business corporations or trade unions. Any attempt to reform political finance must take this fact into consideration."[6]

---

[5] Khayyam Z. Paltiel, "Federalism and Party Finance," in Paltiel et al., *Studies*, no. 1, pp. 1-21.

[6] Paltiel, "Canadian Party Finance," p. 278.

Financing the 1974 Election

Any attempt to make a realistic estimate of the overall amounts raised and spent severally and collectively by political parties and candidates in Canada is seriously hampered by ignorance. Some lacunae in our data are due to faulty reporting procedures. Others are attributable to the looseness of the structures of Canadian political parties; weak coordination and laxness in central direction are reflected in incomplete and overlapping records. The most serious difficulty is the willful refusal of party and public officials to supply information which neither law, custom, nor practice has required of political parties or party fund-raisers and spenders. Even local candidates and their agents have been required to make only minimal declarations. The Canadian investigator, therefore, has been compelled to base his estimates on available official and unofficial information and on his knowledge of past and current party and candidate behavior. The only official data publicly available under legislation governing the 1974 and earlier elections have been the declarations required of local candidates for the House of Commons and their agents. Summaries of these have been made available as "parliamentary returns" some six months after a general election, but only in response to formal requests by members of Parliament. These data are partial, incomplete, and tendentious, and often seriously underestimate the amounts raised and spent by candidates. Furthermore, a large percentage of candidates, about one-quarter in 1974, fails to submit the declarations required by law; none has ever been prosecuted for this negligence, nor has any audit of these declarations ever been made.

Defective as this information has been, at the very least it provided a notion of the amounts spent by individual candidates and of the trend of these expenditures, by party affiliation and by province. Thus, candidate spending in the period since the end of the Second World War rose almost five times and appears to have more than doubled in the course of the last four general elections, from 1965 to 1974.[7] No reports comparable to those required of candidates are available with respect to national, provincial, or regional party organizations operating on the federal scene. Here the

---

[7] Information concerning candidate expenditures as declared under the provisions of Section 63 of the old Canada Elections Act has been derived from the parliamentary returns prepared by the Office of the Chief Electoral Officer. Data for the federal general election of 8 July 1974 are derived from the return dated 26 November 1974 and tabled in the House of Commons on 28 November 1974.

researcher must depend on interviews and contacts with party officials and functionaries and on their goodwill and readiness to make information available. While archival material has been helpful in the study of past elections, the reports of journalists have sometimes had to be consulted for the contemporary period. These can only be judiciously used after proper cross-checking. From time to time the public inquiry—by a judge, parliamentary committee, or royal commission—of some scandal casts a strong if lurid light on aspects of party finance. The reforms discussed below will make the declaration of such information mandatory for all future elections.

The only other public, official information about election costs is derived from data collected by the Canadian Radio-Television Commission (CRTC), the regulatory body which controls the Canadian broadcasting system. The CRTC and its predecessors have been empowered to collect data regarding the amount and cost of time sold to political parties and their local candidates by radio and television broadcasting stations. This information is helpful inasmuch as it indicates trends in media spending. However, the publicly available data fail to distinguish between parties, between candidates, and between production and time costs. These data are partial at best and must be heavily qualified from other sources to be useful.

Bearing these caveats in mind, the author has followed a method which both he and the Advisory Committee on Election Expenses have employed for previous campaigns to arrive at the figure $35 million. This would appear to be a fair conjecture of total spending by political parties and candidates on the 1974 federal general election. The imputed value of free broadcasting time supplied to parties and candidates by the publicly owned Canadian Broadcasting Corporation (CBC) should be added to this sum, along with the unknown cost to local candidates of obtaining a party's nomination. Over and above these sums are the chief electoral officer's expenditures on the process of enumerating voters for the federal election, the polls and constituency machinery, and other election costs, amounting in all to about $29 million for the 1974 election.

Candidate Expenditures in 1974. A comparative analysis of party expenditures at the candidate level may be undertaken on the basis of the avowedly questionable declarations made under the old Canada Elections Act. Of the 1,209 candidates who fought the 1974 federal general election in 264 constituencies, 75 percent, or 914, filed returns. These indicated total expenditures of $10,690,488, that is, 13.4 percent more than the $9,428,728 reported to have been spent by the 840

Table 7-1

DECLARED EXPENDITURES OF CANDIDATES, 1974
CANADIAN FEDERAL GENERAL ELECTION

Political Affiliation	Total Amounts Declared by Candidates	Candidates Filing Returns	Candidates Not Filing Returns	Seats Won	Average Declared per Reporting Candidate	Total Declared by Winning Candidates	Average Declared per Winning Candidate
Liberal	$ 4,961,127	243	21	141	$20,416	$3,279,098	$23,256
Progressive-Conservative	4,215,180	217	47	95	19,425	1,851,989	19,495
New Democratic	1,262,018	210	52	16	6,010	223,234	13,952
Social Credit	138,497	86	66	11	1,610	59,099	5,373
Communist	45,061	58	11	—	777	—	—
Marxist-Leninist	15,798	60	44	—	263	—	—
Independent	40,047	29	34	1	1,381	24,211	24,211
Other	12,760	11	20	—	1,151	—	—
TOTAL [a]	$10,690,488	914	295	264	$11,696	$5,437,631	$20,597

a Figures may not add to totals due to rounding.

Source: Based on the chief electoral officer's report tabled in the House of Commons on 28 November 1974.

Table 7-2

DECLARED EXPENDITURES OF CANDIDATES, 1974 FEDERAL GENERAL ELECTION, BY PROVINCE AND PARTY

Province	Liberal	Progressive-Conservative	New Democratic	Social Credit	Communist	Marxist-Leninist	Independent	Other	Total
Ontario	$1,837,649	$1,907,927	$ 587,047	$ 3,282	$17,498	$ 9,372	$ 7,479	$11,396	$ 4,381,652
Quebec	1,553,521	579,745	36,967	94,483	2,298	3,017	2,099	934	2,273,062
Nova Scotia	228,353	216,131	33,670	2,016	—	7	—	—	480,178
New Brunswick	236,914	115,716	6,286	881	—	30	25,597	—	385,424
Newfoundland	165,080	100,791	3,503	—	—	—	—	—	269,375
Prince Edward Island	66,039	39,961	804	—	—	—	—	10	106,815
Manitoba	145,290	228,851	99,322	2,022	2,660	—	260	—	478,404
British Columbia	347,398	436,645	206,117	10,037	17,473	2,854	2,575	—	1,023,100
Saskatchewan	179,471	241,601	229,872	1,710	1,755	518	1,031	—	655,957
Alberta	179,497	326,028	39,756	24,066	3,376	—	1,006	420	574,151
Yukon	21,917	21,090	5,164	—	—	—	—	—	48,171
Northwest Territories	—	692	13,509	—	—	—	—	—	14,201
National Total [a]	$4,961,127	$4,215,180	$1,262,018	$138,497	$45,061	$15,798	$40,047	$12,760	$10,690,488

[a] Figures may not add to totals due to rounding.

Source: Based on the chief electoral officer's report tabled in the House of Commons on 28 November 1974.

(75 percent) candidates who filed returns after the 1972 elections. Liberal spending at the candidate level rose by almost 7 percent in the two years from 1972 to 1974; Progressive Conservative candidates spent almost 20 percent more, and New Democrats over one-third more, but reported Social Credit spending fell by almost 40 percent in the same period. (The small Liberal rise and the drop in *Créditiste* spending may be accounted for in part by the fact that in both cases fewer candidates submitted reports after the 1974 campaign than had filed in 1972.) Liberals spent over 46 percent of the reported total, averaging $20,416 per candidate; Progressive Conservatives spent just under 40 percent of the total, declaring $19,425 per candidate; 210 New Democrats declared a total of more than $1.25 million, averaging slightly more than $6,000 per candidate; 86 Social Credit candidates averaged a mere $1,610.

Party expectations and spending patterns may be reflected in the distribution of party expenditures at the candidate level. The expenses of Liberal candidates were above the party's national average in Ontario, Quebec, the Atlantic provinces (other than Prince Edward Island), and the territories. Liberal expenditures at the local level in all the western provinces were well below the national mean, and in the case of Alberta fell to almost half the overall average. It should be borne in mind that the expenditures of the 141 winning Liberals were almost two-thirds of the total declared by that party's candidates. Furthermore, very large sums were spent at the constituency level by Liberal cabinet ministers in the large metropolitan centers of English-speaking Canada. Liberal constituency-level expenditures in Quebec appear to have been lower than anticipated owing to the practice of assigning and reimbursing organizers from the provincial campaign committee and treasury.

The highest average spending by Progressive Conservative candidates was in Ontario, Nova Scotia, and Newfoundland. In fact, the largest expenditure reported by any candidate in the 1974 campaign was $108,759 declared by Stephen B. Roman, a prominent mining executive who was the Progressive Conservative candidate in the Ontario constituency of York North. (His successful Liberal opponent, Barney Danson, reported expenses of $41,825.) In Quebec, Progressive Conservative candidates spent less than two-thirds of their party's national average and only 60 percent of what Liberal candidates spent in that province. It should be noted, however, that the three winning Progressive Conservatives in Quebec did spend two-and-a-half times the party's provincial average. Expenses in the Atlantic provinces hovered about the national average. In the West the candidates' declared costs were slightly below the national average for the Progressive Conservative party.

The sharpest deviations from the national means in spending are recorded by the New Democratic party and Social Credit candidates. Almost half of the total declared NDP candidate expenditures occurred in Ontario, but the highest provincial averages, in descending order, occurred in Saskatchewan (about three times the national average), Manitoba, and British Columbia. In the rest of the country, except on Cape Breton Island where the party gained a seat, spending was largely symbolic and aimed at asserting the party's purportedly national character. The large sums spent by NDP candidates in western Canada are related to that party's control of the legislatures and governments of Saskatchewan, Manitoba, and British Columbia and to the advantages of incumbency. To the sums declared by NDP candidates must be added the value to be imputed to the "voluntary" services provided by the organized labor movement, which have not been included in official expense reports until now. In contrast, the *Créditistes* of Quebec spent two-thirds of the total expenditures reported nationally by Social Credit candidates. Only in British Columbia and Alberta, with their remnants of once-powerful provincial organizations, did Social Credit candidate spending approach the party's national average. The pitiful amounts spent by most Social Credit candidates attest to the critical financial shortages under which Social Credit has labored since it lost control of the two far-western provinces.

With some exceptions, largely attributable to regional variations in Canadian political culture, there is a close relationship between spending patterns at the candidate level, the past and present successes of the parties, and their immediate expectations—patterns demonstrated by the differences between over-all national and provincial averages of declared candidate expenditures and the averages reported spent by winning candidates of the several parties. In view of the fact that a considerable proportion of each candidate's resources are supplied directly or indirectly from central party funds, the declared expenditures of candidates tend to reflect the parties' respective assessments of their areas of strength and weakness tempered by the resources which might accrue to a candidate because of his private wealth or personal popularity.[8]

---

[8] Paltiel, "Party and Candidate Expenditures," p. 342.

National Party Receipts and Expenditures. Although the 1974 election was probably the most expensive in Canadian history, the amounts raised by the Liberal, Progressive Conservative, and New Democratic parties at the national level do not appear to have been much greater than in the previous election. On the other hand, the sums spent by the national offices in the last campaign were somewhat larger. In part this is explained by the fact that in 1974 the Liberals did not have as large an inter-election debt to discharge as they had in 1972 and the Conservatives incurred a considerable deficit to meet their planned election budget. The modest NDP budget rose, however, on both the revenue and expenditure sides by about 20 percent. (Social Credit revenues and expenditures were so miniscule as to hardly affect the outcome one way or another.) It would also appear that the provincial campaign committees of the national parties had somewhat greater resources at their disposal than in previous campaigns, but it is at this level that the greatest mystery about campaign funds still abides. Only when more complete information is available concerning the operations of the Quebec section of the Liberal party and the Ontario section of the Progressive Conservative party will a true picture of Canadian election financing at the federal level emerge.

The Liberal party appears to have been plentifully supplied with funds, and ended the campaign with close to a $1 million surplus from the net revenues of the 1974 and 1972 elections.[9] The National Treasury Committee of the Liberal Party of Canada, headed by Senator Richard J. Stanbury, raised approximately $6.2 million for the 1974 general election. Of this sum, $5.5 million was spent, the difference accruing to the surplus from the previous campaign. Unlike the 1972 campaign fund, the 1974 fund did not have to be used to discharge a large debt from the inter-election period. Thus, at the national level the Liberal party spent about $200,000, or about 5 percent, more than in 1972. The National Office used about $1.5 million (compared to $1.3 million in 1972); another $1.75 million was used for general campaign purposes at the national, provincial, and regional levels; and $2.6 million was distributed to candidates to supplement funds raised at the constituency level. The average amount distributed at the local level was somewhat higher in 1974

---

[9] Information concerning the finances of the Liberal Party of Canada at the headquarters and national levels was generously provided by Dr. Blair Williams, the party's national director, and Senator Richard J. Stanbury, chairman of the National Treasury Committee, during interviews which took place in October 1974. In a letter to the author dated 31 October 1974, Senator Stanbury further provided detailed financial reports.

than in 1972. In Ontario, the minimum was about $5,000, the average varied from $6,500 to $7,000, and the highest allocations reached $10,000. In the West the figures were comparable, in Quebec and the Atlantic provinces, considerably higher.

The National Treasury Committee of the Liberal party, under the chairmanship of Senator Stanbury, consists of two representatives from the party organizations in Quebec and Ontario and one from each of the other provinces. The chairman acted as coordinator with the provincial campaign chairmen and was the link with the cochairmen of the National Campaign Committee, Senator Keith Davey and Jean Marchand, minister of transport, who was chief of the party organization in Quebec. Major donors were again approached by Senator John Godfrey, who had headed fund-raising operations in 1972. He was assisted by Joseph Cruden in Ontario (who had the cooperation of about seventy-five canvassers), Maurice Riel and Fraser Elliott in Quebec (who were aided by about forty collectors), and teams of canvassers in British Columbia, Manitoba, and Saskatchewan. Others, such as Senator Harry Hays in Alberta, operated as "lone wolves," exploiting their extensive business contacts for the benefit of the party's national treasury. The principal targets of these groups and individuals were the national offices of national and multinational corporations. Although the party tends to assert officially that its funds are raised in three roughly equal parts from Ontario, Quebec, and the rest of the country, reliable sources at the highest level confirm that Ontario is the main provider of funds and that a sizeable proportion of funds raised in Quebec, particularly in the Montreal area, tends to remain in that province to cover the considerably higher expenses incurred there. This situation is exacerbated by the fact that outside Anglophone areas of Montreal little is raised at the constituency level in the Province of Quebec. Presumably reliable reports from party officials place the expenditure of the head office of the Quebec section of the federal Liberal party at about 50 percent of the amount spent nationally by the national headquarters on advertising and organizational costs.

The expenditures of the Liberal National Campaign Committee in 1974 at the national level are summarized in Table 7-3. On the whole there was a marked similarity between expenditures on the 1972 and 1974 campaigns. The significant differences occurred in spending on the broadcasting media and in the costs of the leader's tour. In 1974 there was a drop in the cost of polls and surveys (although the party probably had some polls taken prior to the dissolution of Parliament which are not included in the campaign

Table 7-3

LIBERAL NATIONAL HEADQUARTERS
CAMPAIGN BUDGET AND EXPENDITURES, 1974

Item	Budgeted	Expended
TV Programming—free time		
Programming	$ 150,000	
Production	50,000	
Total	200,000	$ 196,472
Media		
TV spots	200,000	
TV production	25,000	
Radio spots	150,000	
Radio production	10,000	
Print media	60,000	
Print production	5,000	
Miscellaneous	25,000	
Contingencies	25,000	
Total	500,000	529,000
Ethnic press	—	—
Organization and communications	76,000	73,584
Leader's tour (Less recovery of $64,756)	300,000	243,516
Other travel (see administration)	18,000	—
Other speakers	10,000	2,772
First-time voters (youth)	3,000	1,009
Women liberals	3,000	—
Surveys	85,000	95,000
Administration	142,000	135,246
Contingencies	20,000	11,174
Transfers (to some provinces)	160,000	205,224
TOTAL a	$1,517,000	$1,492,997

a Figures may not add to totals due to rounding.

Source: Liberal Party Campaign Budget, Final Statement of Expenditures as of 31 December 1974 provided by Senator Paul Lafond.

expenses). And the party abandoned the use of the expensive computerized direct mail technique because of the adverse publicity it had brought in 1972. A comparison of the campaign budget with actual expenditures indicates that a decision was made to curtail television advertising in favor of radio. The cost of the leader's tour rose by about 50 percent, largely because of the chartering of a campaign train in addition to the usual aircraft. To the actual cash outlays must be added the enormous financial advantages which accrue to the Liberal party as the party in power. Ministers and their personal staffs exploit their positions to use government aircraft and other travel facilities. Executive and special assistants whose tasks are essentially political rather than administrative serve as organizers, advance men, and speech writers. The governing party also benefits from patronage appointments to boards and councils, in return for which services are rendered by officeholders not subject to the limitations placed on administrators by the public service merit system. Also, the prime minister and the cabinet are the most important newsmakers. The 1974 campaign was shrewdly staged by Senator Keith Davey, the ex-advertising salesman who served as cochairman of the party's campaign committee. Announcements of projects, programs, and grants were timed and tailored to hit the headlines and main newscasts and gain free publicity; the fact that many of these promises have since been shelved only serves to underline their principal purpose. The unrequited advantages of incumbency are tremendous, and their imputed monetary value should be added to Liberal party expenditures.

To round out the picture of Liberal party finances in the last campaign, continuous inter-election expenditures must be discussed. These are covered by special canvasses and fund-raising dinners, two-thirds of the necessary sum being raised in Ontario and about one-third in Quebec. The costs of the Montreal office are covered by Quebec donations, but the National Treasury Committee does not, by and large, support the separate provincial offices of the party. For 1973 the net disbursements of the Liberal Party of Canada amounted to $407,130, while for the eleven months ending 31 July 1974 (the fiscal year of the party was readjusted because of the new Election Expenses Act discussed below) these costs were $392,409. For the year ending 31 July 1975 it is anticipated that maintenance costs will rise to $517,399.

In contrast to the Liberals, who found money easier to come by as polling day approached, the Progressive Conservatives encountered increasing difficulty. To many observers this was due less to the attractiveness of Liberal policies than to growing disenchantment with those advanced by the Conservative leader, Robert Stanfield, in particular his income and price freeze. But whatever the cause, the result for the Progressive Conservative party was a wide gap between the campaign budget and the amounts raised, and a campaign deficit almost as large as the gross Liberal surplus. Overall spending at the national level by the Progressive Conservative party on the 1974 campaign amounted to $4,457,900.[10] In addition, the Progressive Conservative party had the burden of maintaining an expensive well-tuned inter-election organization throughout the eighteen months of minority government, a machine which had to be prepared to launch a campaign at a moment's notice if the government were to fall or Parliament be dissolved at the behest of the prime minister. Thus, during 1973 the expenditures of the party at the national level were no less than $900,195, and noncampaign expenditures in the first part of 1974 were estimated by the party's national director to have been approximately $500,000. To counterbalance these expenditures the party's National Finance Committee raised a total of $3.9 million for the 1974 campaign, as much as had been raised in 1972. This support came from the party's traditional sources in the Canadian industrial and financial community. The Conservatives approached them in much the same way as the Liberals, the principal target for both being the large corporations centered in Toronto, Montreal, and Calgary.

Although the Progressive Conservative party's expenditures at the national level in the 1974 campaign closely parallel those of the 1972 campaign, it is clear that there was an increase of about 10 percent, particularly in advertising costs. The National Campaign Committee distributed $1.7 million to candidates through the provincial campaign chairmen. This sum is considerably below the comparable Liberal total. However, it should be recalled that the party's provincial organizations in Alberta and Ontario are largely self-sustaining and that Progressive Conservative spending in Quebec at the local level is quite low except where the party has had some success in the recent past.

Clearly, the income and expenditures of the socialist-oriented New Democratic party do not approach those of the two major

---

10 The author is grateful to the leader of the opposition, the Honorable Robert L. Stanfield, and the national director of the Progressive Conservative party, John Laschinger, for their help in providing information concerning Progressive Conservative campaign finances in 1974. Mr. Laschinger wrote a detailed letter to the author dated 27 November 1974 which is the basis for the statements here.

Table 7-4

PROGRESSIVE CONSERVATIVE PARTY
NATIONAL CAMPAIGN COMMITTEE EXPENDITURES, 1974

Item	Expenditures
Advertising costs	
Radio bureau (supplying actualities)	$ 23,205
Total media costs (English and French)	
—Production costs	423,163
—Media space and time	1,033,120
Free-time production costs (E & F)	94,273
	1,573,761
Candidates' material (posters, pins, et cetera)	234,832
Costs of in-house print shop	30,986
Total	$1,839,579
Leader's tour	
(less recovery of $87,583)	259,686
Other travel (included above)	(80,482)
Surveys	111,336
Administration	
Salaries	113,784
Phone and telex equipment	147,378
Mailing	21,369
Miscellaneous	264,768
Total	547,299
Transfers to candidates	1,700,000
TOTAL	$4,457,900

Source: Letter to the author from John Laschinger, national director of the Progressive Conservative Party of Canada, 27 November 1974.

parties. Nevertheless the NDP did raise and spend more money in 1974 than in 1972. Preliminary figures demonstrate that the revenues of the NDP federal election fund rose about 20 percent to $371,924 (apart from the recovery of costs from the sale of printed material).[11] The biggest share came directly from affiliated trade unions or through the Committee on Political Education (COPE) of the central labor organization. In conformity with the NDP's bottom-up method of

[11] The New Democratic party has continued its record of unstinting help to the author, with a letter and documents concerning the 1974 campaign from the federal secretary, Clifford Scotton, dated 31 October 1974.

financing, the second largest sum was received from the party's provincial sections. Contributions from individual members (and miscellaneous items) fell slightly. Parallel with the rise in income was an increase of about 10 percent in expenditures, which totaled $353,852. (See Table 7-5.)

Table 7-5
NEW DEMOCRATIC PARTY FEDERAL ELECTION FUND, REVENUE AND EXPENDITURES FOR 1974

Item	Income and Outlays
Revenue	
Contributions, COPE, and trade unions	$234,745
Provincial NDP section quotas	115,000
Individuals and miscellaneous sources	22,178
Total revenue	$371,924
Expenditures	
Candidates deposits	18,600
Organization	
Concentration [a]	134,400
Other assistance	20,800
Leader's tour (net cost)	40,924
Other travel	
Organizers and speakers	9,049
Committee	1,058
Special salaries, additional staff	5,182
Telephone, telex, postage, and express	22,954
Media	
TV and radio, free-time production	56,528
Advertising agency	20,558
Printing (net cost)	21,502
Controverted election (Vancouver East)	1,000
Total expenditures [b]	$353,852

[a] Concentration is a form of saturation canvassing developed by the NDP.

[b] Figures may not add to totals due to rounding.

Source: Letter from Clifford A. Scotton, federal secretary of the New Democratic party, to author, dated 31 October 1974. It should be noted that these are interim figures only. The final audit for the 1974 campaign has yet to be released.

The NDP did not finance any preelection polls during the campaign and it sharply cut its media advertising budget. There was a sharp increase, however, in organizational expenses, particularly for concentrated canvassing at the constituency level in Ontario, British Columbia, and Saskatchewan. To assert its claim to being a national party, the NDP was compelled to provide the official deposits required of candidates in almost 100 constituencies east of the Ottawa River. Lacking the classical branch structure in this vast area, it had to resort to the top-down methods it eschews elsewhere. For general inter-election maintenance purposes, however, the NDP remains faithful to the mass principle of the social democratic parties in Europe. In 1973 and 1974 the regular budget of the party ranged from $223,350 to $279,700. This was covered by the federal office's share of the membership dues, sustaining contributions raised by local branches and forwarded through the provincial sections, a share of the affiliation dues remitted by affiliated trade unions which raise them from the check-off dues of their members, contributions from the indemnities paid to NDP members of Parliament amounting to $600 each, and some miscellaneous sources.

As might be expected of a party which depends on the modest contributions of its partisans, the Social Credit Party of Canada, led by Réal Caouette, collected about $60,000 from approximately 4,000 contributors for the 1974 campaign.[12] Of this amount $9,800 was used to cover candidate deposits in Quebec, Ontario, and Nova Scotia. Television time was purchased for the sum of $19,413, and another $7,250 was used for production costs. The party leader's tour, rental of meeting halls, and the travel of two organizers cost $3,159. Since the party depends on volunteer help, administrative costs (for telephone, postage, and sundries) were a mere $2,166. Maintenance costs were similarly slight. Annual receipts and expenditures for 1972–1973 were $10,145 and $3,897 respectively, and for 1973–1974 (ten months), $8,305 and $7,058. The drop in constituency expenditures discussed in an earlier section testifies to the financial drought which has faced the Social Credit party since it lost control of the provincial governments of Alberta and British Columbia.

Media Expenditures in 1974. The prominence of media spending in the panorama of national party expenditures warrants special atten-

---

[12] I am very thankful to Mme. Judith Richard, chef du cabinet of M. Réal Caouette, M.P., leader of the Social Credit Party of Canada, who went to great efforts to gather information concerning her party's finances in the 1974 campaign which she forwarded to me in a letter dated 10 December 1974.

tion, though, here again, there are gaps in the publicly available data and in the information furnished by the parties.[13]

In contrast to the United States, Canada has a large public broadcasting system as well as a private sector. The publicly owned Canadian Broadcasting Corporation has customarily allocated time free of charge to the political parties on its English and French radio and television networks. Furthermore, the CBC devotes considerable resources and broadcasting time to campaign coverage under the heading of news and public affairs broadcasting. Both the "party politicals" and the CBC-initiated programs are an invaluable, cost-free means of leadership, candidate, and issue exposure. In 1974, the CBC made available to the six registered parties and their spokesmen three hours and forty-four minutes of television time on all the stations of the English television network and just ten minutes less on the French network; similarly, one hour and forty-eight minutes of time were allocated on the English radio network, and somewhat more time (twenty-three minutes more) on the French radio network.[14] The allocation formula is roughly one-third to the governing party and two-thirds to the combined opposition. Thus, in 1974, of the thirty-four time periods available to the parties, the Liberals received eleven, the Progressive Conservatives ten-and-a-half, the NDP six-and-a-half, Social Credit four, the Communist and Marxist-Leninist parties one each. Local constituency candidates also benefited from the free-time provisions of the CBC, which made available to them individually as much as four-and-a-half hours of time on ten radio stations and the Northern Service, the fourteen channels of the English TV network, eight channels of the French TV network, and the Northern Ontario and Northern Manitoba TV networks. The imputed value of this time may be conservatively estimated as little short of $300,000. According to information gathered by the Canadian Radio-Television Commission, the private sector also made available vast amounts of free time on fifty-seven TV channels, 267 AM and seventy FM radio stations.[15] Distributed in roughly the

---

13 For details concerning the use of the broadcasting media in Canadian election campaigns, see Paltiel, *Political Party Financing*, pp. 76-93; and Khayyam Z. Paltiel and Larry G. Kjosa, "The Structure and Dimensions of Election Broadcasting in Canada," *Jahrbuch des Öffentlichen Rechts der Gegenwart*, Neue Folge/Band 19, Tübingen, 1970, pp. 355-82.

14 Canadian Broadcasting Corporation, *Free Time Periods: Federal Election Campaign 1974* (CBC Program Policy Branch, Ottawa, 13 August 1974).

15 "Paid Political Broadcasts—Federal Election—1974," a summary table prepared and sent to the author by Mr. L. Mahoney, chief of the Logs and Monitoring Section, Broadcast Programmes Branch, Canadian Radio-Television Commission, in December 1974.

same proportions as on the public sector to the four largest registered parties, more than seventy-one hours of TV time and more than 276 hours of radio time were allocated free of charge by private stations to parties and candidates. In the absence of a station-by-station breakdown it is not possible to put a realistic value on these announcements and programs. Suffice it to say that the Liberal, Progressive Conservative, and New Democratic parties together spent no less than $347,000 in preparing production material for the free-time broadcasts on public and private radio and television.

A comparison of the data supplied by the CRTC for the 1972 and 1974 campaigns indicates that all parties and candidates spent slightly more for paid political broadcast time in the private sector in the

Table 7-6
STATION RECEIPTS FOR TIME SOLD TO PARTIES AND CANDIDATES, 1974 FEDERAL GENERAL ELECTION

Party/ Candidates	Spot Announcements		Programs		
	Number	Time	Number	Time	Receipts
Radio: 340 stations					
Liberal	49,368	31,448:21	322	2,627:30	$ 692,978
Progressive Conservatives	47,047	37,701:09	222	2,069:00	697,303
New Democratic	9,353	5,996:10	432	2,752:00	141,137
Social Credit	1,815	1,129:55	101	870:00	18,375
Others	973	607:05	19	245:00	9,834
Total radio a	108,558	76,882:40	1,096	8,563:30	$1,559,625
Television: 57 stations					
Liberal	6,469	3,898:31	229	1,741:00	$ 550,469
Progressive Conservatives	6,715	3,870:22	195	1,490:00	532,334
New Democratic	721	454:12	61	455:00	43,932
Social Credit	57	26:10	135	1,780:00	25,341
Others	7	4:30	7	60:00	2,204
Total television a	13,969	8,253:45	627	5,526:00	$1,154,279
GRAND TOTAL a	122,527	85,136:25	1,723	14,089:30	$2,713,905

a Dollar figures may not add to totals due to rounding.

Source: "Paid Political Broadcasts—Federal Election—1974," prepared by Mr. L. Mahoney, chief of the Logs and Monitoring Section, Canadian Radio-Television Commission, December 1974.

most recent campaign. Total expenditures rose to $2,713,905, but spending on TV time fell in favor of AM and FM radio time. In fact, much of the change appears to have been due to a rise in rates, since the amounts of time purchased on all three of the broadcasting media actually declined. Furthermore, there was a sharp drop in program time purchased, and a continuation of the shift detected in earlier elections to the more expensive but allegedly effective "spot" announcements. The Liberals replaced the Progressive Conservatives as the biggest spenders in the broadcast media, both in absolute and relative terms. It is, therefore, surprising to find so large a discrepancy in the figures supplied by both parties with respect to radio and TV production costs. Either the Liberals paid for these from sources other than the National Campaign Committee, or they benefited from the services of advertising agencies who gave the party beneficial rates in anticipation of patronage advertising contracts at the disposal of the party on its expected return to office. A well-informed Ottawa journalist, John Gray, confirms this surmise in the *Ottawa Citizen* of 6 March 1975, in which he reports that of $27 million for advertising placed by eleven government departments in the past year, all but $5 million was contracted to agencies directly associated with the Liberal campaign of 1974. Of this sum, over $8 million went to a Quebec agency—a senior executive of which had headed the ad hoc consortium which handled the Liberal advertising campaign in Quebec.

The New Election Expenses Act [16]

It is clear that the major Canadian political parties did not suffer from any perceptible shortage of funds during the 1974 campaign. What, then, prompted the Liberal government to press ahead with a reform measure? The *Report of the Committee on Election Expenses* tabled in the House of Commons on 11 October 1966 had been allowed to gather dust. Nor was a better fate slated for the proposals of the second report of the House of Commons Special Committee on Election Expenses of 1 June 1971, or Bill C-211 on election expenses introduced by the president of the Privy Council on 16 May 1972,

---

[16] The Election Expenses Act has been published in a consolidated version referred to as the Canada Elections Act, *Revised Statutes of Canada*, Chapter 14 (1st supplement). The bill, known as Bill C-203, was given first reading on 22 June 1973. It was passed by the House of Commons on 3 January 1974 and received royal assent on 14 January 1974. It came into force on the day following the return of the 1974 election writs.

too late in the session of the Twenty-eighth Parliament for it to be enacted. Neither the Progressive Conservatives nor important sections of the Liberals, including the prime minister, were enthusiastic about the project. Scandal and rumor, however, continued to beset the fund-raising process at the provincial and federal levels. In Quebec there were revelations of contacts between prominent Liberal politicians, including a former minister, and supposed underworld characters. In Ontario allegations of funds raised by Conservative collectors from property developers doing business with the provincial government prompted the premier to take steps toward reform at that level. Charges and countercharges concerning the dependence of the two old parties on large multinational corporations headquartered in the United States and the reliance of the New Democrats on American-based international unions helped rouse public opinion.

But the timing and impetus for the new act must be attributed to the 1972 campaigns and election results in the United States and Canada. It is one of the continuing ironies of Canadian history that developments south of the border have had a significant influence on Canadian legislation in the area of campaign finance. Just as the reforms of the Progressive era in the United States affected the shape and timing of the election expense provisions of the Dominion Elections Act of 1908, the Watergate affair has had its impact on the latest statute. Even more important, however, was the outcome of the Canadian federal election of 1972—a minority government in which the Liberals needed New Democratic support in order to retain office. The NDP had been pledged to reform, particularly to the disclosure of the sources and amounts of campaign contributions. The passage of the new act was part of the price it elicited in return for its support of the government.

The Election Expenses Act, which came into effect in August following the 1974 general election, takes the form of a series of amendments to the Canada Elections Act, the Broadcasting Act, and Income Tax Act. Building on principles long inherent in Canadian law, such as the doctrine of agency (investing legal responsibility for the use of money in election campaigns in a single agent), the law aims to reduce spending by parties and candidates by setting limits to certain expenditures, imposing overall spending ceilings, and transferring some costs to the state. In addition, the act provides for subventions to eligible parties and candidates in the form of the reimbursement of costs incurred, and a tax credit system to serve as an incentive for donations. On the other hand, the new legislation requires full disclosure of donors, contributions, and costs higher than a specified minimum, and provides mechanisms for reporting, checking, and publicizing the declarations made by parties and candidates.

Party Ceilings. To be "registered" a party must have at least twelve representatives in Parliament or present fifty or more candidates at a federal election. It is then entitled to the privilege of having its party name on the official ballot after the names of its candidates. Only registered parties are permitted to collect and spend funds through a system of registered official agents. Only registered-party agents or persons authorized by them may incur expenditures aggregating more than $25 in behalf of a party, and all such outlays must be backed by itemized invoices and receipts. Registered parties are permitted to spend up to thirty cents per elector appearing on the preliminary lists of electors in all of the electoral districts in which they present official candidates. If this provision had been in effect at the last federal general election, a party that presented candidates in all 264 federal constituencies would have been permitted to spend up to $4,007,482; together the six "registered parties" could have spent about $16 million.

The act also sets a limit of four weeks on active campaign advertising in the mass media—radio, television, newspapers, and periodicals. Parties which violate the financial limits and the ceilings on advertising will be subject to fines not exceeding $25,000 on summary conviction. For purposes of the act, parties are deemed legal persons subject to prosecution, the actions of their officers and agents being presumed to be those of the parties themselves. (It should be noted that the nomination process does not fall within either the time or financial limits; however, the nomination process and the related costs are relatively unimportant in Canada.)

The only direct financial assistance provided for the federal parties is the reimbursement of half of the actual cost incurred by each party in purchasing its share of the six and one-half hours of broadcasting time which all broadcasting concerns will have to make available for future federal campaigns. However, the federal parties will also be helped indirectly by the subsidies to candidates, since a significant proportion of funds spent at the candidate level has come, in the past, from the central party campaign chests. Furthermore, sums transferred by the parties to their candidates are not to be deemed party expenditures for purposes of the act.

Disclosure of Party Income and Donors. No limitations are placed on the amounts which may be collected by the parties or given by either individual or corporate contributors. But the act takes a major step forward in recognizing the existence of party funds. It requires not only the reporting, disclosure, and publication of all expenditures by parties, but more notably, for the first time in the history of Canadian election expense legislation, demands the reporting of the amounts contributed together with the identity of the givers. Registered parties must appoint professionally qualified auditors with the legal obligation to audit their financial affairs and to submit reports, including information concerning financial receipts, to the chief electoral officer. The chief agent of a party must submit two returns together with the appropriate vouchers with the auditor's reports, one covering the party's regular operations and another the election campaign expenses, within sixty days of the end of its fiscal year or within six months after polling day, respectively, in a form prescribed by the chief electoral officer. The annual return must include: first, the total sums donated to the party by each of the following classes of contributors: individuals, public corporations, trade unions, corporations without share capital, and unincorporated organizations or associations—together with the number of donors in each of these categories; second, the individual contributions in each category, including the amounts given and the name of each giver whose aggregate gifts exceeded $100 in the fiscal period; third, the amounts of money spent on party operating expenses, including the travel costs of the party leader and other party officials; fourth, the total of all other expenditures made by or on behalf of the party.

The declaration concerning election campaign income and expenditures must state funds received for the conduct of the election, the party's administrative costs, the leader's and other officials' travel costs for the campaign, the amounts spent on "election expenses," and the total of other outlays incurred by or on behalf of the party for the election. The new act defines "election expenses" in the following terms:

> (a) amounts paid, (b) liabilities incurred, (c) the commercial value of goods and services donated or provided, other than volunteer labour, and (d) amounts that represent the differences between amounts paid and liabilities incurred for goods and services, other than labour, and the commercial value thereof where they are provided at less than their commercial value, . . . [namely] . . . the cost . . . of promoting or opposing, directly and during an election, a particular registered party, or the election of a particular candidate, and . . . includes (e) the cost of acquiring the use of time on the facilities of any broadcasting undertaking . . .

or of acquiring the right to the publication of an advertisement in any periodical publication for any such purpose, (f) the cost of acquiring the services of any person, including the remuneration and expenses paid to him or on his behalf, as an official agent or registered agent or otherwise, except where such services are donated or provided at materially less than their commercial value, (g) the cost of acquiring meeting space, of provision of light refreshment and of acquiring and distributing mailing objects, material or devices of a promotional nature, and (h) the cost of goods or services provided by a government, crown corporation or any other public agency. . . .[17]

All party reports, returns, and declarations will be public records and open to inspection by any person on request during regular business hours. Failure to file a return or auditor's report, the submission of false or misleading returns, and willful violation of the spending ceilings and limitations on campaigning are offenses and make the party subject to fines not exceeding $25,000 in each case. Party agents and officials are also subject to the regular sanctions of the Canada Elections Act on summary conviction or indictment. Nevertheless, these provisions are weakened by the failure to provide for adequate enforcement machinery. It is left to the rival parties, candidates, the public, the overburdened chief electoral officer, or a commissioner under his supervision, to seek compliance by laying complaints or charges.

Candidate Spending Limits and Subsidies. The act makes a significant advance regarding spending at the constituency level and financial assistance for qualifying candidates. Overt campaign advertising on the mass media is limited to the last four weeks prior to polling day. Reporting, audit, and disclosure requirements similar to those that apply to the parties are imposed on the local candidates and their agents with respect to their constituency campaign receipts and expenditures, and are subject to the sanctions of the act.

Ceilings on the total expenses of each candidate are linked to the number of electors and, in some cases, to the geography of constituencies. The limitation is one dollar for each of the first 15,000 names on the constituency's preliminary list of electors, fifty cents for each of the next 10,000, and twenty-five cents for each elector in excess of 25,000. Thus, a candidate in a constituency with 80,000 eligible voters could spend up to $33,750. Had these ceilings been in

---

17 Ibid., section 2.

effect in the 1974 election, the permissible expenditures per candidate would have ranged from $11,312 plus personal travel expenses, in the Yukon, to $44,395 in the largest riding of York-Scarborough. The candidates of a party which presented nominees in all 264 constituencies might have spent collectively $6,941,932 plus their permissible personal traveling costs (a maximum of $2,000 per candidate). With 1,209 candidates, as in 1974, the total allowable spending at the local level would amount to well over $30 million.

If one adds to these figures the sums which would have been permitted to each registered party under the act, each party with a full slate would have been allowed to spend, at both the local and national levels, no less than $11 million, and all parties and candidates would have been allowed a combined spending total of about $45 million.

To help meet these anticipated costs, a public subsidy is provided in the form of the reimbursement of a portion of the costs of candidates who gain at least 15 percent of the votes actually cast in a constituency. A qualifying candidate is entitled to receive whichever is the lesser sum, either reimbursement for his actual costs, or the first-class postage of a one-ounce item to each elector on his constituency's preliminary list (currently eight cents per ounce), plus eight cents for each of the first 25,000 voters on the list, and six cents for each name over 25,000. In addition, in twenty-one large and remote constituencies, candidates who qualify will be repaid their actual traveling costs, or one cent multiplied by the square mileage of the riding, or $3,000, whichever is least. All candidates conforming to the act's provisions will also receive up to $250 to cover their auditor's fee, and will be reimbursed the $200 deposit required of all candidates. The various reimbursements will be made by the receiver-general of Canada from the Consolidated Revenue Fund on receipt of a certificate from the chief electoral officer that the candidate has complied with the requirements of the statute.

In an electoral district of 80,000 voters, a candidate with permissible expenditures of $33,750 would be entitled to the reimbursement of about a third of his costs, that is, $12,150. In 1974, 613 candidates—260 Liberals, 229 Progressive Conservatives, ninety-seven New Democrats, twenty-six *Créditistes*, and one independent— received more than 15 percent of the vote in their respective constituencies. Had the law been operative for the last election, close to $5 million would have been reimbursed to candidates from the public treasury.

Disclosure by Candidates. The stringent record-keeping and auditing requirements imposed on parties extend to the candidate level. And similar provisions apply to the names, numbers, class of donors, and amounts contributed. To prevent the subterfuge of using the local riding association as a cover for donors and gifts, the act requires that all remittances of over $100 from such bodies to candidates be reported in a manner similar to that demanded of the candidates themselves. A summary of the election expenses return and the auditor's report must be published in a newspaper circulating in the constituency concerned. Furthermore, the constituency returning officer must forward a copy of each auditor's report, return, and candidate declaration to the chief electoral officer in Ottawa; it is also incumbent on him to preserve the original documents, receipts, and vouchers for six months, and to permit any elector to inspect them and make copies on payment of a nominal fee, after which the documents may be destroyed or returned to the candidate on demand.

In order to facilitate control and further limit spending, the act forbids persons other than registered parties and candidates or persons authorized to act in their names from incurring election expenses as legally defined, from the date of the issuance of the writ for an election to the day immediately following the day of the poll. This prohibition is particularly directed against the use of the media other than by parties. But it would be a defense against any prosecution if the outlays were made in good faith simply to promote certain views on public policy issues or the aims of associations and of organizations not of a partisan political character. Violators would be subject to fines not exceeding $5,000.

Broadcasting Provisions for Parties. The act takes a step forward in the equitable allocation and provision of broadcasting time to political parties, but the clauses extending the principle to candidates were dropped during the passage of the bill through Parliament. No similar provisions are made for the print media, other than a clause subject to sanction that space must be sold at the lowest rate charged for an equal amount of equivalent advertising space in the same issue or any other issue of the periodical published in the election period. A parallel clause applies to broadcasting time.

Each broadcaster is obliged to make available *for sale* at each general election a total of six-and-one-half hours of prime broadcasting time to registered parties. The allocation of this time among the parties will be made by the Canadian Radio-Television Commission during the four weeks beginning Sunday the twenty-ninth day before polling day and ending on Saturday the second day before polling day. The registered parties will recover half the cost of the broadcasting time utilized and purchased by them from the Consolidated Revenue Fund calculated at the regular standard rate charged for such time, as certified by the CRTC. No distinction is made between television and radio except for the definition of prime time— 6 P.M. to midnight in the case of TV; 6 A.M. to 9 A.M., 12 P.M. to 2 P.M., and 4 P.M. to 7 P.M. for radio. Nor does the act tackle the thorny question of "spot announcements" versus program time. Finally, the act provides that network operators as distinct from individual stations must provide a number of program periods free of charge to the registered parties, to be allocated after consultation with their representatives and the CRTC.

Given the existence of more than 400 commercial broadcasting undertakings in Canada operating in a variety of metropolitan, urban, and rural settings, it is not possible to estimate the potential value to the registered parties or the cost to the public treasury, of the subsidies provided for broadcasting time. Clearly, the parties' resources will limit their use of broadcasting time, and it is unlikely that parties other than the Liberals and the Progressive Conservatives will take full advantage of the proviso. The NDP and the *Créditistes* will benefit only as far as their limited funds will allow. It must be noted that no repayments are included for production costs or for candidate time costs. Using 1974 expenditures as a guide, the value of broadcasting assistance to all parties may be conservatively estimated at $1.5 million.

Tax Credit for Contributions to Parties and Candidates. The act also attempts to stimulate donations to parties and candidates through an income tax credit for contributions to their operating and/or campaign funds. In any taxation year, a taxpayer may deduct from the federal income tax he would otherwise owe a substantial proportion of the amount donated during the year to a registered party or to a candidate at an election to the House of Commons: 75 percent of the amount given if it does not exceed $100, $75 plus 50 percent for amounts exceeding $100 but less than $550, $300 plus one-third of the amount by which the sum given exceeds $550, with a maximum tax credit of $500 for aggregate donations of $1,150 per annum. To claim the tax credit, appropriate verifiable receipts must be submitted in a prescribed form.

Conclusion

There is no doubt that recent political events in Canada and the United States, as well as the absolute rise in campaign costs, stimulated the enactment of the reforms contained in the Election Expenses Act. It breaks new ground by requiring the disclosure of campaign giving and instituting such devices as the tax credit system. But it retreats from the proposals of the Advisory Committee on Election Expenses, which would have totally freed the parties from the cost of broadcasting time. More seriously, it fails to deal with the problem of campaign donations from foreign-domiciled corporations and individuals, a curious omission in the light of current Canadian opinion and the recommendations of the advisory committee. It might have been well, too, to provide the political parties with a measure of direct financial support to make up for the losses which may ensue from the new disclosure provisions, and to reduce their dependence on questionable sources of funds. No doubt the enforcement machinery could have been strengthened through tighter drafting.

However, an important first step has been taken toward a more responsible party system. That this is but a first step is underlined by the fact that the act requires the chief electoral officer to report to the Speaker of the House of Commons on the election expenses of the registered parties after the first general election to which the act applies. On the basis of this report, a standing committee will consider the appropriateness of the limits set by the act. It is to be hoped that it signifies a willingness to entertain further reform in this crucial area of Canadian public life.

8
THE MEASUREMENT OF PUBLIC OPINION

Lawrence LeDuc

Gauging the mood of the electorate was an important preoccupation of politicians and analysts alike during much of the period preceding the 1974 election. The Liberals' near-defeat in 1972, coupled with the resurgence of the Conservatives in Ontario and the strong showing of the New Democratic party (NDP) in that year, had created an atmosphere of volatility in Canadian politics unmatched since 1962. High inflation and the poor economic outlook contributed to this general climate. All political parties were particularly attuned to the necessity of correctly assessing public opinion, given the political uncertainties and the knowledge that an election might occur at any time. The Conservatives' determination to force an early election and the NDP's reluctance to do so during much of the Twenty-ninth Parliament were symptomatic of the parties' readings of the public mood. The Conservatives, sensing themselves on the threshold of power, anxiously sought the combination which would turn the prevailing climate of opinion to their advantage. The Liberals, shaken by the failure of the 1972 "land is strong" campaign, brought back former Liberal strategist Keith Davey to run the next campaign. The NDP wavered uncertainly between support and condemnation of the minority Liberal government. In all, it was a time when the accurate reading of public opinion was a crucial element of political strategy, and when opinion measurement would play an important role in any campaign.

The Setting

Opinion measurement in Canada is complicated by the sheer size of the Canadian nation and the diversity of its population. A single national survey sample can provide only the most rudimentary indication of political trends in a nation where regional climates of opinion are frequently at variance with national patterns. Canada's population of slightly over 22 million is distributed unevenly across the ten provinces and the Yukon and Northwest Territories (see Table 8-1).[1] The population increased by 18 percent over the past decade, with the largest increases occurring in Ontario and in the western provinces of Alberta and British Columbia. Canadians have also become a more urban people in recent decades, with nearly three-quarters of the population now residing in areas classified as urban in the 1971 census. Canada's two major language groups (see Table 8-2) do not coincide precisely with these geographic divisions, although the vast majority of the French-speaking population is concentrated in the Province of Quebec; the rest are found mainly in the province of New Brunswick and, to a lesser extent, in parts of Ontario, Manitoba, and Nova Scotia.

The diversity of population and conflict of regional interests are reflected extensively in Canadian political life. A 1973 Gallup poll (Table 8-3) disclosed that many Canadians feel that their part of the country has not derived its share of benefits from confederation. In different ways, "western alienation" and "Quebec separatism," both much-discussed factors in Canadian politics in recent years, are symptomatic of this malaise. John Meisel found in a 1968 survey that 26 percent of the French-speaking population of Quebec believe that Quebec will one day separate from Canada (see Table 8-4). The independence-minded *Parti Québécois* obtained 30 percent of the popular vote in the 1973 Quebec provincial election that decisively returned Premier Bourassa's Liberals to power.

The existence of regional climates of opinion is an important underlying characteristic of the Canadian political setting. In some instances it can mean the creation of issues which are unique to a particular part of the country or to a particular subgroup of the population. In others, it implies that issues of national importance carry different connotations in different regions. Economic issues in particular, which were so important in the 1974 election campaign, often assume different forms from one region to the next. Unemployment—considered by many the most significant issue in the 1972 election—is seldom uniform throughout the country. Similarly inflation, the prime topic of the 1974 campaign, carries a variety of regional nuances. High grain prices, for example, which mean

---

[1] Population estimated June 1973. All demographic information cited in this chapter is derived from materials published by Statistics Canada.

Table 8-1
POPULATION OF CANADA, BY PROVINCE [a]
(in thousands)

Newfoundland	541	2.4%
Prince Edward Island	115	0.5
Nova Scotia	805	3.7
New Brunswick	652	2.9
Quebec	6,081	27.9
Ontario	7,939	35.7
Manitoba	998	4.6
Saskatchewan	908	4.3
Alberta	1,683	7.5
British Columbia	2,315	10.1
Yukon & N.W. Territories	58	0.3
Total Canada	22,095	100.0%

[a] Estimated 1 June 1973.
Source: Statistics Canada.

Table 8-2
DISTRIBUTION OF LANGUAGE GROUPS
(in percents)

	Mother Tongue	Language Spoken Most Often
English	60	67
French	27	26
Other	13	7

Source: Statistics Canada.

prosperity to the prairie wheat farmer, often are at the root of skyrocketing costs for the Ontario livestock breeder. Much the same situation has existed with regard to oil and gas from Alberta. So, too, the fortunes of political parties and political leaders are subject to sharp regional distortion. The Liberal party, which has virtually swept all before it in Quebec in recent federal and provincial elections, remains unable to win a single parliamentary seat in Alberta, just as the Conservatives, with substantial strength in the West and in the maritime provinces, have been unable to make any real breakthrough in Quebec. Prime Minister Pierre Trudeau found

Table 8-3

RESPONSES TO GALLUP QUESTION:
"Which, if any, region of Canada would you say
has benefited least from confederation?"

Region	Percent Naming Own Region
Atlantic provinces	52
Quebec	30
Ontario	6
Western provinces	45
(N = 723)	

Source: CIPO, *The Gallup Report,* 28 November 1973.

Table 8-4

**CANADIAN OPINION OF LIKELIHOOD
OF QUEBEC SEPARATION, 1968**
(in percents)

"Will Quebec Separate?"	Quebec (French-speaking)	Total Canada
Yes	26	19
No	47	60
Don't know	27	21
	(N = 632)	(N = 2,767)

Source: John Meisel, "The 1968 Election Study," in Ronald Manzer, *Canada: A Socio-Political Report* (Toronto: McGraw-Hill, 1974), p. 165.

in 1972 and 1974 that much of his personal popularity was concentrated in central Canada.

These observations, many of which are readily evident to those who have followed Canadian politics closely in recent years, form an important backdrop to any discussion of opinion measurement. Unlike Britain, where the swing of votes toward or away from the governing party has until recently tended to be fairly uniform throughout the country, Canada usually experiences several countervailing trends simultaneously. Largely for the same reason, it is virtually impossible in Canada to extrapolate, as forecasters do for Britain, the distribution of parliamentary seats from any single indicator of a national trend. This is further attributable to the fact that constituencies in Canada are not strictly equal in population and

Table 8-5
REGIONAL VARIATION IN MAJOR ECONOMIC INDICATORS

Unemployment Rates, May 1974 (in percents)		Consumer Price Index, April 1974 (1961 = 100)	
Vancouver—Victoria	5.5	St. John's, Nfld.	154.3
Southern British Columbia	5.6	Halifax	149.9
Alberta	6.9	Saint John, New Brunswick	150.8
Saskatchewan	3.4	Montreal	151.6
Manitoba	3.6	Ottawa	158.4
Northern Ontario	4.5	Toronto	154.2
Southwestern Ontario	4.4	Winnipeg	152.4
Eastern Ontario	4.0	Saskatoon—Regina	144.6
Toronto area	3.8	Edmonton—Calgary	151.3
Montreal area	5.8	Vancouver	152.4
Quebec (Eastern townships)	7.3		
Quebec (Gaspe area)	10.3		
New Brunswick— Prince Edward Island	8.8		
Nova Scotia	6.8		
Newfoundland	14.4		

Source: Statistics Canada.

that the minor parties, strong in some areas, are weak or nonexistent in others. Thus, in 1972, with 36 percent of the total vote the NDP was able to capture eleven of British Columbia's twenty-three seats, while the Liberals, with a comparable 34 percent of the vote in Nova Scotia, gained but one of that province's eleven seats. For similar reasons the 1972 election produced a virtual deadlock in parliamentary seats in spite of the Liberals' 4 percent edge in the total vote. It is not surprising that few analysts are willing to venture predictions of parliamentary outcomes, even when sound national forecasts of political trends are available.

Polls and Surveys in Canada

The art and science of survey research is closely associated with nearly every stage of modern elections in most Western countries, and Canada is no exception. Political scientists depend heavily on postelection surveys for explanations of electoral behavior and polit-

Table 8-6

DISTRIBUTION OF POPULAR VOTE AND PARLIAMENTARY SEATS IN CANADIAN ELECTIONS, 1968–1974, BY PROVINCE

		1968		1972		1974	
		Vote	Seats	Vote	Seats	Vote	Seats
Newfoundland	Lib.	43%	1	45%	3	47%	4
	PC	53	6	49	4	44	3
	Other	4	—	6	—	9	—
Prince Edward	Lib.	45	0	40	1	47	1
Island	PC	52	4	51	3	49	3
	Other	3	—	9	—	3	—
Nova	Lib.	38	1	34	1	41	2
Scotia	PC	55	10	53	10	48	8
	NDP	7	—	12	—	10	1
	Other	—	—	1	—	—	—
New	Lib.	44	5	43	5	47	6
Brunswick	PC	50	5	45	5	34	3
	NDP	5	—	5	—	8	—
	Other	1	—	7	—	11	1
Quebec	Lib.	53	55	49	56	54	60
	PC	21	4	17	2	21	3
	SC	16	15	24	15	18	11
	Other	10	—	10	1	7	—
Ontario	Lib.	46	64	38	36	45	55
	PC	32	17	39	40	35	25
	NDP	21	6	21	11	19	8
	Other	1	1	2	1	1	—
Manitoba	Lib.	41	5	31	2	27	2
	PC	32	5	42	8	47	9
	NDP	25	3	26	3	25	2
	Other	2	—	1	—	1	—
Saskatchewan	Lib.	27	2	25	1	31	3
	PC	37	5	37	7	36	8
	NDP	36	6	36	5	31	2
	Other	—	—	2	—	2	—
Alberta	Lib.	35	4	25	—	24	—
	PC	50	15	58	19	62	19
	NDP	9	—	13	—	9	—
	Other	6	—	4	—	5	—
British	Lib.	42	16	29	4	33	8
Columbia	PC	20	—	33	8	42	13
	NDP	33	7	35	11	23	2
	Other	5	—	3	—	2	—
Total	Lib.	45	154	39	109	43	141
Canada	PC	31	72	35	107	35	95
	NDP	17	22	18	31	16	16
	Other	7	16	8	17	5	12

Source: For 1968 and 1972: *Reports of the Chief Electoral Officer;* for 1974: Canadian Press.

214

ical change. Major postelection surveys were undertaken in Canada in 1965 and 1968 and have provided much important data for students and teachers of political science. A third such study is currently in progress for the 1974 election.[2] In recent years journalists in Canada have also made extensive use of preelection polls of a number of different types conducted by private polling firms. These vary quite widely in size, scope, and methods, and are used to monitor electoral trends, to predict outcomes, and to probe specific issues. The Canadian Gallup affiliate, the Canadian Institute of Public Opinion, has conducted national surveys in Canada for years, and its findings are syndicated to many Canadian newspapers. Some newspapers organize their own surveys, particularly at the local or constituency level, and these, again, vary widely in scope and level of sophistication. Both major television networks, the public CBC and the independent CTV, organized and reported national surveys during the course of the 1974 election campaign, and some local stations did the same at the local level. Private surveys of a variety of different types have also found increasing acceptance in Canada in areas ranging from the collection of market research data for business firms to social surveys sponsored by government departments. Political parties have also employed polls and surveys more extensively in recent years to assess party strength and to assist in shaping electoral strategies. It was widely rumored at the time that Prime Minister Pearson's decision to call the 1965 federal election in the hope of winning a parliamentary majority was based on the optimistic reports of private polls commissioned by the Liberal party. Similarly, several key aspects of Liberal and Conservative strategy in the 1974 election were shaped at least in part by early polls conducted privately for the national parties. A number of Canadian firms, many quite small, conduct specially designed surveys for private clients. Several large American firms, particularly Harris and

---

[2] The 1974 study currently in progress is directed by Harold Clarke, Jane Jenson, Lawrence LeDuc, and Jon Pammett, and is supported by the Canada Council. It is based on a national sample of 2,574 respondents. The 1968 study, based on 2,767 respondents, was directed by John Meisel, and the 1965 study, based on 2,118 respondents, was directed by Philip Converse, John Meisel, Maurice Pinard, Peter Regenstreif, and Mildred Schwartz. Some of the findings of these studies are reported in John Meisel, *Working Papers in Canadian Politics* (Montreal: McGill-Queen's Press, 1973); Mildred Schwartz, *Politics and Territory: The Sociology of Regional Persistence in Canada* (Montreal: McGill-Queen's Press, 1974); and Richard Rose, ed., *Comparative Electoral Behavior* (N.Y.: Free Press, 1974). The data from the 1965 and 1968 election studies were made available by the Inter-University Consortium for Political Research. Neither the original collectors of the data nor the consortium bear any responsibility for the analyses or interpretations of the data in this chapter.

Market Opinion Research, have also done important private work in Canada in recent years.

Thus, the conduct of survey research in Canada touches upon a variety of fields and a wide range of objectives. Surveys differ considerably in the techniques which they employ and in the level of accuracy and reliability which they can be expected to maintain. Large quota samples, for instance, permit detailed breakdowns of population by region and by various demographic groupings at relatively low cost, and are therefore favored by some firms even though no precise estimates of sampling error can be computed for samples of this type. Others, to whom the calculation of error is more critical, will opt for smaller probability samples at the national level.[3] A level of accuracy that is acceptable to the market researcher may be unacceptable to the political party mapping its electoral strategy. Polls can therefore rarely be classed as accurate or inaccurate in any absolute sense, but rather must be matched against a reasonable set of expectations. These in turn will be determined by the techniques employed and by the environment in which the survey is conducted. Because of the size of the country, survey research in Canada tends to be expensive. Most researchers will therefore tend to choose the least expensive methods which will meet a particular set of goals. Thus, surveys which appear to be of varying quality sometimes only reflect differences of purpose.

The record of accuracy of opinion polls in Canada is generally uneven, but in many respects differs little from established patterns in other countries. Based on national samples in the 700–1,200 range, Gallup forecasts have usually fallen within their advertised limits of sampling error. Notable "failures" were Gallup's overestimates of the strength of the Liberals in 1957 and in 1965 (see Table 8-7). In

---

[3] For samples which approximate a simple random probability design, the following represents a conservative estimate of the 95 percent confidence interval (2σ) for various sample sizes.

Reported percentage	Sampling error in percent, by size of sample or group					
	2000	1000	700	500	300	100
50	3	4	5	6	8	14
30 or 70	3	4	5	6	7	13
20 or 80	2	4	4	5	6	11
10 or 90	2	3	3	4	5	8
5 or 95	1	2	2	3	4	

Source: Leslie Kish, *Survey Sampling* (N.Y.: Wiley, 1965), p. 576.

Quota samples, still quite widely used in polling in Canada, are subject to errors which are not directly measurable but which will more frequently exceed the levels shown. The use of these samples is discussed in some detail in F. F. Stephan and P. J. McCarthy, *Sampling Opinions* (N.Y.: Wiley, 1958).

Table 8-7
DIFFERENCE BETWEEN GALLUP PREDICTIONS
AND ACTUAL ELECTION RESULTS, 1945–1974
(in percentage points)

	Liberal	Progressive-Conservative	CCF-NDP	Others
1945	−2	+2	+1	−1
1949	−2	+1	+2	−1
1953	+1	0	0	−1
1957	+7	−5	−1	−1
1958	0	+2	−2	0
1962	−1	+1	−2	+2
1963	−1	−1	+1	+1
1965	+4	−3	0	−1
1968	+2	−2	+1	−1
1972	0	−2	+3	−1
1974	0	0	0	0

Source: Author.

1972 the Gallup forecast was extremely accurate for the Liberals, but overestimated the strength of the NDP by 3 percentage points and underestimated the Conservatives by 2 percentage points. Like many polling organizations, Gallup has refined its procedures over the years, attempting to improve its accuracy and to avoid the repetition of past mistakes. It now continues polling late into the campaign and bases its final prediction on slightly larger samples. The final Gallup report for the 1974 election was published on 6 July, two days before the election, and was based on 1,374 interviews conducted on 2 July.

As is the case with most polling organizations, the Gallup affiliate frequently finds that its forecasts are treated with greater skepticism by political practitioners than by the newspapers that publish them. Usually, the Gallup surveys report a high percentage of "undecided" respondents, a fact which tends to produce the most guarded interpretations of Gallup findings. A Gallup survey taken in February 1974 which included the standard poll question, "If a federal election were held today, which party's candidate do you think you would favor?" placed 34 percent of the respondents in the "undecided" group, by far the largest single category in the survey.[4]

---

[4] CIPO, *The Gallup Report*, 6 February 1974.

Even the final election-eve forecast, which later proved to be extremely accurate, reported 15 percent of the electorate "undecided."[5] Gallup follows the practice of eliminating undecided respondents and calculating percentages on the smaller base, assuming that the undecided respondents will distribute among the parties in approximately the same proportions as other respondents. Politicians are often inclined to read great significance into this "undecided" category, particularly in times of apparent volatility in the electorate. An increase in the number of "undecided" voters can be viewed by leaders of all parties as a "favorable" trend in some circumstances and frequently produces conflicting interpretations of the same poll. Interpretation of Gallup surveys is also affected somewhat by the conventional wisdom, widely accepted among Canadian politicians, that Gallup surveys consistently underestimate the Conservative vote. It is hard to account for the origins of this notion, although Table 8-7 does show that in each election since 1962 Gallup *has* underestimated the Conservative vote by small margins. But before 1962 there is no clear pattern. The belief is sometimes justified with the contention that the "undecided" category contains a disproportionate number of potential Conservative voters. There is no evidence to support this hypothesis, but the belief itself often produces cautious interpretations of the polls, particularly those showing a Liberal lead.

In addition to these characteristics of the Gallup forecasts, one should not ignore the fact that they deal only with national voting percentages and not with the distribution of parliamentary seats. Gallup's samples are too small and the regional variation in Canada too great to permit even the most cautious extrapolation of seats from the Gallup percentages. And, of course, in the minority government atmosphere of 1974, the distribution of seats rather than the popular vote was of greater interest to most observers.

Gallup's limitations, however, have not applied to all polling activities in Canada. Peter Regenstreif, who has covered elections for the *Toronto Star* and other newspapers since 1958, has not shown the same hesitation to predict the distribution of parliamentary seats as have other analysts, although he has never achieved high levels of accuracy in his predictions. Working with national samples much smaller than Gallup's, generally in the range of 200 to 500 respondents, Regenstreif has aimed at gauging the "mood" of his respondents rather than compiling statistical estimates. In a book published in 1965, Regenstreif himself classified his work as "more

[5] Ibid., 6 July 1974.

art than science."[6] Because he does not employ probability sampling techniques, tests of statistical significance cannot be applied to Regenstreif's samples. And he has occasionally hedged his seat predictions in close elections by classifying as many as thirty seats as "doubtful."

In spite of these limitations, Regenstreif has enjoyed several notable successes, largely because of the intensiveness with which he surveys each region of the country. He correctly predicted the decline of the Diefenbaker government to minority status in 1962 and the rise of the *Créditistes* (Social Credit party) in Quebec the same year. But together with other pollsters, Regenstreif overestimated Liberal strength in 1965, and since then his predictions have been somewhat more cautious. He now predicts a "range"of seat distributions rather than exact figures. But given the vagaries of parliamentary outcomes in Canadian elections, this has not led to improved forecasts. On the eve of the Trudeau sweep of 1968, he forecast a possible range of Liberal seats of 128 to 145 and a Conservative range of 75 to 93.[7] The actual result—155 Liberal and 72 Conservative seats—serves only to illustrate the difficulty of making such estimates from national poll data. Throughout his career, Regenstreif has been generally accurate in his forecast of overall election trends, but markedly less accurate in his prediction of the distribution of parliamentary seats. His in-depth analyses of each region of the country, however, provide an important complement to the national forecasts. Regenstreif has increasingly supplemented his own work in recent years with the Gallup forecasts and other large sample surveys done by private firms.

Canadians display a healthy skepticism toward all polls, and few experts were willing to make firm predictions on the eve of the 1974 election in spite of the fact that the trend of Gallup and several other polls was quite clear. Mindful of the several factors that render prediction difficult in Canadian elections, some analysts cheerfully dismissed the utility of all predictions. A few days before the election, one newspaper commentator said, typically:

> One problem with election surveys is most pronounced in close election contests in which a swing of a few percentage points can change the election outcome. The acknowledged margin of error in most polls is so high that the indicated result can be a victory for either of the two major parties. . . . Uniform national swings are rare, so it is silly to base

---

[6] Regenstreif, *The Diefenbaker Interlude* (Toronto: Longman's, 1965), p. ix.

[7] *The Toronto Star*, 22 June 1968.

predictions on behaviour that doesn't occur. It is clear that regional or local polls can have more validity than national ones, but now comes the hardest problem of all—the undecided voters. Some of them are indeed undecided but many simply use the term to avoid telling pollsters their preferences. . . . Adding to the uncertainty of opinion surveys is the undoubted last minute vote switching that some people engage in, often in an irrational way, that no survey could predict.[8]

Others sought to make the published predictions cover the widest possible range of outcome. This *Time* magazine report of the final Gallup survey was fairly typical of journalistic speculation on election eve:

As it turned out, the final campaign polls, which appeared to point to another Liberal minority, or possibly a majority Government, held out some hope for the Tories. For such was the balance of the Canadian electoral equation that within the spread of the last minute Gallup poll, a Tory Government was still possible.[9]

The 1974 Election

Political Issues. It became virtually a cliché during the 1974 election campaign that inflation was the most important issue; by the same token, it was nearly impossible to find a survey respondent who did not mention this issue in polls reported during the campaign. The exact meaning of inflation as a political issue was considerably less clear. Nevertheless, it is evident that inflation replaced unemployment as the most important problem in the eyes of the voters well before the 1974 campaign began. In a private national survey undertaken in October 1973, a full year after the 1972 election, 43 percent of the respondents named inflation as the most important problem facing Canada (see Table 8-8). The same survey found many Canadians increasingly pessimistic and apprehensive about the general economic outlook. The Conservatives' determination to force an early election and their decision to focus their campaign heavily on the inflation issue, then, were well grounded in public opinion and were, at least in part, dictated by the findings of private polls (see Figure 8-1). One such poll, commissioned by the Conservatives at the

8 "What the Polls Can't Tell Us," *Ottawa Journal*, 5 July 1974.
9 "More of the Same?" *Time* (Canada edition), 15 July 1974.

Table 8-8

RESPONSES (OCTOBER 1973), BY REGION, TO THE QUESTION:
"What is the most important problem facing Canada today?"
(in percents)

Problem	Total Canada	Maritime Provinces	Quebec	Ontario	Prairie Provinces	British Columbia
Inflation (2) [a]	43	41	46	39	46	42
Unemployment (1)	22	30	28	19	16	20
Environment & pollution (3)	15	14	12	16	13	19
Taxation	14	14	12	16	13	10
U.S. investment in Canada	7	5	5	8	6	7
English/French relations in Canada (4)	4	4	4	4	6	3
No opinion	2	1	2	1	1	2
	(N = 4,980)	(N = 444)	(N = 1,411)	(N = 1,812)	(N = 799)	(N = 514)

[a] Numbers in parentheses indicate rank order in 1972 survey.

Source: Elliott Research Corp. and the International Business Studies Research Unit, University of Windsor.

Figure 8-1

RESPONDENTS WHO FEEL THAT A DEPRESSION IS LIKELY
WITHIN THE NEXT TWO OR THREE YEARS, 1965–1973

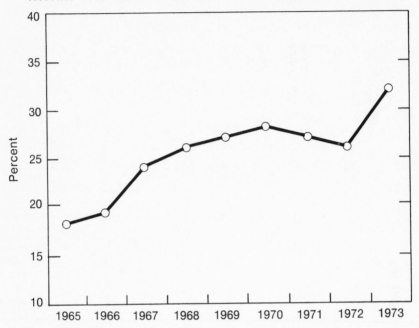

Source: Elliott Research Corp. and the International Business Studies Research Unit, University of Windsor.

beginning of the campaign, was reported to have shown inflation as the primary concern of 91 percent of the sample. But the proposed Conservative program of wage and price controls received a mixed reception in many quarters, possibly damaging the credibility of the Conservative anti-inflation campaign. Nevertheless, the postelection view, supported by many journalists, that emphasis on controls was a key factor in the failure of the Conservative campaign, may somewhat overestimate the impact of this issue. A Gallup poll published in June 1973, a year before the election, found that 61 percent of a national sample *approved* of wage and price controls as an anti-inflationary measure.[10] The poll showed little regional variation, the lowest level of support for the proposal being 51 percent in the maritime provinces. Another Gallup poll, published in January 1974, found that 64 percent of the survey respondents across the nation

---

[10] *The Gallup Report*, 2 June 1973.

were "willing to accept" wage and price controls. Again, the lowest level of support for the measure was in the maritime provinces (54 percent), but there was little indication in any region of serious opposition to the proposal.[11] A private Liberal poll taken at the beginning of the campaign was reported to show 79 percent of the electorate in favor of some form of controls. Postelection surveys may, of course, shed greater light on the significance of the wage-price controls issue, but these data would tend to suggest that the policy itself was not highly unpopular in the beginning. On the other hand, it is possible that the Conservatives' handling of the policy during the campaign and the dissension that it provoked in the party ranks may have damaged Conservative leader Robert Stanfield's credibility as a leader, an area that we shall deal with in somewhat more detail later. Regenstreif, in the regional surveys he undertook during the campaign, found that the wage and price controls policy was cited negatively by respondents in western Ontario, and that this response was at least partly linked to the question of leadership. He reported that voter opposition to the Conservative wage and price controls proposal was "significantly higher [in western Ontario] than in Western Canada or in Toronto" and that it "was contributing to the Liberal upsurge." [12] But he does not report statistics that can be compared with the preelection surveys. However, a survey undertaken during the campaign by Complan Research Associates on behalf of CTV found that 44 percent of voters sampled were "opposed" to temporary wage and price controls (see Table 8-9) and that the Liberals were thought to have "the best policy to control inflation" by 49 percent of the electorate (see Table 8-9). The official Liberal position, that inflation was an "international problem" largely beyond the reach of domestic controls, appears also to have had some base in public opinion. A Gallup poll conducted at the beginning of the campaign found that only 9 percent of a national sample viewed Canada's anti-inflation policies as inferior to those of other countries (see Table 8-9).

While discussion of inflation and of the Conservative policy proposals dominated much of the campaign, it is important to recall that other issues, including several of long-term importance, formed part of the backdrop of Canadian politics in 1974. In addition to these, a host of regional and local factors intervened from time to time to make "national" issues less national than they sometimes

---

[11] Ibid., 12 January 1974.

[12] "Wage Price Controls No Help to Stanfield in Western Ontario," *The Toronto Star*, 18 June 1974.

Table 8-9

PUBLIC ATTITUDES TOWARD THE PROBLEM OF INFLATION

Question	Response	
A. Do you favor a temporary wage-price freeze?	Yes	35%
	No	44
	No opinion	21
	(N = 3,200)	
B. Which party has the best inflation-control policy?	Liberals	49
	Conservatives	24
	NDP	19
	All other a	8
	(N = 3,200)	
D. Compared to other countries, how is Canada doing in controlling inflation?	Better than most	32
	About the same	50
	Not as good	9
	Don't know	10
	(N = 1,000)	

a Includes "no opinion."
Source: For questions A and B: Complan Research Associates (for CTV), 16 June 1974; for question C: *The Gallup Report*, 12 June 1974.

seemed at first glance. Agriculture Minister Eugene Whelan's pro-farmer stance was credited by many postelection analysts as the source of the strong Liberal upsurge in certain parts of the country, notably rural Ontario. His enforcement of the ban on beef imports from the United States, in the face of strong U.S. government opposition, received much newspaper coverage during the campaign, and it also dovetailed neatly with the rising tide of Canadian nationalism in recent years (see Figure 8-2). No longer an Ontario phenomenon, a desire for greater Canadian independence of American influence, particularly in the economic sphere, now extends to most parts of the country and has become a factor, if not an overt issue, in many areas of Canadian politics, both federal and provincial.

Like the issue of relations with the United States, the question of English-French relations within Canada may not stand high on a list of problems or "issues" at any particular time (see Table 8-8), but it, too, touches many aspects of contemporary Canadian political life. Thought by some analysts to have been one of the main undercurrents in the 1972 election campaign, the issue of "bilingualism" resurfaced on several occasions during 1974. The issue was rekindled by the independent candidacy of Leonard Jones, mayor of Moncton, New Brunswick, and by the introduction of the controversial Bill 22

Figure 8-2

PUBLIC ATTITUDES TOWARD U.S. INFLUENCE IN CANADA

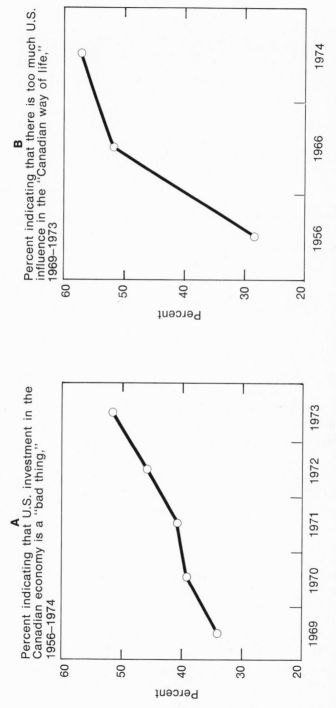

A

Percent indicating that U.S. investment in the Canadian economy is a "bad thing," 1956–1974

B

Percent indicating that there is too much U.S. influence in the "Canadian way of life," 1969–1973

Source: For A: Elliott Research Corp. and International Business Studies Research Unit, University of Windsor; for B: CIPO, *The Gallup Report*, 8 May 1974.

by the Liberal government in Quebec. Both of these events caused ripples in other parts of the country as well, largely because of the sensitivity of many Canadians to the bilingualism issue. Regenstreif found in his survey of prairie voters in early June that, "while inflation is the overwhelming issue, the language question in Quebec is having some impact." [13] Indeed, Premier Bourassa's bid (Bill 22) to make French the *only* official language of Quebec and to limit enrollment in English-speaking schools in the province had touched a nerve that was still sensitive in many regions of Canada. The cautious response of the federal government to the issue may have limited its potential damage to the Liberal campaign, but the timing of the bill was clearly not an asset to federal Liberal candidates. Even in the Province of Quebec it was clear that the aims of Bill 22 had only limited public support, as indicated in a survey conducted by the Quebec Institute of Public Opinion on behalf of three Quebec newspapers (see Table 8-10). And although a Gallup poll taken at about the same time reaffirmed the support of most Canadians for the basic principle of bilingualism (see Table 8-11), it was clear that measures such as Bill 22 had considerable explosive potential in some parts of the country.

Images of Political Leaders. It is often difficult in Canadian politics to separate matters of substance from matters of style. It was not chance that led the Conservatives to emphasize the issue of inflation throughout the campaign. Virtually all polls, both public and private, suggested that this was the area of the government's greatest vulnerability. Neither was it chance that led the Liberals to counter throughout the campaign with emphasis on the "issue" of leadership. Private polls continually reaffirmed the wide edge that Pierre Trudeau enjoyed over Robert Stanfield in personal popularity. A Gallup poll, published at the beginning of the campaign, found that Trudeau held a margin of 24 percentage points over Stanfield as the man "who would make the best Prime Minister for Canada" (see Table 8-12). Significantly, Trudeau's position was strongest in Ontario and Quebec, but he enjoyed a personal margin over Stanfield in virtually every part of the country, even in provinces where the Liberals have been extremely weak in recent years. This same poll found that the proportion of voters who "approved" of the way that Prime Minister Trudeau was handling his job had risen to 48 percent, an increase of

---

[13] "Prairie Voters Are United in Disgust at Rising Prices, but Divided on the Remedy," *The Toronto Star*, 7 June 1974.

Table 8-10
PUBLIC ATTITUDES IN QUEBEC TOWARD LANGUAGE ISSUES

Question	Response	
What should the official language be?	French only	16%
	French first and English second	41
	Both French and English	42
	No opinion	1
Should French-speaking parents retain the right to send their children to English schools?	Yes	79
	No	16
	No opinion	5

(N = 1,259)

Source: Quebec Institute of Public Opinion.

Table 8-11
RESPONSES, BY REGION, TO GALLUP QUESTION:
"Do you think that French/English should be a compulsory subject in all grades of public school in English-speaking/French-speaking Canada?"
(in percents)

Responses	Atlantic Provinces	Ontario	Quebec	Western Provinces	Total Canada
French					
Yes	60	57	88	39	61
No	26	37	9	57	34
No opinion	14	6	3	4	5
English					
Yes	78	76	84	69	76
No	15	18	14	27	19
No opinion	8	6	2	4	5

(N = 1,000)

Source: The Gallup Report, 12 June 1974.

14 percentage points over his 1969 rating.[14] Clearly, in a campaign of uncertain outcome, Trudeau was the Liberal party's best asset.

It has not always been so. While there is little question that Trudeau's bright new image underwrote the solid Liberal majority of

---

[14] In the 1974 poll, 48 percent approved, 34 percent disapproved, and 18 percent had no opinion. *The Gallup Report*, 1 May 1974.

1968, many analysts felt that his declining popularity contributed heavily to the Liberals' near-defeat of 1972. Part of the problem was most certainly the fact that the public image of Trudeau had changed perceptibly between 1968 and 1972. Political commentator Larry Zolf, in a satirical commentary on the changing Trudeau image, said that he had gone from "philosopher king" to "Robespierre" to "Marie Antoinette" to "Generalissimo Ky" (1972) over the course of the four-year majority Parliament.[15] Indeed, the caricature of Trudeau as Marie Antoinette was a favorite with newspaper cartoonists during 1972. Stanfield's public image proved to be steadier and more durable during most of this period.

In 1968, when both Trudeau and Stanfield were fresh faces on the Canadian federal political scene, the contrast of images presented to the public was remarkably clear. Political scientists Gilbert Winham and Robert Cunningham observed that "Stanfield tried to create the image of quiet competence, of a plain man talking plain sense about policy decisions facing Canadians. Trudeau on the other hand built his image around the excitement of a new kind of politics, and pressed home the themes of change, dynamism, and youth."[16] John Meisel, in his postelection survey in 1968, measured a number of the contrasting qualities of the Trudeau and Stanfield images (see Table 8-13). But the times were favorable to Trudeau's jet-age, "new politics" image and to the Liberal party, particularly in central Canada. By 1972, however, the Trudeau image had seriously eroded, and economic and political conditions in the country had changed markedly. The 1972 election result recorded the low ebb of both the Liberal and the Trudeau fortunes. The fact that Trudeau's popularity had steadily declined was likewise recorded in the polls.

But an image that had changed as much as had Trudeau's over this four-year period could readily be changed again. Following the 1972 election, two factors combined to bring about a substantial change in Trudeau's public image and in his personal popularity. The first of these was the minority Parliament itself. Trudeau could no longer be the aloof (to some, arrogant) leader of an impregnable majority, but rather was forced into the role of a minority prime minister, clinging to a narrow parliamentary plurality and fighting for his political life. The margin was thin—the slightest misstep could bring down his precarious government and precipitate another election. Some actually thought that he might resign after the 1972

---

15 Larry Zolf, *The Dance of the Dialectic* (Toronto: Lewis & Samuel, 1973).
16 G. Winham and R. Cunningham, "Party Leader Images in the 1968 Election," *Canadian Journal of Political Science*, vol. 3 (1970), p. 43.

Table 8-12

RESPONSES, BY REGION, TO THE GALLUP QUESTION:

"Regardless of any political feeling you may have, and just thinking of the individuals, which man do you think would make the best prime minister for Canada, Pierre Elliott Trudeau or Robert Stanfield?" (in percents)

	Atlantic Provinces	Ontario	Quebec	Prairie Provinces	British Columbia	Total Canada
Trudeau	38	51	49	37	44	46
Stanfield	26	18	16	32	28	22
Other	2	4	6	5	7	4
Don't know	35	27	29	26	21	28
(N = 1,047)						

Source: *The Gallup Report,* 4 May 1974.

Table 8-13

PERCEPTIONS OF TRUDEAU AND STANFIELD, 1968

Trudeau	Stanfield

Most Frequently Cited Qualities (Rank Order)

Trudeau	Stanfield
Intelligence, competence (1)	Reliability, responsibility (1)
Knowledge, education (2)	Intelligence, competence (2)
Honesty, sincerity, frankness (3)	Honesty, sincerity, frankness (3)
Progressive (4)	Experience (4)
Age, youth (5)	Personality (5)
Personality (5)	

Percent of Respondents Who Agree That Trudeau/Stanfield Is:

Intelligent	88%	Honest	77%
Progressive	80	Fair-minded	76
Tough-minded	73	Intelligent	76
Fair-minded	72	"Too conservative"	72
Able to handle Quebec	69	A man of integrity	71
Honest	69	"Too slow"	67
Capable of solving French-		Progressive	54
English problems in Canada	61	Better suited to provincial	
Charming	58	than federal politics	49
Arrogant	46	Soft on French Canada	35
"Conservative"	33	Quick to make promises	34
Inadequately concerned with		Capable of solving French-	
moral standards	30	English problems in Canada	21
Too rigid	23	Influenced by Dalton Camp [a]	19
"Pro-Communist"	15		

(N = 2,767)

[a] Former president of the Progressive Conservatives who opposed Diefenbaker's continuation as party leader in 1967.

Source: Meisel, "The 1968 Election Study"; data courtesy of the Inter-University Consortium for Political Research.

Figure 8-3

RESPONSES TO THE GALLUP QUESTION: "WOULD YOU
SAY YOUR OPINION OF PRIME MINISTER TRUDEAU
HAS GONE UP OR DOWN IN THE PAST THREE MONTHS?"
1968–1973

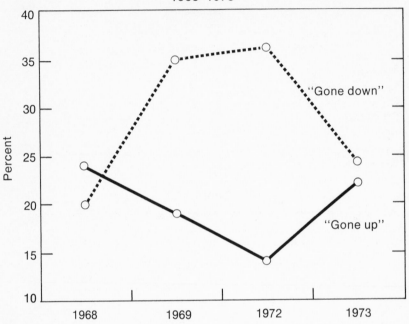

Source: *Gallup Report*, 14 April 1973.

election rather than meet the minority Parliament. But once in session, the political circumstances of this Parliament were so different from those of the preceding one that they could not help but mold a new image of Trudeau in the public mind. In Zolf's satirical lexicon, he now became "Mackenzie King," the master of parliamentary manipulation.[17] This post-1972 minority setting itself provided the key to improving a badly damaged public image, making possible the second main factor leading toward change. This was the decision on the part of Trudeau and Liberal party strategists to consciously attempt to change or reshape the Trudeau image. Following the 1972 result, Trudeau announced that he had "received a message from the Canadian people," and his advisers strived to overcome the old Trudeau image. Evidence of this change was seen

---

[17] Zolf, *Dance of the Dialectic.*

extensively in the 1974 campaign when one journalist after another observed that Trudeau was "different." Campaigning extensively in 1974 with his wife and young family, Trudeau had, in the words of *Toronto Star* correspondent Tony Westell, "changed from being a new politician with new ways into an old pol who pleases the crowds in the old ways." [18] This observation, made very early in the campaign, was evidence of the new Liberal strategy. Private Liberal polls had shown that an important factor in the Liberal debacle of 1972 was a widespread perception of Trudeau as arrogant, remote, and disinterested, but they also disclosed an improvement in Trudeau's popularity throughout the minority Parliament and following the defeat of his government in Parliament. Senator Gil Molgat, Liberal party president, observed: "He's taken a kicking, eaten some humble pie, and shown he can change, and now he's back fighting to win. People will like that." [19]

Presumably they did, and the public opinion polls documented a recovery in Trudeau's personal popularity (see Figure 8-3) from its low ebb of 1972. More importantly, they recorded the public's conviction that Trudeau *had* changed, in ways that were generally seen as positive. A Gallup poll taken early in 1973, only a few months after the October 1972 election, disclosed that 57 percent of a national sample felt that there had been a change in the prime minister. The survey also disclosed that the most commonly perceived direction of this change was that he had become less arrogant, more open, and more communicative (see Table 8-14).

By contrast, the public image of Trudeau's opponents appeared to change remarkably little. David Lewis, leader of the New Democratic party, had captured the popular imagination with a sparkling campaign in 1972, but conditions were much less favorable to his party following the defeat of the minority government. Réal Caouette, leader of the Social Credit party, retained much of his appeal to rural Quebec voters. And Robert Stanfield, leader of the opposition Conservatives, projected perhaps the steadiest and least changing personal image of all. But the very qualities that had hampered Stanfield in 1968 were seen by many preelection observers in 1974 as a decided potential asset to the Conservatives. Indeed, the Conservatives, having deemphasized the position of the party leader in the past two campaigns in favor of a "team" approach, placed much more emphasis on Stanfield's personal leadership quali-

---

[18] "A Different Pierre Trudeau Is Fighting This Time to Win," *The Toronto Star*, 25 May 1974.

[19] "A Different Pierre Trudeau," *The Toronto Star*, 25 May 1974.

Table 8-14

**PUBLIC PERCEPTION OF CHANGES IN THE IMAGE
OF PRIME MINISTER TRUDEAU, 1973**

"After the October election, Prime Minister Trudeau said that he
had 'received a message from the Canadian people.' Just from
what you have heard or read, do you think that Mr. Trudeau has
changed his attitude at all since the election?"

Yes	57%
No	38
No opinion	5

(If 'yes') "In what way?"

Less arrogant; more humble; easier to get along with; trying to make amends for his errors; more human; calmed down	35% [a]
Seems to care more about people; thinks more of the common man; realized he was not communicating enough with voters	30
Changed his mind on some policies; more aware of problems such as unemployment and welfare abuse; pays more attention to the West; Throne Speech showed a different approach	14
Has to listen more to Opposition; to other points of view; knows he's out of office if he doesn't	13
All other reasons	6
Can't say why	13

(N = 725)

[a] These percentages add up to more than 100 percent because of multiple
mentions.
Source: *The Gallup Report*, 21 February 1974 and 24 February 1974.

ties in 1974. This was partly to counter the appeal of Trudeau and
partly to attempt to take advantage of dimensions of the Stanfield
image that were suddenly more valuable in times of high inflation
and political uncertainty. Private Conservative polls had shown that
the most positive dimensions of Stanfield's image were those of
honesty, integrity, sincerity, and competence. Thus, even though his
overall personal popularity fell well behind that of the prime minister,
these qualities could well be exploited and developed in the 1974
campaign. As journalist Richard Gwyn observed at the opening of
the PC campaign, "The Conservative campaign . . . features two
themes, each reinforcing one another—Stanfield the decent, likeable
person whom Canadians can trust, and Stanfield the bare knuckle
politician whom Canadians can also trust to tough it out when
needed." [20] As the campaign developed, the images and issues became increasingly inseparable in the minds of voters and analysts
alike.

20 "This Time Around, Bob Bares His Knuckles," *The Toronto Star*, 25 May 1974.

The Problem of Minority Government. The results of the 1972 election forced Canadians, for the third time in four elections, to grapple with the problems of minority government in Ottawa. In spite of the seeming permanence of a multiparty system in modern Canadian federal politics, there is ample evidence that a large part of the electorate views the situation of a government commanding only a plurality of parliamentary seats with some unease. It is a commonplace of recent political analysis in Canada to note that there exists a strong preference for majority governments in the British tradition of parliamentary politics and a corresponding latent feeling that minority government represents sickness rather than health in the political system.

There is ample survey evidence to support at least the first of these assertions. Both major postelection studies to date (in 1965 and 1968) disclose that the majority of voters favor the concept of majority government and that they consider the matter "important" (see Table 8-15). A poll taken by Complan Research Associates for CTV one month before the election found that 72 percent of respondents wanted a majority government. It does not automatically follow from these findings, however, that voters will abandon their normal voting behavior in order to secure a parliamentary majority. Nor does it follow that majority government is a truly important political issue as compared with the other contemporary issues of Canadian politics.

In fact, it is quite likely that the survey figures by themselves may somewhat overstate the importance of the majority government

Table 8-15
VOTER PERCEPTIONS OF THE IMPORTANCE OF
MAJORITY GOVERNMENT, 1965 AND 1968
(in percents)

Opinion	1965	1968
Very important	60	69
Fairly important	19	16
Not very important	21	15
	(N = 2,128 a)	(N = 2,257 a)

a Weighted. Both years exclude "no opinion" responses and nonvoters. The form of the question differs slightly between the 1965 and 1968 surveys.
Source: For 1965: P. Converse, J. Meisel, M. Pinard, P. Regenstreif, and M. Schwartz, "The 1965 Election Study"; for 1968: Meisel, "The 1968 Election Study." Both surveys courtesy of the Inter-University Consortium for Political Research.

question. The majority government issue is only infrequently mentioned by survey respondents in response to open-ended questions. It is also worthwhile to recall that the Liberal government in 1965 was, after all, unsuccessful in obtaining its sought-after majority, in spite of the indications in the survey data at the time that this was considered an important election issue. The results of that election were, in fact, remarkably close to those of the 1963 election—which leads to the rather obvious speculation that very little, if any, change in actual voting behavior occurred as a direct result of the minority government setting. It should not be inferred from the opinion distributions alone that widespread changes in voting behavior could or did take place, either in 1965 when a majority government was not elected or in 1968 when it was. Another question asked in the 1965 postelection survey yields a more realistic proportion of the electorate who might under some circumstances have been amenable to switching their vote to a party capable of securing a majority.[21] But there is little evidence in the two postelection studies that actual switching did in fact take place on any substantial scale.

The Canadian preference for majority governments does not necessarily imply deviations in voting behavior, nor an unwillingness to accept minority governments. Seemingly in contrast to the above patterns, a Gallup poll in 1973 found that a majority of respondents felt that the minority government had been "good for the nation" (see Table 8-16). Other polls throughout this period strongly suggest that an election to resolve the parliamentary impasse was neither desired nor widely expected, save in the event that the government should suffer a defeat in Parliament. In fact, Liberal strategy both before and after the defeat of the budget in Parliament was based on the assumption, documented in private polls, that voters generally were not favorable to an early election.

While there is much survey evidence of the long-standing voter preference for the concept of majority government, and a corresponding dislike of frequent elections, there has been relatively little measurement of voter attitudes toward various types of minority situations, coalition politics, the position of the minor parties, or the qualities of minority government in general. Some will undoubtedly

---

[21] Estimated at about 21 percent on the basis of cross-tabulation of the general question on majority government against the question: "If you believed that a party could form a majority government, but you did not ordinarily vote for that party, how likely would you be to vote for it in order to have a majority government—very likely, somewhat likely, or not very likely?" This question was not asked in the 1968 survey. Converse et al., *1965 Election Study;* data courtesy of the Inter-University Consortium for Political Research.

Table 8-16

RESPONSES TO THE GALLUP QUESTION:

"Canada has had a number of minority governments in Ottawa during the past ten years or so—that is, a Parliament in which the party in power has no clear-cut majority over all other parties. On the whole, in your opinion, do you think that a minority government is good or bad for the nation?"

Response	Percent
Good	54
Bad	27
Qualified	3
No opinion	16
(N = 713)	

Source: *The Gallup Report*, 25 April 1973.

see the 1974 result as reflecting a determination on the part of voters to install a strong majority in Ottawa. The Gallup finding that many voters saw the minority Parliament as "good for the nation" should, however, give pause to those who would make such an interpretation. Similarly, some interpretations will suggest voter determination to "punish" the opposition parties for precipitating the election, a theme that the Liberals attempted to exploit somewhat in the campaign. But there is equally little evidence to support this conclusion. It is also the view of some that the NDP was damaged by its support of the Liberals for a long period, a fear that undoubtedly led to the election itself. But there is evidence of a generally positive perception of the NDP's role in the Twenty-ninth Parliament, as well as of the voters' dislike of frequent elections as a means of resolving this type of impasse. A Gallup poll published in October 1973 uncovered a feeling that the Liberals had lost ground since the previous election, while the NDP was seen as having improved its position.[22] This, of course, represents the exact opposite of the actual 1974 election result.

While it is doubtful that Canadians voted for majority government per se in 1974, it is indisputable that the minority government setting made a stronger impression on voters than comparable earlier

---

[22] Fifty-three percent of those interviewed felt that the Liberals would get fewer votes in a new election, while only 19 percent felt that they would get more. Forty-three percent, on the other hand, felt that the NDP would improve, as opposed to only 18 percent who saw that party losing support. Opinion was divided regarding the prospects of the Conservatives. *The Gallup Report*, 24 October 1973 and 31 October 1973.

Table 8-17

PUBLIC ATTITUDES TOWARD THE
MINORITY PARLIAMENT, 1973

Question	Response	
A. Do you expect a federal election within the next year?	Yes No No opinion (N=1,044)	35% 48 17
B. Will the NDP continue to support the government?	Yes No No opinion (N=723)	68 13 19
C. Should minority government carry on, or call an election as soon as possible?	Carry on Call election No opinion (N=1,044)	64 28 8
D. If government falls, should Stanfield be called upon to form a government or should an election be called?	Call on Stanfield Call election No opinion (N=725)	29 57 14

Source: *The Gallup Report,* for question A, 29 December 1973; for question B, 3 November 1973; for question C, 26 December 1973; for question D, 7 February 1973.

Table 8-18

PUBLIC ATTITUDES TOWARD NDP SUPPORT OF
THE MINORITY LIBERAL GOVERNMENT

"It has been suggested that the Liberal Government is complying with NDP proposals simply to avoid an election, and not because of policy convictions. Do you think this is true, partly true, or untrue?"

True	27%
Partly true	38
Untrue	16
No opinion	19

(N=1,037)

(If 'true' or 'partly true') "Do you think they are justified in doing this?"

Yes	61%
No	31
No opinion	8

(N=674)

Source: *The Gallup Report,* 20 February 1974.

situations had. The Pearson minority governments of the sixties had fallen only a few seats short of majorities and had faced a badly splintered opposition in Parliament. They had been able to behave, therefore, in many respects as if they held a majority. The Trudeau minority, on the other hand, was precarious (with its two-seat plurality) and had to contend with a vigorous New Democratic party group's demands as a quid pro quo for support, and with a newly awakened opposition Conservative party across the aisle. The day-to-day give and take of this situation in Parliament was more than sufficient to keep the minority government setting in the mind of the public. But, while there is past evidence of only the most limited "majority government effect" on voting behavior in Canadian elections, the possibility remains that even a small shift of votes away from the NDP as a result of such an effect can be of considerable importance in a close election.

The Election. It is always difficult to assess the impact of a campaign on the outcome of an election. Political scientists generally tend to minimize the importance of campaign activities, speeches, rallies, and so on, while journalists are often prone to overestimate it. It can generally be shown, however, that campaigns may have a "reinforcing" effect, providing motivation and commitment to voters who already identify with a party and whose support is likely if not certain, and that they may have an impact on the "undecided" or "uncommitted" voter. However, as a rule, only a small proportion of votes are actually won or lost in a campaign. By comparative standards, Canadian election campaigns tend to be long, largely because of the substantial amount of time required to register voters spread over large land area. The likelihood that events or circumstances might at least marginally influence a result is, therefore, increased.

A Gallup poll, taken just before the government's defeat on the budget in early May 1974 and published on 5 June, showed the Liberals with 40 percent of the vote compared to the Conservatives' 33 percent and the NDP's 21 percent.[23] But, more importantly, the poll also showed that more than a third of all voters surveyed were "undecided," suggesting that the campaign itself might prove to be more important than would normally be the case.[24] As noted earlier,

---

[23] *The Gallup Report*, 4 June 1974.

[24] As noted earlier, polls measuring vote intention in Canada are prone to a high proportion of "undecided" responses. Because some analysts view "undecided" respondents as more favorable to the Conservatives, the high proportion in the Gallup poll was viewed in some quarters as a favorable omen for that party.

the Conservative decision to emphasize the issue of inflation and the Liberal decision to concentrate on the "issue" of Trudeau's leadership each reflected the respective parties' carefully measured assessments of their strengths and weaknesses. With hindsight there can be little doubt that the campaign as a whole favored the Liberals, although its effect on the overall result is still debatable. A private Conservative poll taken two weeks before election day showed that inflation had dipped to 52 percent as the issue of greatest importance, while the issue of leadership promoted by the Liberals, though nonexistent in previous surveys, was cited by 43 percent. Certainly, the Conservative handling of the wage and price controls proposal, coupled with the Liberal emphasis on Trudeau, accounted for at least part of this change. The release in the midst of the campaign of the latest Statistics Canada figures showing record increases in the cost of living seemed to damage the Liberals far less than their opponents might have had reason to expect.

The overall success of the Liberal campaign is seen in the fact that 60 percent of the respondents to the preelection Gallup poll expected the Liberals to win the election, a distinct reversal of the pessimistic assessment of the Liberals' position in the same poll of the previous October. And the Liberals made steady gains as the "undecided" category declined to its election-eve low of 15 percent.

These fairly clear patterns, however, fail to capture the regional variation in party strength which is such an important feature of Canadian politics. It was generally agreed that the Conservatives stood little chance of making serious inroads into the Liberal stronghold of Quebec and that the Liberals would prove incapable of dislodging the solid Conservative strength on the prairies. It also appeared that little change was in prospect in the Atlantic provinces. Short-term swings, if they materialized at all, were expected only in Ontario, where the Conservatives had made sharp gains in 1972, and in British Columbia, where provincial factors appeared to endanger the eleven NDP seats won in 1972. As the campaign developed, the polls began to disclose the gain in Liberal strength in Ontario that afterward would tell much of the story of the 1974 election. On 5 July Regenstreif wrote, citing a large (1,623 respondents) Ontario survey conducted by Canadian Facts, Ltd., for the *Toronto Star*, that the Liberals enjoyed a clear lead across Ontario, in distinct contrast to their 1972 performance in that province.[25] This poll suggested that Liberal gains were most likely to occur in the Hamilton-

---

[25] "Ontario Lead Held by Liberals, Poll Indicates," *The Toronto Star*, 5 July 1974.

Figure 8-4

GALLUP PREDICTIONS, FEBRUARY 1973–JULY 1974

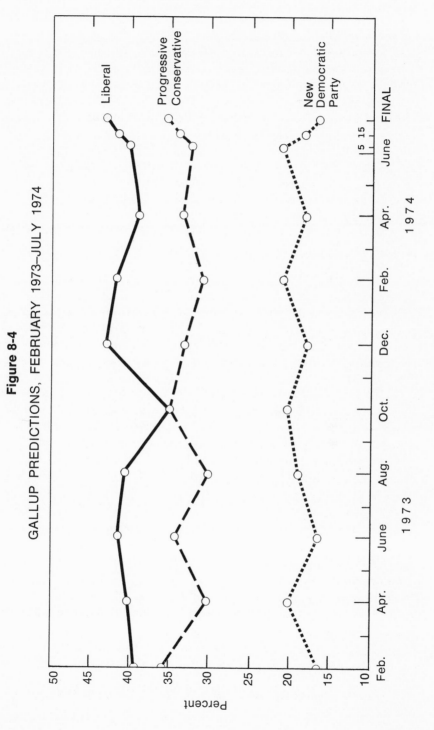

Niagara region in southwestern Ontario and, to a lesser extent, in metropolitan Toronto.

Given these relatively clear trends in the campaign, one might have expected the election result to have been entirely predictable. This was far from the case. Gallup turned out to be extraordinarily accurate in its estimates of the popular vote, not only for the Liberals but for each of the parties. But the predictions based on these figures were nevertheless cautious. Regenstreif, citing his own interviews, the Gallup figures, and the Canadian Facts' Ontario survey, predicted a Liberal minority—"a win but not a romp." Again, Regenstreif's forecasts illustrate the difficulty of translating poll figures in Canada into a distribution of parliamentary seats: he predicted a range for the Liberals of 118 to 130 seats (they actually won 141), 100 to 112 for the Conservatives (who won 95), and 23 to 26 for the NDP (who won 16). He predicted that Social Credit's 1972 total of 15 seats could be "cut in half" (they won 11).[26]

There were, in fact, few if any actual predictions of the Liberal majority result, in spite of the accuracy of the Gallup percentage figures. Other polls tended to show the Liberals lower than Gallup, with a CBC poll estimating their popular vote at 34 percent and a CTV poll at 38 percent. In a telecast on 4 July, the CBC announced that its poll showed a Progressive Conservative minority government to be "a strong possibility," and the following night amended this statement to emphasize that this result was only one "possibility," a Liberal minority being an equally likely outcome. Interestingly, both television polls purported to have discovered a last-minute trend away from the Liberals, thus causing more uncertainty in their predictions. Gallup, on the other hand, indicated throughout a clear trend to the Liberals, and Regenstreif noted that the Liberal lead, which had faltered in previous elections, had held up right to the end. Many analysts tended to accept the belief that the polls were too generous to the Liberals, and so were cautious in their predictions. CTV actually revised its estimate of Liberal strength downward for this reason, thereby adding somewhat to the error in its prediction.

Regardless of the record of accuracy and relative sophistication of particular polls, in 1974 there was a marked tendency to interpret findings with utmost caution. Most often this had the effect of portraying the Conservatives as somewhat stronger than they ultimately proved to be and created an aura of uncertainty about the

---

26 "The Polls' Message—A Liberal Win," *The Toronto Star*, 6 July 1974.

result and expectations of a close contest. The fact that the most reliable poll figures clearly revealed the Liberal strength did not seem to appreciably affect these attitudes.

Conclusion

To the political scientist, an election is a convergence of a number of long-term and short-term factors which produces a particular result. There is little doubt that in Canada the long-term factors have been favorable to the Liberal party for over a generation. The Liberals have been out of power for only a five-year period since 1935, and surveys uniformly indicate that more voters identify with them than with any other party. The volatility of Canadian politics in recent years, however, coupled with the substantial differences in regional patterns, has tended to place greater emphasis on the short-term factors that can influence elections. It would have seemed that many of these forces were favorable to the Conservatives in 1974; indeed, the concern with inflation and economic uncertainty alone might have led observers to expect an improvement in Conservative fortunes. But it is evident that other short-term factors beyond these must also enter the 1974 calculus. Such elements as Trudeau's personal popularity, the conduct of the campaign, and the uncertainty of the period of minority government all appear to have played some role in the outcome. Neither was the trend to the Liberals uniform. The Conservatives improved their position in no fewer than five provinces and retained a lead over the Liberals in two others. The fact that the substantial Liberal gains in the province of Ontario were not matched throughout the country should cause doubts about any explanations of the election outcome that emphasize a single factor, particularly a short-term factor. Preelection polls, however, are inclined by their very nature to suggest short-term explanations and therefore should be treated carefully in this regard by the serious student of politics. Only by attempting to place poll findings in long-term perspective is it possible to achieve a more sophisticated level of analysis of contemporary Canadian electoral politics.

9

THE MASS MEDIA IN THE 1974 CANADIAN ELECTION

Frederick J. Fletcher

In Canada, as in other industrial democracies, the mass media have played an increasingly important role in election campaigns in this century. Party politicians have had to develop new techniques of electioneering to keep pace with such developments as the decline of the partisan press, the emergence of radio in the 1930s, and the development of television in the 1950s. Expenditures on political advertising, especially on radio and television, have grown steadily.[1] And, increasingly, election campaigns have become contests for the attention of the news media, which provide free exposure and greater credibility than partisan advertising. Candidates recognize that the mass media provide most people with much of their campaign information. In fact, research suggests that the news media, through their selection and presentation of news, can shape the images of candidates, help determine the main campaign issues, and influence the tone of the election.[2]

The impact of the mass media campaign on the outcome of any election is often subtle, however, and difficult to assess. Voting studies show that few voters actually switch from one party to another during

This study could not have been completed without the assistance of many people in the news organizations who provided both information and opinions, nor without the help of my research assistants, Jay Kaufman, Daphne Gaby, Dan Butler, Ian Box, Richard Bellaire, Laurent Dobuzinskis, and James R. Williams, all of York University. Needless to say, the analysis and interpretations are my own.

[1] For discussions of these developments, see Khayyam Z. Paltiel, *Political Party Financing in Canada* (Toronto: McGraw-Hill, 1970), pp. 76-91; W. H. Kesterton, *A History of Journalism in Canada* (Toronto: McClelland and Stewart, 1967), Chapters 4 and 6-8; Colin Seymour-Ure, *The Political Impact of the Mass Media* (London: Constable, 1974), Chapter 8.

[2] For a good summary of the literature, see Seymour-Ure, *Political Impact of Mass Media*, Chapters 1, 2, and 8.

a campaign and that mass media messages influence only some of those. As one recent study of the Canadian mass media put it, "newspapers can't swing elections any more. . . ."[3] It can be argued, however, that the increasing urbanization of Canada's electorate, the entrenchment of a multiparty system, and other factors have increased the fluidity of Canadian voting behavior and therefore enhanced the importance of campaigns. Certainly the opinion polls have shown a greater proportion of undecided voters in recent years.[4] The system is such that it takes only a slight shift in votes to change the outcome of Canadian federal elections. And there is a good deal of evidence to suggest that the campaign, by influencing turnout rates and some of the undecided voters, can swing an election.[5]

The impact of the media on the politicians is more easily discerned. Although local candidates can ignore the media and concentrate on canvassing and other forms of person-to-person communication, the national party organizations rely heavily on the mass media to transmit their electoral appeals. As a result, campaigns are generally run with careful attention to the media. To a significant extent, the party leaders time their announcements and draft their speeches with an eye on what they think will attract media attention. They try to come up with something new every day to keep reporters interested and they stick with themes that seem to be catching on in the media; feedback from the reporters and commentators is much more immediate than feedback from the public. In addition, attempts are made to provide attractive "visuals" for the cameras. In short, the public content of the campaign is shaped to a substantial degree by a complex process of interaction between the parties and the media.[6]

The 1974 Canadian federal election campaign was marked by charges of media bias, allegations that reporters had allowed themselves to be manipulated by Liberal party media strategy, and an unusual amount of self-criticism on the part of journalists. The

---

[3] Canada, Special Senate Committee on the Mass Media, Report, 3 vols. (Ottawa: Information Canada, 1970), vol. 1, p. 8; hereinafter cited as Davey Committee Report.

[4] See, for example, Lawrence LeDuc, "The Measurement of Public Opinion," in this volume, pp. 217-218.

[5] See Jay G. Blumler, "Mass Media Roles and Reactions in the February Election," in Howard R. Penniman, ed., Britain at the Polls (Washington, D. C.: American Enterprise Institute, 1974), p. 150, and Seymour-Ure, Political Impact of Mass Media, pp. 203-204.

[6] For a brief discussion of this process in another Canadian context, see Frederick J. Fletcher, "Between Two Stools: News Coverage of Provincial Politics in Ontario," in Donald C. MacDonald, ed., Government and Politics of Ontario (Toronto: Macmillan, 1975).

issues raised by these controversies are examined in this chapter, as are the Canadian system of campaign communication, the media strategies of the parties, and the amount, form, and content of campaign news coverage and advertising. The campaign is viewed here primarily as a contest for news media attention.

The Canadian Mass Media System

The Canadian mass media system is marked by cultural dualism, a significant degree of public ownership, the absence of a national press, and a substantial communications overflow from the United States. These characteristics stem in large part from two facts: most of Canada's relatively small population (about 21 million) lives in clusters along a narrow band about 100 miles wide north of the U.S. border; and this population is divided along linguistic lines. The country's 6 million French-speaking citizens have their own media system. The publicly owned Canadian Broadcasting Corporation (CBC), which provides radio and television service in both French and English, was founded in 1932 to provide a nationwide alternative to the spillover from American radio stations in a situation in which Canadian private enterprise could not compete.[7] Television followed the same pattern, though a private network became economically feasible a few years after CBC television was formed.

Canada has no truly national newspapers or news magazines (unless one counts the four to six pages of Canadian news which appear in the Canadian edition of *Time*). The *Toronto Globe and Mail* is the most national of Canada's newspapers but it sells fewer than 7,500 copies outside of Ontario (some 3 percent of its total circulation). Transportation costs make a truly national newspaper economically unfeasible, according to Ross Munro, publisher of the *Edmonton Journal* and current president of the Canadian Press (CP), a cooperative news-gathering and distribution agency owned collectively by the nation's daily newspapers.[8] The burden of presenting a national picture of political events thus falls on CP and on the national news broadcasts of the CBC and the privately owned CTV television network. The broadcast networks maintain correspondents across the country and also rely on Broadcast News (BN), a sub-

---

[7] The first private network, Canadian Television (CTV), did not come into being until 1961.

[8] *Toronto Star*, 5 December 1974. On CP, see Davey Committee Report, vol. 1, pp. 229-235.

sidiary of CP, which provides both teletype and tape services to the networks and to more than 300 private radio and television stations.

The CBC English-language television service feeds more than fifty CBC-owned or affiliated television stations in all ten provinces, while the French network serves seventeen stations, eleven in Quebec, where 80 percent of Canada's Francophones live, and six in major centers across the country. CBC radio provides English-language service in all the provinces and French service in all but two. CTV, which operates exclusively in English, has some seventeen affiliated stations covering most of the country. In addition, there are several radio news services and regional radio and television networks.

The national news available to most Canadians is that presented on the radio and television networks or provided to local newspapers by CP (or, in a few cases, by their own correspondents). The CP does a generally good job of covering the country despite its meager resources (some 200 reporters, writers, and editors), but editors often choose not to use materials which lack a local angle. The networks are the most truly national news outlets. For Anglophones, there are the CBC national news (average audience, 2 million) and the CTV national news (average audience 1.2 million). Their news staffs are smaller than those of the U.S. networks (about twenty each) and their newscasts shorter.[9] Both newscasts run for twenty minutes daily at 11 P.M. (though CTV carries only thirteen minutes of news because of commercials). The CBC also provides extensive radio news on three national newscasts per day and a weekly Sunday magazine. The most popular broadcast, the 8 A.M. world news, has an average audience of about 650,000.

Radio-Canada, as the CBC is known to French-speaking Canadians, presents two national television newscasts daily at 7 P.M. and 10:30 P.M., to an average audience of about 800,000 and several radio newscasts. The major one, at 8 A.M., has an average audience of about 300,000. Although both the radio and television services operate with a handful of reporters, they do maintain correspondents in major centers across the country.

The French and English news services of the CBC are completely separate in personnel and content. Although CP translates material for its members, the French media tend to rely heavily on their own personnel. Most Quebec news outlets concern themselves primarily with Quebec issues and project a strong Quebec identity.

---

[9] Data on audience sizes and staff deployment were supplied by network officials. For the U.S. networks, see Timothy Crouse, *The Boys on the Bus* (Toronto: Ballantine Books, 1973), Chapter 7.

Except for reporters posted in Ottawa, the French newspapers of Quebec do not maintain a single correspondent outside the province (whereas a few large English-language dailies do have bureaus in Quebec). The CBC French service is the only Quebec-based outlet with correspondents across Canada. As a consequence of these patterns, the two language groups often get quite different pictures of Canadian politics, even of the same event. For example, the near-defeat of the Liberal administration of Prime Minister Pierre Elliott Trudeau in 1972 was widely interpreted in the Quebec press as a rejection of French-Canadian influence in Ottawa, while English-language journalists blamed it on economic factors and the lackluster Trudeau campaign.[10]

The inescapable proximity of the United States has also been a major influence on the Canadian mass media system. Many Canadians are concerned about the fact that more than 75 percent of the magazines sold in Canada are published in the United States, that a high proportion of the foreign news in Canadian newspapers comes from American sources (for example, CP relies heavily on the Associated Press), and that many Canadians are regular viewers of U.S. network news.[11] There is also concern that two of the bestselling magazines in Canada, *Reader's Digest* and *Time*, are controlled from outside the country and carry over much of their content from their U.S. editions. This is especially true of *Time*.[12] This massive U.S.

---

[10] See Paul Stevens and John T. Saywell, "Parliament and Politics," in J. T. Saywell, ed., *Canadian Annual Review of Politics and Public Affairs 1972* (Toronto: University of Toronto Press, 1974), pp. 74-75.

[11] See W. Brian Stewart, "The Canadian Social System and the Canadian Broadcasting Audience," Frank W. Peers, "Broadcasting and National Unity," and Frederick Elkins, "Communications Media and Identity Formation in Canada," in Benjamin D. Singer, ed., *Communications in Canadian Society* (Toronto: Copp Clark, 1972), pp. 39-66 and 202-230. See also Frank Peers, "Oh Say, Can You See?" in Ian Lumsden, ed., *Close the 49th Parallel, Etc.* (Toronto: University of Toronto Press, 1970), pp. 135-156, and Joseph Scanlon, "Canada Sees the World through U.S. Eyes: One Case Study in Cultural Domination," *Canadian Forum*, September 1974, pp. 34-39.

[12] On 23 January 1975, the Canadian government introduced legislation to amend the Income Tax Act to end current special provisions which permit advertisers to claim income tax deductions for advertising in the Canadian editions of *Time* and *Reader's Digest* (as well as several smaller foreign-owned publications). The bill, which is expected to become law in the fall and to take effect 31 December 1975, applies to Canadian-editions rules established for other foreign-owned magazines in 1965. To qualify for deductions, publications will have to be 75 percent Canadian-owned, free of licensing arrangements with foreign companies, and "not substantially the same" in content as foreign publications. The precise meaning of the last clause has yet to be clarified. The bill also provides for the withdrawal at some future date of the right of Canadian businesses to deduct the costs of advertising on foreign radio and television stations. The

presence has meant that Canadians are often more aware of American issues than of Canadian issues; indeed, many Canadians will tune out Canadian political broadcasts to watch entertainment shows on nearby U.S. stations. And there has been an emulation effect, with political parties borrowing campaign techniques and reporters press practices from the United States.

Another important aspect of the Canadian mass media system is the heavy concentration of ownership of the private outlets. Nearly 80 percent of Canadian dailies are members of newspaper groups, and a few large chains dominate the field. The three largest chains account for about half of total daily circulation. Nearly half of the private radio and television stations are also group-owned. While there is concern about this concentration, it has resulted in the development of cooperative news bureaus which supplement CP. Both the Southam and Thomson groups maintain Ottawa bureaus, for example.[13]

In spite of the difficulties cited here, Canada does have a highly developed and pervasive mass media system, made up of some 114 daily newspapers with a total circulation of about 5 million, more than 1,000 other newspapers, about 100 television stations (many with numerous booster stations), some 450 radio stations, and a few mass-circulation magazines. A survey taken in 1969 found the presence of the media to be pervasive: 96 percent of a national sample reported owning a television set and 98 percent at least one radio, and 88 percent reported subscribing to at least one newspaper.[14]

The Canadian System of Campaign Communication. Among the distinctive features of the Canadian system of campaign communication are the tradition that party leaders must campaign in all regions, the combination of free broadcast time and paid advertising, and the dominant role played by members of the parliamentary press gallery in campaign coverage. Recent trends, not unique to Canada, include the growing importance of television and the impact of that development.

Canadian campaigns are relatively intense affairs lasting about eight weeks. Traditionally, it has been mandatory for party leaders to tour the country at least once. As Howard A. Scarrow observed

---

fundamental rationale for the measures is that these outlets drain off millions of dollars in advertising from Canada, but provide little Canadian content. See Bill C-58, 23-24 Elizabeth II, 1974-75, and Canada, House of Commons, *Debates*, vol. 119 (1st session, 30th Parliament), pp. 5591-5604 and 5607-5621.

13 On chain ownership in Canada, see Davey Committee Report, vols. 1 and 2.

14 Davey Committee Report, vol. 3, pp. 11-12.

fifteen years ago, "The articulate interests which are identified with particular geographic areas must be satisfied by the party which hopes to be a successful vote getter, and to appeal to these interests there is no adequate substitute for the candidate's personal appearance within the area. . . ." [15] In 1974 local editors still criticized leaders who failed to put in an appearance. The practice of touring ensures that party leaders and the reporters traveling with them will be exhausted by election day and keeps speech writers busy developing "local angles" (though it also permits speeches to be recycled as the road show moves on).

Free-time political broadcasts are a well established tradition, initiated by CBC radio more than twenty-five years ago. Though, according to Canadian Radio-Television Commission (CRTC) regulations, "licensees are not obligated to offer free time for broadcasts of a partisan political nature to political parties and candidates," [16] many private stations have followed the example of the CBC radio and television services. Where free time is offered, the allocation among parties and candidates must be "on an equitable basis" as defined by the CRTC: each recognized party must get a share of any free time, and the time must be allocated roughly on the basis of party standings in the House of Commons at dissolution. In 1974, for the first time, parties without seats were recognized if they had nominated candidates in one-fourth of the constituencies (sixty-six) in the previous election. As a result, the Communist and Marxist-Leninist parties qualified. The allocations are set by negotiation between the parties and the broadcasters, but appeals may be made to the CRTC, which is usually able to resolve them without recourse to legal authority.

While the parties and candidates gain considerable benefit from the free time, they also engage in extensive advertising campaigns, spending up to 40 percent of their election budgets on purchasing time and space and producing advertising copy, tapes, and films. The CBC will not accept political advertising as a matter of policy, and the regulations forbid parties and candidates from advertising on American stations. But there are many private Canadian radio and television stations, newspapers, and magazines eager for the advertising dollar.

---

[15] Howard A. Scarrow, "Communication of Election Appeals in Canada," *Journalism Quarterly*, vol. 36 (1959), p. 219.

[16] Canadian Radio-Television Commission Circular 197, "Broadcasting Guide for Canadian Elections," Ottawa, 14 May 1974. The CRTC is an independent regulatory agency which operates under the authority of the Broadcasting Act of 1968.

Television has played an increasingly important role in the communication of campaign appeals since the 1957 election, the first in which it was extensively used. Political image-makers believe that it reaches more voters, especially more uncommitted voters, and has more impact than other media.[17] The major change in the use of television since 1957 has been in program content. Virtually all of the 1957 broadcasts were talks by leaders or other party spokesmen, an extension of radio techniques and a result of the parties' lack of sophistication and the broadcast regulations. The rules, which initially prohibited cartoons, jingles, dramatizations, and films of rallies, have been progressively loosened, permitting the parties in recent elections to draw on their advertising consultants for the most sophisticated techniques available.[18]

The importance of television news has also increased significantly since 1957, to the point where party strategists regard it as the major channel of opinion formation. The television stress on party leaders has, because of the medium's importance, led to a similar emphasis in the other media. Although a team approach to campaigning is well-suited to a parliamentary system—in which the party leader is only first among equals—such an approach ran into problems in 1968, when the Conservatives tried it, and again in 1972, when the Liberals attempted it. As Anthony Westell, Ottawa editor of the *Toronto Star*, put it in 1972, "Cabinet ministers cannot serve as political substitutes for the [prime minister]. The media do not report them to anything like the same extent. . . ."[19] The same observation applies with even greater force to the opposition leaders and their front-bench colleagues.

Despite the best efforts of the television networks, the system of campaign communication in 1974 did not include a national debate. In fact, there has been no public debate among party leaders since the one and only television debate of 1968. Despite the fact that many people had considered the 1968 debate dull,[20] the CBC and CTV made a joint proposal to the parties in 1974, but negotiations broke down over format. Network officials agreed that the pattern

[17] John Meisel, *The Canadian General Election of 1957* (Toronto: University of Toronto Press, 1962), pp. 65-81, 109-110 and 163.

[18] Ibid., pp. 163-164, and *Broadcasting and Cable Television Regulatory Handbook*, Peter S. Grant, compiler and annotator (Toronto: Law Society of Upper Canada, 1973), vol. 1.

[19] *Toronto Star*, 28 September 1972.

[20] See Stevens and Saywell, "Parliament and Politics," in Saywell, ed., *Canadian Annual Review for 1968* (Toronto: University of Toronto Press, 1969), p. 50.

of negotiations suggested that major party leaders believe a free-for-all debate on television is too risky.

The Press Gallery and Campaign Coverage. The key "gatekeeper" role [21] played by the members of the parliamentary press gallery in the day-to-day reporting of national politics carries over to election coverage. Most of the reporters who cover national elections are drawn from the approximately 125 members of the gallery and provide not only most news reports but also a high proportion of the commentary. While they may not be a cohesive group, divided as they are by such factors as region, language, age, and ideology, these full-time political observers all live and work in Ottawa, use the same sources of information, and interact with one another regularly. As a result, there often does emerge among them a loose consensus derived, as one reporter has put it, "from the nonstop caucus of newsmen in the Gallery lounge. . . ." [22]

It has been suggested that the gallery helped to create Trudeau's landslide in 1968 and then played a major role in his near-defeat in 1972. Many observers traced Trudeau's rise to the Liberal party leadership to media attention, and there has been even wider agreement that the so-called "Trudeaumania" of the 1968 campaign—the squealing girls and political groupies attracted to Trudeau's public appearances by his carefree bachelor antics—was media created. Certainly, the media reported Trudeau's every unconventional act in 1968, though it is unclear whether reporters were hungry for a hero, as some have suggested,[23] or simply hungry for colorful copy.

More important for events in 1974, however, was what happened after the 1968 election. Numerous observers have suggested that the gallery became disillusioned with the prime minister in the months after the election and that by 1971 there was what one reporter has called a "burning animosity" towards him.[24] Reporter Larry Zolf, in a satiric but serious book, argues that this animosity stemmed from Trudeau's manifest belief that most reporters are poorly educated and ill-informed and his tendency to "put down" reporters whose questions he deemed ignorant, his technocratic style of government,

---

[21] On the gatekeeper concept, see David Manning White, "The 'Gatekeeper': A Case Study in the Selection of News," *Journalism Quarterly*, vol. 27 (1950), pp. 383-390.

[22] June Callwood, quoted in Borden Spears, "Canadian Newspaper Practice," in the Davey Committee Report, vol. 3, p. 205.

[23] Stevens and Saywell, "Parliament and Politics [1968]," pp. 50-51.

[24] John Burns, "Dogging the Campaign Trail to Check on the Press," *Toronto Globe and Mail*, 21 June 1974.

which many reporters thought dull and not newsworthy ("strictly bread and no circuses"), and his attempts to keep his private life private.[25] Others have argued that Trudeau ran an "empty vessel" campaign in 1968 which permitted reporters to read their own preferences into his highly general statements, so that disillusionment was inevitable when his administration had to make hard decisions.[26]

Zolf goes so far as to suggest that some reporters, anxious to defeat Trudeau in 1972, worked to make the other party leaders more credible. For example, he alleges that some broadcast reporters began "to edit out the interminable Stanfield 'pauses' from their tapes and films. A crisp new Stanfield, not quick but not slow, was presented to the eyes and ears of Anglophonia [English Canada]." [27] Whatever the truth of this allegation, Robert Stanfield, leader of the opposition Conservative party, did well in the 1972 campaign in the contest for media attention, aided by a sympathetic press and a new speech writer with a talent for one-liners, while the Trudeau cabinet— in Zolf's words, "the best management team in the country"[28]— was running a dull campaign. The media had tagged Trudeau as arrogant, aloof, and inaccessible in the period before 1972, and the polls suggest that a large segment of the electorate agreed.[29] Whatever the impact of the media on the outcome, there is little doubt that gallery members carried the hostilities and sympathies they had developed between 1968 and 1972 into the election coverage.

What was the situation in 1974? One reporter, John Burns, a gallery member from 1969 to 1971, joined the campaign tour to find out. His conclusion at midcampaign was that "the animosity, while still there, seems greatly diminished." He found reporters still professing great hostility to the prime minister but "by and large the mood is more tolerant than it was." [30] Burns suggested several reasons for the new mood: an infusion of young reporters "who joined the Ottawa gallery too late to be caught up in the love-hate syndrome that set in once the passions of 1968 began to cool," a mellowing of the older hands, primarily as a result of a reassessment triggered by Trudeau's near-defeat in 1972, and greater willingness on the part of the prime minister to treat the press with at least a modicum

25 Larry Zolf, *Dance of the Dialectic* (Toronto: James, Lewis and Samuel, 1973), pp. 21-35.
26 Stevens and Saywell, "Parliament and Politics [1968]," pp. 45-51.
27 Zolf, *Dance of the Dialectic*, p. 55.
28 Ibid., p. 40.
29 See, for example, LeDuc, "Measurement of Public Opinion," p. 231.
30 Burns, "Check on the Press."

of respect. Anthony Westell, a senior gallery member, commented in an interview that by 1974 reporters had become self-conscious about their hostility to Trudeau and were making more of an effort to resist it in their news coverage.[31] Nevertheless, the campaign began with a general press preference for Stanfield over Trudeau. As one reporter put it in midcampaign, "Most [English language] newspapers favor the Conservatives. Most reporters like Conservative leader Robert Stanfield best among the leaders. Yet Trudeau so far has won the media campaign. He has a true politician's flair for self-dramatization."[32]

The 1974 Campaign

The Media Strategies of the Parties. In their quest for effective communication of campaign appeals, the parties adopted somewhat different media strategies. The Liberals, aware of the hostility of much of the campaign press corps, developed a strategy designed to obtain maximum coverage with a minimum of confrontation between the prime minister and reporters. The Conservatives and New Democrats, lacking the attention-getting advantages of the governing party, which can make news easily through policy announcements, ceremonies, et cetera, sought to provide as many media contacts as possible.

The Liberal strategy, crafted by Senator Keith Davey, a media expert, was the most controversial. Its aim was to get the media to communicate the party's appeals with as little distortion as possible. This meant creating a situation in which the reporters would cover Trudeau's activities without being able either to interrogate him or to spend much time analyzing what he was doing. Knowing the imperatives of the reporters' craft, the Liberals fed them what they needed, a steady flow of "good copy"—colorful, simple, dramatic,

---

[31] Interview with Anthony Westell, *Toronto Star* Ottawa correspondent, Ottawa, November 1974. Also interviewed for this study were (in order of reference in the text): Ray Chaisson, CBC television news resources manager, Toronto; Craig Oliver, CTV national news producer, Toronto; A. Pineau, Radio-Canada, Montreal; William Donovan, CBC radio national news supervisor, Toronto; Frances Cutler, CBC public affairs producer, Ottawa; Clark Davey, *Toronto Globe and Mail* managing editor, Toronto; Arch Mackenzie, CP Ottawa editor, Ottawa; David Ablett, *Vancouver Sun* Ottawa correspondent, Toronto. Robert McConnell, *Vancouver Province* editor, Vancouver, and Andrew Garrett, CP editor, Toronto, were also interviewed. All the interviews were conducted in November 1974. References to these respondents in the text are from the interviews unless otherwise noted.

[32] Richard Gwyn, "The Boys on the Bus Are Being Used," *Toronto Star*, 18 June 1974.

new. As veteran Ottawa correspondent Anthony Westell put it, "In this election Trudeau (and Senator Davey) acted cynically to give reporters what they wanted. They ran a carefully orchestrated campaign in which they gave them a colorful whistle stop tour through the Maritimes, Margaret [the prime minister's young wife] as a beautiful person, Trudeau as a fighting politician, and then a series of policy announcements, all designed to feed the hunger for something to write."

By keeping the prime minister away from reporters and hot-line shows, party strategists were able to avoid the incidents of past campaigns in which Trudeau had offended segments of the electorate by refusing to suffer fools gladly. The same policy was extended to other ministers. Interviews were agreed to only under controlled conditions. Instead, reporters were provided with colorful "happenings" and hard news which they could not ignore. A series of complex policy announcements, prepared by a committee of party and government officials and approved by the cabinet, kept the opposition off balance and the reporters busy. Ten such announcements were released during three weeks in June. Reporters were given the statements (sometimes as long as fifty pages) only a few hours in advance of their public announcement and were briefed under controlled circumstances (on a plane or bus) and given little opportunity for analysis. By the time critical reports could be prepared, which often took three or four days, the next announcement was dominating the news. In at least one instance, an announcement was timed to upstage a major speech by Stanfield. While many of the policies have yet to be implemented, they served their purpose in the contest for media attention.

The policy announcements, the prime minister's personal flair, the star appeal of his wife, and the various happenings organized by the party all operated to keep the media spotlight on Trudeau. This strategy of concentrating on the prime minister was based on the very clear poll findings that he was the party's major asset. Surveys showed that he generated the greatest reaction of all the leaders among the voters and the strategy was to magnify his strengths and, by avoiding uncontrolled situations, minimize the possibility that he would throw away votes by making caustic remarks in trying situations. He kept carefully to his prearranged plans and refused to comment on issues as they arose. As will be seen, the Liberal strategy was generally successful.[33]

[33] For details of the Liberal strategy, see Stephen Clarkson, "The Liberal Party and Pierre Trudeau: The Jockey and the Horse," in this volume.

The Conservative media strategy was based on the need for maximum exposure. As with the Liberals, the emphasis was on the party leader. Strategists hoped that Stanfield's personal leadership qualities could counter those of Trudeau, and they tried to emphasize his image of honesty, integrity, sincerity, and competence. The most obvious aspect of the strategy was Stanfield's general accessibility to the press. In one nine-day stretch in May, he held nine news conferences, gave seven broadcast interviews, and appeared on four open-line shows.[34] This was typical of the campaign as a whole. The party chose to concentrate most of its efforts on the inflation issue and, therefore, on its wage and price controls proposal. However, this policy was attacked from the very beginning of the campaign by the labor unions and the New Democratic party (NDP), as well as by the Liberals. The result was that Stanfield had little to announce when he appeared before the press and was constantly responding to criticisms of the proposal, both from outside the party and from within, explaining contradictory interpretations of the proposals given by Conservative candidates, and announcing exceptions and qualifications. As a result, he was generally unable to take the initiative and was either presented in the media as on the defensive, or ignored because, as reporters and editors saw it, he was not saying anything new.

The NDP also relied heavily on news coverage to get its message across. Such a policy was even more imperative for NDP leader David Lewis than for Stanfield, since the New Democrats had little money for paid advertising. In one fourteen-day period, Lewis held nine news conferences, gave nine broadcast interviews, and appeared on four open-line programs.[35] The news conference approach, which is much cheaper than organizing rallies and other such events for the press to cover, worked well early in the campaign, but the party announced no new proposals and interest dwindled. The media considered the attacks on government subsidies to corporations and high corporate profits, which had been very successful in getting attention in 1972, as "old hat" and appeared to find the NDP proposal for a two-price system for Canada's basic commodities, which proposed domestic prices lower than world prices, too complex for easy reporting. The NDP attacked the Conservative wage and price controls proposal and the Liberal budget but had no clear alternative proposals. As will be seen, the party got good coverage in quantitative

[34] Geoffrey Stevens, "A Simple Strategy," *Toronto Globe and Mail*, 4 June 1974.
[35] Ibid.

terms but the coverage was much less favorable than in 1972. As one NDP candidate put it, "In 1974, there was less to say and there was too much repetition. The lack of new material gave reporters time to comment on small crowds, lack of excitement in the campaign, and poor organization."[36] The NDP had lost the initiative it had gained in 1972.

The Social Credit party lacked funds, was caught by the election unprepared, and suffered from the ill health of its major campaign attraction, party leader Réal Caouette. Caouette is one of Canada's best political orators, and his restricted campaign weakened the party in the contest for media attention. The party received little attention outside its Quebec stronghold.[37]

News Coverage of the 1974 Campaign. In order to obtain a general picture of press coverage, a systematic content analysis of the front pages and editorial pages of a sample of twelve issues of sixteen Canadian daily newspapers was undertaken. The newspapers selected represented Canada's five major regions and included the three major French-language dailies. All of the large circulation prestige papers were included and the sixteen accounted for nearly half of the total daily newspaper circulation in Canada. The survey was confined to front pages, editorial pages, and special election pages for practical reasons and because their contents reflect the best judgments of editors regarding what news is important and what issues are worth commenting on. Front pages also have high readership.[38] (See Table 9-1 for a list of the newspapers surveyed.) No such systematic survey was possible for radio and television newscasts, but it was

---

[36] Michael Copeland in a speech at Bethune College, York University, Toronto, 10 October 1974.

[37] For details, see Michael Stein, "The Social Credit Party in the Canadian General Election of 1974," in this volume.

[38] In selecting newspapers for analysis, an attempt was made to include the major newspapers in each region, considering both circulation and reputation. *Le Devoir*, for example, has a small circulation but is highly influential. The inclusion of papers from smaller centers in Ontario was intended to provide some indication of coverage outside the major centers. The twelve issues were chosen by the constructed week sampling method which ensures that papers are drawn from each day of the week in roughly equal numbers. On this and other aspects of content analysis, see Wayne A. Danielson, "Content Analysis in Communication Research," in Ralph O. Nafziger and David M. White, eds., *Introduction to Mass Communications Research* (Baton Rouge: Louisiana State University, 1963), pp. 180-206. Saturday newspapers were excluded on the grounds that they contain mainly features. Few Canadian dailies publish Sunday editions. On front page readership, see Davey Committee Report, vol. 3, p. 78.

possible to obtain a general picture of their coverage from interviews and published accounts.[39]

How much attention did the news media pay to the campaign? The figures in Tables 9-2 and 9-3 make it clear that there was considerable coverage. Although no systematic data are available for 1972, the impression of media personnel is that in 1974 newspaper coverage declined but that television coverage increased. Newspaper editors tended to view the 1974 campaign as dull, but television news executives, with larger staffs and better technical facilities than in 1972, seemed to be excited by the challenge of covering the campaign.

The broadcast networks offered substantial coverage. During the final five weeks, when coverage was highest, the three television networks each carried more than 200 minutes of election news. The CBC English service national news devoted about 25 percent of its air time to the election, the CTV national news about 50 percent, and the CBC French service somewhat more than half. The French service had assigned most of its reporters to the election and could cover little else. CTV presented two one-hour news specials, some special election reports on its morning show "Canada AM," and some interviews with leaders on its interview show "Question Period." In line with his media strategy, Trudeau refused to appear. News coverage combined reports on the leaders with reports from regional crews and featured weekly reports on how the leaders were doing. The news specials included leader and regional reports and summaries of two national polls commissioned by the network. The CBC English service presented ten election specials, amounting to 330 minutes of air time. Nine half-hour programs included two on specially commissioned national polls and one each on the campaigns in British Columbia, Quebec, and Ontario, and interviews with each of the four party leaders. There was also a one-hour preelection wrapup. The CBC French network presented most of its coverage—mainly leader coverage and regional reports—on the national news, supplemented by a preelection special in which the five regional reporters presented a coast-to-coast review of the campaign.

The two CBC radio networks devoted a total of more than thirty-eight hours of newscasts to the campaign. The French service offered a special five-minute broadcast at 8:30 each morning and four

---

[39] Editorial decisions at the national networks and at the major newspapers often produce similar news lineups for the national news broadcasts and the front pages. Indeed, interviews suggest that there is a good deal of mutual influence.

Table 9-1

CHARACTERISTICS OF DAILY NEWSPAPERS SURVEYED

Newspaper	Circulation	Ownership	Traditional Partisanship	1974 Endorsement
WEST				
Vancouver Sun (e) [a]	241,821	F P Publications	Liberal	Conservative
Edmonton Journal (e)	148,733	Southam	Liberal	Conservative
Regina Leader-Post (e)	61,030	Sifton	Liberal	Lib.-Cons.[b]
Winnipeg Free Press (e)	137,118	F P Publications	Liberal	Liberal
ONTARIO				
Hamilton Spectator (e)	133,144	Southam	Conservative	None
London Free Press (m & e)	125,288	Indep.	None	Conservative
Ottawa Citizen (e)	91,523	Southam	Liberal	Liberal
Ottawa Journal (e)	84,940	Indep.	Conservative	Conservative
Thunder Bay Chronicle-Herald (e)	25,740	Thomson	None [c]	None
Toronto Star (e)	502,963	Indep.	Liberal	Conservative
Toronto Globe and Mail (m)	265,077	F P Publications	Conservative [d]	Conservative
QUEBEC				
La Presse (Montreal) (e)	178,533	Indep.	Liberal	Liberal
Le Devoir (Montreal) (m)	36,380	Indep.	Liberal [e]	Liberal
Le Soleil (Quebec) (e)	150,346	Indep.	Liberal	None
Montreal Star (e)	174,522	Indep.	Liberal	Liberal
EAST				
Halifax Chronicle-Herald (m)	67,955	Indep.	None [f]	None

[a] Newspapers marked (e) are published in the evening, those marked (m) in the morning.

[b] The editorial position of the *Regina Leader-Post* was that either the Liberals or the Conservatives would be a satisfactory governing party and that a minority situation in which the NDP held the balance of power would be highly undesirable.

[c] Although generally Conservative in orientation, Thomson newspapers usually avoid explicit partisanship.

[d] Although conventional wisdom is that the *Globe* is a Conservative paper, it supported the Liberals in the federal elections of 1963, 1965, 1968 and 1972.

[e] *Le Devoir* is at best a very fickle Liberal supporter. It has often supported the Liberals but could as accurately be classed as Independent.

[f] Although generally Conservative in orientation, the *Halifax Chronicle-Herald* has avoided explicit endorsements in federal elections for a decade or more.

Source: *Editor and Publisher International Yearbook—1974* (New York: Editor and Publisher, 1974); W. H. Kesterton, *A History of Journalism in Canada* (Toronto: McClelland and Stewart, 1967), Chapter 5; John Saywell, ed., *Canadian Annual Review for 1968* (Toronto: University of Toronto Press, 1969), pp. 43-44; John Saywell, *Canadian Annual Review of Politics and Public Affairs 1972* (Toronto: University of Toronto Press, 1974), pp. 44-45.

Table 9-2

NONCOMMERCIAL BROADCAST TIME DEVOTED TO 1974 CAMPAIGN ON NATIONAL NETWORKS, IN MINUTES [a]

Form	Networks				
	CBC-TV (French)	CBC-TV (English)	CTV	CBC Radio (French)	CBC Radio (English)
Free time	201	224	161	131	102
News and specials [b]	535	530 [c]	320	1364	953
Totals	736	774	481	1695	1061

[a] These figures apply to the final five weeks of the campaign.
[b] These figures include only national news broadcasts and specials.
[c] The national news component of this figure is an estimate.
Source: Calculated from Canadian Broadcasting Corporation, *Free Time Periods: Federal Election, 1974* (Ottawa: CBC Program Policy Branch, 13 August 1974) and from figures supplied by the Canadian Radio-Television Commission and by network officials.

one-hour phone-in shows, each featuring a representative from one of the established parties. The special reports were prepared by reporters in each of the regions and presented regional issues and reactions to the campaign to supplement coverage on the regular newscasts, which tended to focus on the party leaders. The English service supplemented its regular newscasts with five one-half-hour election specials on its public affairs program, "Sunday Magazine." These included regional reports, constituency profiles, commentaries on continuing issues, and reports on how the election was being covered in the media. There was also a special one-hour preelection broadcast which attempted to sum up the campaign.

There were sharp differences among the newspapers surveyed in the amount of attention they paid to the campaign. While some 20 percent of the front-page stories in the overall sample were devoted to the campaign, the proportions varied from 6 percent to 33 percent (see Table 9-3). Western papers tended to be below average and French papers above average in both front-page and editorial-page attention. For example, the western papers fell below the average of one editorial for each two editions surveyed; only 44 percent of their editions ran campaign editorials. The figure for the Quebec papers was 58 percent. These findings are in line with the widely held view that the French-language press values political commentary more highly than the English-language press. It is possible that western editors were reflecting a general alienation from national politics that has flared up in the West recently. The Ottawa dailies provided their government-oriented readers with a good deal of editorial comment, while the *Halifax Chronicle-Herald* continued a long tradition, shared by many smaller Canadian dailies and generally accepted by broadcasters as well, of avoiding editorial comment on partisan issues.

The relatively low level of attention paid to the election by the newspapers, in spite of their substantial investment in covering it, seems to have reflected a widely held view that the election was unnecessary or undesirable and the campaign dull. The phrase "the election nobody wanted" cropped up in editorials and columns in dozens of dailies across the country. Many editors shared the opinion expressed in the 10 May *Hamilton Spectator* that the election was being held at a bad time (July) when many voters would be on vacation and public attention to politics low, that the campaign would be expensive and wasteful in a time of inflation, and above all, that the election was futile because no party was likely to win a majority. That the latter view was widely held is yet another example of the fallibility of editorial writers.

The Quebec papers in particular regarded the election as a waste of time and money (as the *Montreal Star* noted on 9 May). There was no significant competition for Liberals in Quebec, which led to a feeling that the election would be decided elsewhere. *Le Soleil* found itself "wondering whether Quebeckers really feel involved at all" and commented on the campaign: "The politicians speak to the press and use it. The press replies to the politicians. The public itself is absent." [40] Lack of public involvement was also reported in other regions. The Quebec papers, in fact, paid less attention to the election than to provincial politics, which were particularly volatile at the time, with charges of corruption in government, labor unrest, and, especially, the government's controversial Bill 22, which involved regulations to require businesses in the province to operate in French and to restrict access to English-language schools in Quebec.[41] Assessing the campaign coverage in Quebec up to 28 June, *Globe and Mail* correspondent Hubert Bauch commented that "the language issue has been hogging the headlines and dominating the editorial

---

[40] "Les politiciens parlent à la presse et l'utilisent. La presse répond aux politiciens. Le public, lui, est absent." *Le Soleil*, 29 June 1974.

[41] For useful discussions of the issues surrounding Bill 22, see Edward McWhinney, "Bill 22 'Relatively Modest and Politically Balanced,'" and "Seven McGill Law Professors Raise Objections to Bill 22," *Montreal Star*, 1 June and 19 July 1974.

Table 9-3

ATTENTION TO THE 1974 CANADIAN GENERAL ELECTION IN SIXTEEN DAILY NEWSPAPERS

Newspaper	Front-Page Stories on Election		Days Election Was Main News Item on Front Page [a]	Days in Which at Least One Election Editorial
	%	(N)		
WEST				
Vancouver Sun	14	(13)	3	5 (4) [b]
Edmonton Journal	14	(10)	2	5 (4)
Regina Leader-Post	33	(25)	5	5 (5)
Winnipeg Free Press	13	(20)	3	6 (6)
ONTARIO				
Hamilton Spectator	23	(18)	3	4 (3)
London Free Press	14	(10)	3	8 (5)
Ottawa Citizen	18	(14)	3	9 (4)
Ottawa Journal	19	(20)	4	8 (4)
Thunder Bay Chronicle-Herald	15	(12)	5	6 (0)
Toronto Star	26	(27)	5	4 (2)
Toronto Globe and Mail	21	(17)	1	6 (4)

QUEBEC

La Presse (Montreal)	28	(17)	3	7 (6)
Le Devoir (Montreal)	27	(22)	4	7 (6)
Le Soleil (Quebec)	19	(12)	3	5 (5)
Montreal Star	6	(5)	5	9 (5)

EAST

Halifax Chronicle-Herald	29	(28)	3	1 (1)
Mean	20	(17)	3.4	6 (4)

[a] Twelve issues of each newspaper were analyzed.
[b] The figure in parentheses is the number of issues in which the main editorial dealt with the election.

263

pages." [42] The highly political *Le Devoir* appeared to take the view that the election was an important event which a responsible newspaper should cover, but that the language issue was more significant.

The British Columbia newspapers also gave the election relatively low priority and, in addition, tended to view it in provincial terms. To a significant extent, the election was portrayed as a referendum on the NDP provincial government which had come to power in 1972, after twenty years of Social Credit rule. The NDP had won eleven of the province's twenty-three seats in 1972, and these were watched carefully for signs of a backlash against the administration of Premier Dave Barrett.

As the campaign progressed, many editorialists complained that the parties were not only running dull campaigns but also failing to articulate real issues. *La Presse* commented that no party was offering a credible solution to the country's major problem, inflation, and that therefore the election was futile. [43] Some editors saw little difference between the two major parties. Others, however, viewed the election as an opportunity to end the balance of power role played by the NDP. On 10 May the *Regina Leader-Post* commented, "This [minority government] could not go on forever, as more and more Canadians seemed to realize the reins of power were, in fact, being wielded by a representation which did not have the support of a majority of the Canadian voters." Editorial writers who took this view saw the election as a chance for one of the major parties to win a majority of seats.

On the whole, the newspapers presented the election as dull and largely irrelevant to the major problems facing the country. Nevertheless, voter turnout was substantial for a summer election, perhaps as a result of the broadcast media coverage. Some 75 percent of eligible voters went to the polls in 1974, a turnout down only slightly from 1972 (77 percent) and 1968 (76 percent). [44]

As far as form of coverage is concerned, the newspapers for the most part trod well-worn paths, supplementing reports on the leaders with regional reports, as in the broadcast media, but providing more coverage of local candidates and issues. The best coverage tended to appear in those papers which had special election pages, such as "Le

---

[42] "Dailies Reflect Ennui," *Toronto Globe and Mail*, 29 June 1974.

[43] Quoted in ibid.

[44] Turnout rates for 1968 and 1972 are from Canada, *Report of the Chief Electoral Officer, 29th General Election, 1972* (Ottawa: Information Canada, 1973), p. xi. The 1974 figures are from the *Toronto Globe and Mail*, 11 July 1974 (CP). On the role of media coverage in influencing turnout, see Blumler, "Mass Media Roles," pp. 140-143.

8 Juillet" in *La Presse* or "Election '74" in the *Toronto Star*, plus regular summaries of the campaign, profiles of major leaders, and commentary on the issues raised. Some, like the *Toronto Globe and Mail* and the *Regina Leader-Post*, made attempts at analysis of key issues, but critical reporting and comprehensive analysis were often lacking.

Perhaps the most innovative coverage of the election appeared on the CBC English-language television network. For example, the CBC news staff compiled a list of all Liberal campaign promises and calculated the cost of implementing them at some $3 billion. This estimate became an issue in the campaign. In addition, critical reports were presented on the Liberal housing and transport policy announcements. The national news also carried features on party financing, the role of women in the parties, the part played by the families of leaders in the campaign, and apartment-dwelling voters. According to Ray Chaisson, resources manager for CBC television news, the goal was "to be more than simply a conduit for party propaganda." Television news also benefitted from technological advances which permitted more rapid transmission of reports from outlying areas.

The Contest for Media Attention. If the national campaign was indeed a contest for media attention, it is reasonable to conclude that the Liberals "won" the campaign. They had a slight edge in the broadcast media and were clear victors in the press. The closeness of the contest on national radio and television may be explained in large part by the fact that the networks kept a running count of the air time devoted to each party. CBC officials reported that, while they made no attempt at partisan balance on individual newscasts, they did seek a reasonable balance over the whole campaign. The CTV national news "does not operate its election coverage with a stopwatch," as Craig Oliver put it, but it did keep a count. Few newspapers used rulers to assess their campaign coverage, though CP did keep a word count to check party balance in its output.

Despite an unsympathetic press corps, the Liberals dominated the front pages of Canada's newspapers during the campaign. The Liberals were the subject of at least one front-page story in 48 percent of the editions surveyed, compared to only 34 percent for the Conservatives (see Table 9-4). The Liberals obtained more coverage than the other parties in twelve of the sixteen dailies surveyed and were tied with the Conservatives in three others. The Conservatives led in only one paper and actually trailed the Liberals in four of the five newspapers which endorsed them. The Liberals had an even greater

Table 9-4

ATTENTION TO PARTIES AND LEADERS
ON THE FRONT PAGES OF SIXTEEN DAILY NEWSPAPERS
DURING THE 1974 ELECTION CAMPAIGN
(in percents)

	Stories [a]	Headlines [b]
PARTIES		
Liberal	48	52
Conservative	34	32
NDP	27	12
Social Credit	6	3
Other	1	3
	(N = 192)	(N = 60)
LEADERS		
Trudeau	54	43
Stanfield	32	35
Lewis	19	20
Caouette	4	2
	(N = 192)	(N = 113)

[a] The percentage here is a percentage of editions in which there was at least one story on the party or the leader. Only stories longer than four paragraphs were counted. Percentages do not add to 100 because more than one party or one leader could be mentioned in any edition.

[b] Percentages are based on the total number of headlines in which a political party or party leader was mentioned.

edge in the front-page headline count, especially in Ontario, the major battleground of the election, where thirteen of the eighteen partisan front-page headlines referred to the Liberals. The Liberals' margin was most obvious in the two Toronto papers, both of which endorsed the Conservatives. The Liberals were the subject of 71 percent of the *Globe*'s partisan headlines and of 63 percent of the *Star*'s.

The pattern of attention paid to the party leaders was quite similar to that given the parties in general. Prime Minister Trudeau was the subject of a front-page story in 54 percent of the issues surveyed, compared to 32 percent for Stanfield, 19 percent for Lewis, and 4 percent for Caouette. Of the party leaders, Trudeau received the most attention in fourteen of the sixteen papers. Perhaps the distribution of attention in front-page pictures is most telling. Of the seventy-eight pictures surveyed, thirty-two were of Trudeau (41 percent), nine more than Stanfield (30 percent), and thirteen more than

Lewis (24 percent). The prime minister was especially prominent in Ontario, where he appeared in 55 percent of the front-page election pictures turned up by the survey. In fact, Lewis was pictured more often than Stanfield in both Ontario and the West.

The Liberals won a less conclusive victory in the contest for attention in the broadcast media. Taking the five networks together, 906.5 minutes of air time were devoted to stories about the Liberals, compared to 814 minutes for the Conservatives and 622 minutes for the NDP (see Table 9-5). Thirty-two percent of the air time devoted to the election on network news programs was devoted to the Liberals. If only the three major parties are taken into account, Liberals were the subject 39 percent of the time, the Conservatives 35 percent, and the NDP 27 percent. In general, the distribution of attention proved to be similar to the distribution of the popular vote in the previous election (1972), except that the NDP and Social Credit received higher proportions of air time than of votes. (For details, see Table 9-6.)

The distribution of attention among the parties was similar on the two French-language networks and virtually identical on the three English-language services, but differed along linguistic lines. The French services gave greater attention than the English networks to Social Credit and to minor parties, primarily the *Parti Québécois*, a Quebec separatist party that urged voters to boycott the federal election. The distribution of attention on the French networks is accounted for in large part by the fact that 80 percent of their audience is in the province of Quebec. Their patterns of attention may be seen as a compromise between the campaign in Quebec and the national campaign. The NDP, for example, received significantly less attention on the French networks, but its share of time on those two services still exceeded its share of the national popular vote in 1972 and was more than twice its share of the Quebec vote. The Conservatives' share of attention on the French services fell short of their share of the 1972 national vote but exceeded their share of the Quebec vote by about 50 percent. On the other hand, the Liberals and Social Credit, the dominant parties in Quebec in 1972, received considerably less attention than their popular vote might have justified. The English networks virtually ignored Social Credit. These regional differences were also reflected in newspaper coverage. The NDP was particularly prominent in the West, where the party controls three provincial governments, but was given less attention in Quebec. Social Credit received little coverage outside Quebec.

Table 9-5

ATTENTION TO PARTIES ON NETWORK NEWS BROADCASTS (MINUTES)[a]

Party	**Network** CBC-TV (Fr.)	CBC-TV (Eng.)[b]	CTV	CBC Radio (Fr.)	CBC Radio (Eng.)	Total
Liberal	174	65	53.5	402	212	906.5
Conservative	138	65	50	363	198	814
NDP	93	55	43	270	161	622
Social Credit	90	c	c	205	25	320
Other	40 [d]	c	c	124 [e]	c	164
Total	535	185	146.5	1364	596 [f]	2826.5

[a] Since coding was done by each network according to its own rules, comparisons must be made with care. The period covered is the final five weeks of the campaign.

[b] The figures for CBC-TV (Eng.) are estimates. Exact figures were unavailable.

[c] Figures were not kept or were unavailable but were estimated to be negligible.

[d] Includes 12 minutes on the *Parti Québécois*.

[e] Includes 20 minutes on the *Parti Québécois*.

[f] These figures include all of the national radio news broadcasts and specials. Some 347 minutes were coded nonpartisan and were excluded from the table.

Source: Calculated from information provided by the networks.

Table 9-6

RELATIVE ATTENTION TO PARTIES ON NATIONAL NEWS BROADCASTS, 1974,
COMPARED TO POPULAR VOTE BY PARTY, 1972 [a]

(in percents)

Party	CBC-TV (Fr.)	CBC-TV (Eng.)	CTV	CBC Radio (Fr.)	CBC Radio (Eng.)	Total	Popular Vote, 1972 Canada	Popular Vote, 1972 Quebec
Liberal	32.5	35.1	36.5	29.5	35.6	32	38	50
Conservative	25.7	35.1	34.1	26.6	33.2	29	35	18
NDP	17.4	29.7	29.4	19.8	27.0	22	18	7
Social Credit	16.8	—	—	15.0	4.2	11	8	25
Other	7.4	—	—	9.1	—	6	1	—
	(N=535)	(N=185)	(N=147)	(N=1,364)	(N=596)	(N=2,827)		—

(Network spans CBC-TV (Fr.), CBC-TV (Eng.), CTV, CBC Radio (Fr.), CBC Radio (Eng.))

[a] Percentages based on figures in Table 9-5; see notes to that table for explanations of data.

Source: Same as Table 9-5, plus Canada, *Report of the Chief Electoral Officer, 29th General Election, 1972* (Ottawa: Information Canada, 1973), p. XIX.

These patterns of attention reflect a variety of factors, such as party activity in the various regions, the news judgments of editors and news directors, and the concern for balanced coverage. For example, the NDP did not mount a very active campaign in Quebec and therefore provided little local news to cover. Social Credit concentrated most of its activities in Quebec and did not really run a national campaign. CBC officials had been worried that the Conservatives would get little coverage in Quebec because of their limited prospects there, but they did in fact find enough news to provide reasonably balanced coverage. The English networks treated the NDP as a major national party, giving it almost as much coverage as the two traditional parties. The two primary factors supporting this news judgment seem to have been the NDP's strong showing in 1972 and its balance-of-power role in the minority Parliament. The overall prominence of the Liberals can probably be accounted for by the traditional advantage of incumbent governments in getting media attention, as well as by the party's well-designed media strategy.

The quality of coverage given each party is more difficult to assess than the quantity. Here too, however, the Liberals appeared to have had an edge. Given the difficulties of measurement, no systematic count of favorable and unfavorable items could be made for this study.[45] However, a general assessment reveals that much of the coverage of the Conservative and NDP campaigns was negative —reports on their disorganization and, in the case of the Conservatives, dissension within the party. The Liberals suffered some unfavorable coverage, especially with respect to allegations of illicit patronage leveled against Labor Minister John Munro, which were reported first on 29 June and received national coverage for two or three days thereafter. On the whole, however, the front page coverage of the Liberals reflected the party's campaign plans. Early in the campaign, it focused on the prime minister's whistle-stop tour of the maritime provinces, then on 5 June it switched to the series of ten policy announcements made by Trudeau between 5 June and 28 June. Most of these policy announcements made front-page headlines and, in general, they were reported straight without critical analysis, though there was some analysis in following editions, usually on inside pages. The broadcasters found it hard to provide any critical analysis. The train tour provided effective pictures which television could not ignore, and the policy announcements provided hard news which had to be reported. In contrast, the Conservative

---

45 The major problem is that such coding requires the analyst to guess at the motivations of writers and editors and the reactions of specific audiences.

campaign suffered from a low-key start which got little major media coverage, and its central theme—the need for a temporary program of wage and price controls—was constantly under attack from the NDP, the major labor unions, the Liberals, and, perhaps more damaging, from within the Conservative party itself. As a result, the Conservatives projected a less favorable image than did the Liberals.

Editorial Endorsements. On the other hand, the Conservatives did win the contest for newspaper editorial endorsements, at least among the country's major English-language dailies. Among the dailies in our survey, six endorsed the Conservatives and five the Liberals, three of which were in Quebec (see Table 9-1). However, three traditionally Liberal papers, the *Toronto Star*, the *Vancouver Sun* and the *Edmonton Journal* endorsed the Conservatives in 1974. The *Toronto Star*, long identified as a voice of reform within the Liberal party, had endorsed the Conservatives for the first time in its history in 1972. The *Edmonton Journal* had also deserted the Liberals in 1972, for the first time in many elections. The *Toronto Globe and Mail*, traditionally a Conservative paper, had switched to the Liberals in 1963, rejecting the decaying administration of John Diefenbaker, and had endorsed the Liberals in the following three elections. In 1974, however, it supported the Conservatives, surprising many who thought that its new publisher, Richard S. Malone, previously publisher of the staunchly Liberal *Winnipeg Free Press*, would solidify the shift to the Liberals. The *Winnipeg Free Press* and two other traditionally Liberal papers, the *Ottawa Citizen* and the *Montreal Star*, stayed with the party but voiced strong reservations. There were no major defections from Conservative to Liberal, though *Le Devoir* awarded the Liberals a lukewarm endorsement in 1974 after a period of snappish neutrality. Most of the newspapers that had abandoned the Conservatives in the Trudeaumania of 1968 had returned in 1972; the remainder drifted back in 1974.

On the whole, explicit editorial endorsements came late in the campaign and were remarkably lukewarm. On 5 July, for example, the *Winnipeg Free Press* endorsed the Liberals as "the best of three poor choices," remarking that it had considered supporting the Conservatives because the party promised action to combat inflation but had become convinced during the campaign that the wage and price control proposal was little more than a slogan. Most Conservative endorsements gave the party's willingness to fight inflation as the major reason for supporting it, while Liberal supporters claimed that Trudeau and his cabinet offered superior leadership.

The drift away from Trudeau in the English-language press appeared to involve several factors, such as the general disenchantment of the working press with Trudeau, a feeling that Stanfield deserved a chance in office, and the view that Trudeau had been the right leader to deal with problems of French-English relations in 1968 but that he was less able than Stanfield to cope with the economic issues of 1974. A more specific factor may have been a feeling among major Liberal newspapers, like the *Toronto Star*, the *Winnipeg Free Press* and the *Vancouver Sun*, that they were being ignored by Trudeau. The *Star* commented in 1972 (19 October), in explaining its endorsement of the Conservatives: "We do this reluctantly and only because we believe a strong protest is necessary to make the Liberal party re-examine its policies in these crucial times."

How important are editorial endorsements? Although they do influence the morale of party activists and the issues stressed by party leaders, their direct influence on voting is probably marginal. Most voters have already made up their minds by the time endorsements appear and, in any case, seem unaware of them.[46] In 1974, the tide of endorsements swept toward the Conservatives, but the voters drifted in the other direction. In greater Toronto, for example, where all three major dailies and an important chain of weeklies endorsed the Conservatives, the Liberals took twenty-one out of twenty-six seats, a gain of seven over 1972.

Party and Leader Images. In all probability, then, the images of the parties and leaders presented in news reports were more important than editorial endorsements. In the 1974 campaign, the news coverage stressed leaders. In our survey of front pages, for example, we found only 24 percent of election stories dealt with a party without mentioning its leader. The Liberal coverage was particularly leader-oriented. Just twenty-six front-page stories (14 percent) on the party or its candidates failed to mention the prime minister. Indeed, there were thirty items on Trudeau which did not mention the party. In contrast, there were thirty-four stories (31 percent of the total) which mentioned the Conservatives but omitted mention of Stanfield (and only five in which he was the subject apart from the party) and thirty-one (36 percent) in which the NDP was covered apart from

[46] See Davey Committee Report, vol. 3, p. 78, and Colin Seymour-Ure, *The Press, Politics and the Public* (London: Methuen, 1968), pp. 84-94.

Lewis. In the broadcast media a conscious attempt was made to reduce the stress on the leaders in favor of regional reports and features. Nevertheless, each of the three major leaders was on the national news two to three times per week on the CBC English service and more often on the other networks. For example, the CTV national news covered each of the three leaders about three nights in five. Most news organizations felt constrained to provide coverage of the leaders as a first priority and often lacked the resources to do much else.

In terms of the election's outcome, perhaps the most important development in media image making was the shift in the portrayal of Trudeau. The term arrogant, which had so often been applied to him in 1972, appeared only infrequently in our survey. The prime minister's old image as a flip and trendy man of the world was over-shadowed by a new image, that of a concerned, hard-working, and businesslike leader. This change in media image, in large part a result of Liberal campaign strategy, appears to have been accompanied by a change in public perceptions of the prime minister.[47] Stanfield's image as a methodical, hard-working, honest, but perhaps not quite "with it" leader appeared to be little changed from previous elections. Lewis continued, as in 1972, to be portrayed as a hard-hitting, eloquent, and impassioned leader with little real chance to win. Caouette virtually vanished from the national scene, his old image as a fighting orator blurred by underexposure.

As far as party images are concerned, the Liberals and Conservatives continued to be presented as establishment parties whose images derived mainly from their leaders. Social Credit tended to be viewed as irrelevant, an anachronism "destined for the ashcan of history," as the *Montreal Star* commented on 2 July. Although still portrayed in some smaller dailies as a "far out" radical party, the NDP was generally taken seriously, at least outside Quebec, until coverage fell off in the last few weeks of the campaign, when reporters and editors apparently began to feel that "the essence of the election story [was] the fight between the Liberals and the Tories. . . ."[48]

The visual images of the leaders presented by the media may have had a major influence on public perceptions. The most damaging photos of the campaign were clearly those of Robert Stanfield, who was pictured in newspapers across the country fumbling a football,

---

[47] LeDuc, "Measurement of Public Opinion," Table 8-14.
[48] Burns, "Check on the Press."

walking about with a Liberal party sticker on his back and wearing his trousers inside his cowboy boots out West. The football picture caused some controversy when it was noted that Stanfield had caught eight or nine tosses during the game at an airport in North Bay, Ontario, and had dropped only a couple. Canadian Press editors had had a choice of shots and chose to show him fumbling.[49] It can be argued that this choice reflected normal news judgment on the grounds that a celebrity dropping a football is more interesting than a celebrity catching one. But it has also been suggested that the photo had an important symbolic value for many reporters and editors who believed that Stanfield was fumbling the campaign.[50] In any case, these photos contrasted with photos of Trudeau doing a flip on a trampoline (successfully), striding purposefully up streets, gesturing dramatically, and so on. Lewis and Caouette were usually pictured more conventionally. It is fair to say that on the whole, relying on the whistle-stop tour and his photogenic wife and family, Trudeau got much better visual treatment than the other leaders in the press. It is generally believed that this was true on television as well.

Issues in the News Media. A major aspect of the campaign is the contest among the parties to determine the issues around which the election will revolve. The priorities of the parties are reflected in their advertising and free-time broadcasts and in the speeches of party leaders. Reporters feel bound to report what the parties are saying, but they also wish to avoid being mouthpieces for the parties. Thus, they try to approach speeches and announcements skeptically and to select from the materials produced by the parties the issues they think are new or significant. The issues stressed in news coverage represent the outcome of this process of media-party interaction. In 1974, the Conservatives sought to make inflation the prime issue and to suggest that only they were offering leadership on it. The Liberals countered by emphasizing leadership as the major issue, stressing that inflation was simply the current problem.

On the face of it, the Conservatives won the issues contest (or, at least, were most in tune with media priorities). In all the media, the economy was clearly the dominant issue. The results of our content analysis make this quite clear as far as the press is concerned. Inflation was the most frequently mentioned issue, appearing at least

---

49 Ibid.

50 Crouse, *Boys on the Bus*, pp. 51-72, notes that reporters and editors often use seemingly insignificant incidents such as this to express a general conclusion. This view of the football picture was expressed in several interviews with campaign reporters.

once on 28 percent of the front pages examined. It was the most prominent issue in all sixteen papers surveyed. It was followed by references to wage and price controls (16 percent), to the economy in general (13 percent), and to the comparative capacities of the party leaders (12 percent). When all economic issues were taken together, it was found that at least one such issue was mentioned on 46 percent of the front pages examined. Leadership issues were second in prominence, mentioned on 22 percent of front pages, and national unity issues (those involving French-English relations and the grievances of the eastern and western provinces against central government policies) third, appearing on 15 percent of the front pages (see Table 9-7). Although no systematic evidence is available,

Table 9-7
KINDS OF ISSUES STRESSED IN DAILY NEWSPAPERS DURING THE 1974 GENERAL ELECTION CAMPAIGN, BY REGION

Kind of Issue	Region				Canada
	West	Ontario	Quebec	East	
Percentage of Editions in Which Issue Was Mentioned in at Least One Front-Page Story					
Economic [a]	40	40	27	67	46
Leadership [b]	15	23	10	33	22
National unity [c]	13	12	15	8	15
	(N = 48)	(N = 84)	(N = 48)	(N = 12)	(N = 192)
Percentage of Editions in Which Issue Was Mentioned in at Least One Editorial					
Economic	35	36	35	— [d]	36
Leadership	10	19	27	—	19
National unity	6	13	19	—	13
	(N = 48)	(N = 84)	(N = 48)	—	(N = 180 [e])

[a] Stories and editorials dealing with inflation, wage and price controls, unemployment, excess corporate profits, the state of the economy, and the federal budget were included under economic.

[b] Stories and editorials dealing with the competence of the parties and their leaders, internal divisions in the parties, and charges of corruption were included here.

[c] Stories and editorials dealing with federal-provincial relations, French-English relations, and western and eastern grievances were included here.

[d] The *Halifax Chronicle-Herald* carried only one editorial on the election in the issues surveyed and was omitted here.

[e] The twelve issues of the *Halifax Chronicle-Herald* were omitted.

some observers have suggested that economic issues were less prominent on television than in the press, primarily because they are hard to present visually.

As the campaign progressed, it appeared that the Liberal attempt to draw attention away from economic issues was meeting with some success. Inflation declined significantly as an issue during the campaign. Mentioned on 38 percent of the front pages early in the campaign (9–22 May), it was mentioned on only 16 percent of the front pages during the last ten days of the campaign. In fact, the only economic issue which did not decline in visibility as the campaign progressed was the Conservative campaign theme of wage and price controls, which appeared on 11 percent of the front pages in May, built gradually through the campaign, and appeared on 20 percent of the front pages during the last ten days. However, throughout the campaign, much of the attention devoted to wage and price controls was negative, taking the form of attacks by labor union spokesmen and the other parties. Emphasis on the comparative leadership skills of the party leaders increased slightly during the campaign (from 10 percent in May to 13 percent in July), while emphasis on the question of majority government increased sharply (from only one percent of the front pages in May to 17 percent in the final period). Both these trends could be seen as favoring the Liberals. The shifts in emphasis in the broadcast media seem to have been similar to those in the press. It is interesting to note that poll results suggest that the decline in the visibility of inflation in the press was paralleled by a decline in the importance attached to it by the public, and that the increase in press emphasis on leadership and majority government was also matched by trends in popular opinion.[51] It seems likely that the media played a role in these shifts in public perceptions.

There is always some question in Canadian elections about the extent to which the campaign is national, given the strength of political regionalism. In 1974 there were significant regional variations in emphasis, but the major themes of the campaign appeared to be national. For example, inflation was the dominant issue in all regions, perhaps because it was a problem common to all of them. But there were important differences in emphasis, as Table 9-8 shows. Economic issues other than inflation got more attention in the *Halifax Chronicle-Herald* (the sole eastern paper in the survey) than elsewhere. The major emphasis was on unemployment, which was

---

[51] See LeDuc, "Measurement of Public Opinion," p. 238.

Table 9-8

RANKING OF ELECTION ISSUES BY PRESS ATTENTION, BY REGION

Issue [a]	Region				Canada
	West	Ontario	Quebec	East	
Frequency of Mention in Front-Page Stories					
Inflation	1	1	1	1	1
Wage and price controls	4	2	2	4	2
The economy (general)	3	4	3	2	3
Leadership	5	3	9	6	4
Corporate ripoff (excess profits)	6	4	6	7	5
Western alienation	2	10	9	8	6
French-English relations	11	7	3	—[b]	7
Frequency of Mention in Editorials					
Inflation	1	1	1	—[c]	1
Wage and price controls	2	2	2	—	2
The economy (general)	4	2	6	—	3
Leadership	9	4	3	—	3
Party competence	4	6	4	—	5
Majority government	3	9	5	—	5
French-English relations	—	5	5	—	7
Corporate ripoff (excess profits)	6	7	9	—	8

[a] In all, twenty-four issues were identified in our survey.

[b] The dash indicates that the issue was not mentioned in the editions surveyed.

[c] The *Halifax Chronicle-Herald* discussed three issues in the one election editorial which turned up in the survey: inflation, wage and price controls, and majority government.

mentioned on three of twelve front pages in Halifax, but which was completely absent from front pages elsewhere. This emphasis, which was noted for other eastern papers in a *Toronto Globe and Mail* survey of press coverage, is not surprising, given that the Atlantic provinces are the most economically depressed in Canada and consistently have the highest rates of unemployment.

The special interests of the western provinces and Quebec were also reflected in front-page coverage. Western alienation, a set of grievances involving freight rates, control over natural resource development, and tax policy, was the second ranking issue in the western papers. In Quebec, French-English relations ranked third. French-English issues, such as the Conservative party's rejection of the candidacy of the anti-French major of Moncton, were also emphasized on the French-language services of the CBC, while western issues got more attention on the English services. In Ontario, the major battleground of the election, leadership issues received more press attention than elsewhere. These regional variations in press coverage corresponded in general terms to regional differences in public perceptions of relative issue importance.[52] On the whole, however, the differences were differences of emphasis within the framework of a national campaign.

Assessing the campaign coverage overall, it appears that, although the Conservatives were favored on the editorial pages, the Liberals were the clear victors in the contest for attention and in the crucial area of image-making. The NDP lost some of the momentum it had gained in the 1972 campaign and Social Credit virtually vanished from the scene outside Quebec. The newspaper coverage emphasized issues favoring the Conservatives—such as inflation—throughout the campaign, but in the final weeks, there was increased attention to Liberal-oriented issues, such as leadership and majority government. The visual coverage of the campaign clearly favored the Liberals and, if the widely held view that the election boiled down to a choice between leaders is correct, the fact that Trudeau projected a more attractive visual image may have been crucial to the outcome.

Free-Time Broadcasts and Commercial Advertising. The parties did not, of course, have to rely solely on the news media to communicate their campaign appeals. Besides general mailings, rallies, and canvassing, they used free-time broadcasts and paid advertising. In the 1974 campaign, the parties had access to nearly fourteen hours of free time on the national networks (nearly ten hours of it on the three television networks), plus about 280 hours of time on local radio stations and some eighty-five hours on local television channels. In addition, the parties purchased more than 1,650 hours of paid time for radio and television advertisements. In all, Canadians were

---

[52] See LeDuc, "Measurement of Public Opinion," Table 8-8.

Table 9-9

NATIONAL FREE TIME CAMPAIGN BROADCASTS,
BY NETWORK AND PARTY, 1974 GENERAL ELECTION
(minutes) [a]

Party	CBC-TV (Fr.)	CBC-TV (Eng.)	CTV	CBC Radio (Fr.)	CBC Radio (Eng.)	Total
Liberal	65	70	53	42	33	263
Conservative	62	70	53	40	30	255
NDP	38	42	27	25	21	153
Social Credit	24	28	28	16	12	108
Other [b]	12	14	—	8	6	40
Total	201	224	161	131	102	819

[a] The times given here are rounded to the nearest minute or, in some cases, are close approximations of actual air time.
[b] Communist party and Marxist-Leninist party.
Source: Same as Table 9-3.

subjected to more than 2,000 hours of political propaganda during the 1974 campaign.[53]

The free-time broadcasts have been an important part of Canadian political campaigns for many years. The parties are allocated time on the basis of their standings in the House of Commons at dissolution. (For 1974 allocations, see Table 9-9.) The broadcasts, prepared by the parties, were presented during the last four weeks of the campaign in prime time (between 7 and 10 P.M. on television and at noon and 6 P.M. on radio). The television broadcasts were generally thirty minutes long and shared by two or more parties, while radio presentations featured one party and ran either three or four-and-one-half minutes, by a single party.[54]

While smaller than those for entertainment programs, the audiences for political broadcasts were reasonably large. The CBC radio English-language service estimates that the noon broadcasts had an

[53] See Khayyam Z. Paltiel, "Campaign Financing in Canada and Its Reform," Chapter 7 in this volume, Tables 7-1 and 7-6, and Richard Gwyn, "Now, for the Real Decisions," *Edmonton Journal*, 2 July 1974. Data were also provided by the CRTC and the networks.
[54] Information provided by Frances Cutler, CBC public affairs producer, Ottawa.

average audience of about 100,000 and the evening broadcasts about 300,000. On CBC English-language television, the free-time broadcasts presented during the rating period had audiences ranging from about 500,000 to 763,000, with an average of 636,000. About 20 percent of the people actually watching television at the time tuned in the free-time broadcasts. A free-time broadcast with segments by all the major parties on 5 July (8:30–9 P.M.) drew 763,200 viewers, down from 2,554,000 for the preceding program, the American situation comedy, "All in the Family." The audience for the program immediately following, a variety show, jumped back to 1,780,000. The one-hour preelection news special drew an audience of about 1,400,000.[55]

The CBC survey also measured audience reaction to its programs, using an "enjoyment index." The indices for the political broadcasts were relatively low, generally in the fifty to sixty-five range. In contrast, the indices for election news specials tended to be in the high sixties or low seventies, while the national news had an average score of eighty-one. There were no significant differences in the enjoyment indices for the various party segments. In short, the programs drew relatively high audiences, considering that they generally were in competition with entertainment programs. Nevertheless, they could not compete with news programs in terms of numbers of viewers or degree of positive response.[56]

Despite the substantial amount of free time available, the parties presented some $2.7 million worth of paid radio and television programs and spot announcements during the 1974 campaign. The total advertising campaign consisted of some 108,558 spot announcements and 1,096 programs on radio (worth $1,559,625) and 122,527 spot announcements and 1,723 programs on television (worth $1,154,279), all on the privately owned stations.[57] With the exception of local advertising and an eight-page color supplement distributed by the Conservatives in the weekend magazines of most Canadian dailies, the major advertising thrust was in the electronic media.

The two major parties dominated the air waves. Between them, the appeals of the two major parties took up 86 percent of the paid radio time and 80 percent of the paid television time. In terms of money spent, the ranking was: Liberals, 45.8 percent, Conservatives, 45.3 percent, NDP, 6.8 percent, Social Credit, 1.6 percent. In general,

---

[55] John Dvorak, "Summer Panel Report for the Week of July 5-11, 1974," Internal Memo, CBC Toronto, 31 July 1974.

[56] Ibid.

[57] For details, see Paltiel, "Campaign Financing in Canada," Table 7-6.

the major parties had significantly greater access to the media for their campaign appeals than did the minor parties.[58]

For each party, the general content of free-time broadcasts and advertisements was similar. The Liberal strategists believed that Trudeau was the party's strongest selling point and therefore focused almost exclusively on him. According to Richard Gwyn, "Liberal strategists were impressed by American surveys which show that TV newscasts have a high public credibility. So their ads look like TV news clips." [59] In fact, each advertisement was a clip from a Trudeau campaign speech, showing him making a point about housing, leadership, economic policy, or some other current issue; sometimes he was shown responding to a heckler. The Conservatives, too, used the simulated news documentary technique, but chose man-in-the-street interviews and a broader range of campaign scenes than the Liberals. One half-hour free-time broadcast showed Stanfield in a variety of campaign and noncampaign settings. The Conservatives also used more gimmicks—graphics, art work, quick cuts, lively music—and more messages with no direct leader reference (for example, a film of a "Slinky" toy climbing stairs as an announcer read increases in the consumer price index for recent years). Inflation and the need for action on it, but not specifically wage and price controls, were stressed.[60] The NDP followed its usual pattern of presenting mainly discussions and talks. They focused on the cost-of-living issue, with some references to the disadvantages of wage and price controls, and on the activities of the major food chains, but the advertising campaign failed to generate much interest.[61] In general, the radio advertisements were nonvisual versions of the television materials.

Issues and Controversies. News coverage of the 1974 campaign was unusually controversial. Conservative party spokesmen complained that the media were being taken in by the sophisticated strategy employed by the Liberals and that Conservatives were being treated unfairly. Many journalists also had misgivings about the way in which the Liberal campaign was being handled and about the uncritical reporting of many partisan pronouncements. The Conservatives made two major allegations: that their spokesmen were

---

[58] It should be noted that the entire system of campaign broadcasting has been changed by recent legislation which will be in effect for the next federal election. For a discussion of the new rules, see Paltiel, "Campaign Financing in Canada."

[59] Gwyn, "Now, for the Real Decisions."

[60] Val Sears, "Selling the Leaders," *Toronto Star*, 31 May 1974.

[61] Jo Surich, "Purists and Pragmatists: Canadian Democratic Socialism at the Crossroads," in this volume.

Table 9-10
CONSERVATIVE PARTY TABULATION OF AIR TIME
DEVOTED TO THREE PARTY LEADERS ON
TWO NETWORK NEWSCASTS, 6–20 JUNE 1974

	Newscast	
Leader	CBC national news	CTV national news
Trudeau	21 mins. 1 sec.	16 mins. 50 secs.
Stanfield	13 mins. 9 secs.	13 mins. 20 secs.
Lewis	13 mins. 34 secs.	12 mins. 14 secs.

Source: *Toronto Globe and Mail*, 22 June 1974.

receiving less media attention than Liberal spokesmen and that campaign reporters were allowing themselves to be manipulated by the Liberals. The charges of unfair treatment which received most publicity were those directed against the national television news on the CBC English service. An examination of these charges and the responses to them illustrates the general issues.

According to figures compiled by Stanfield's press secretary, Rod MacQueen, Trudeau received substantially more coverage than the other leaders during the period 6 to 20 June (see Table 9-10). The Conservatives were particularly unhappy with the CBC coverage of Stanfield's tour of the western provinces, 19 to 21 June, which had received only twenty-four seconds of attention on the CBC national news, compared to four minutes, fifty-three seconds on the CTV national news. Worse yet, Trudeau's western tour, 12 to 14 June, had been given eleven minutes, fifty-five seconds of CBC coverage.[62] The Conservatives lodged an official complaint with the CBC and party officials met with network spokesmen to discuss the issue. The CBC did not dispute the figures, but pointed out that they took no account of the quality of the coverage (whether it was favorable or unfavorable). For example, MacQueen had included reports of a possible scandal involving a Liberal cabinet minister and critical reports on the potential costs of Liberal campaign promises in the Liberal totals, despite their unfavorable implications. The CBC also noted that assessments of balance should be made for the entire campaign, since events may cause temporary imbalances. (Some observers noted a distinct increase in CBC coverage of the Conservative campaign after the complaint.) Nevertheless, one nationally

[62] *Toronto Globe and Mail*, 22 June 1974.

syndicated columnist, Charles Lynch, accused the CBC of having declared the Liberals reelected before the election.[63] This charge is somewhat ironic, since the major Liberal complaint against the CBC was that it had issued a statement misinterpreting its own poll results and suggesting a potential Conservative minority government.[64]

Political bias is not the only possible explanation of the imbalance in CBC coverage during June, nor even the most likely. Three other factors can be suggested: the decision by the CBC national news staff to report the campaign critically, problems in the Conservative campaign, and the Liberal media strategy. The decision to report the campaign critically led naturally to an emphasis on government party promises. However, this would not have produced a significant imbalance had the Conservatives run a parallel campaign. There were many Liberal policies to report and analyze, but few from the Conservatives. A CBC spokesman commented that the "general coverage strategy would have worked well if the Conservatives had presented a positive platform. But they always seemed to be reacting." Reporters had trouble pinning Stanfield down on the specifics of the wage and price control proposal and ended up deciding that it was little more than a slogan, too amorphous to analyze. A specific reason for low coverage on the western tour was that a promised major announcement in Calgary, for which the CBC had brought in a mobile unit at considerable expense, had failed to materialize.

The main reason for the imbalance, however, was the Liberal campaign. Douglas Fisher, a former M.P. and veteran political commentator, put the argument this way:

> There is an easy explanation why the CBC national TV news got out of whack in favour of Trudeau over the two-week span which the Tories have complained about. The PM and wife Margaret . . . and the so-called or alleged policy statements he has been making on housing, transportation, welfare, seemed to provide the CBC news editors with more solid stuff to snippet into their newscasts than Bob Stanfield was providing daily for his attendant CBC cameras and crew.
>
> Of course, the Trudeau stuff, like the Stanfield and Lewis capers, is plotted and manufactured for just the purpose of catching the TV news. This time the Liberals are doing it much better.[65]

---

[63] "People's Network Tells All," *Edmonton Journal*, 2 July 1974.

[64] See LeDuc, "Measurement of Public Opinion," p. 240.

[65] "PC Complaint about CBC Not Minor," *Halifax Chronicle-Herald*, 29 June 1974.

The Conservatives responded to arguments of this sort by suggesting that reporters had been remiss in allowing themselves to be manipulated by the Liberal campaign.

The complaint regarding the failure of the press to see through the Liberal strategy was made during the campaign and repeated by Stanfield in a postelection television interview:

> One of the interesting things I found [in connection with the election] was the way the journalists sort of laid down and let Mr. Trudeau walk all over them and allowed him to conduct exactly the kind of controlled . . . campaign that he wanted to conduct, and I just got the impression that the journalistic corps was for the most part, with some exceptions, rather frightened.[66]

Some reporters agreed with Stanfield's charges. *Globe and Mail* columnist Geoffrey Stevens, for example, accused the Liberals of adopting a "strategy designed specifically to protect Mr. Trudeau from legitimate questioning. . . ."[67] Others, however, suggested that the charges were mainly a reflection of Conservative frustration at not having run a more effective media campaign themselves.[68] Clark Davey, managing editor of the *Globe and Mail*, took the view that Stanfield himself was "dealt with very gently" during the campaign, especially with respect to the wage and price control proposal. He reported a general feeling that it had been impossible to pin Stanfield down to specifics on his major proposals: "His style is such that his greater accessibility (as compared to Trudeau) did not help reporters get at his ideas in any clear way."

Referring to the prime minister's inaccessibility to the press and the Liberal strategy of providing reporters with regular "happenings" and releases, some reporters called the Trudeau campaign a "Nixon-style" affair. One Ottawa correspondent commented that "Trudeau's script could have been written by Joe McGinniss," author of *The Selling of the President 1968*.[69] Certainly the Trudeau campaign did use many of the tactics employed by Richard Nixon in 1968 and 1972 (though not, as far as is known, harassment of journalists).

---

[66] Robert L. Stanfield, in a letter published in the *Toronto Globe and Mail*, 1 November 1974, quoting his own remarks in television interview a few days earlier.

[67] Stevens, "A Simple Strategy."

[68] See "The Fault, Dear Bob . . .," *Toronto Globe and Mail*, 29 October 1974.

[69] Interview with David Ablett, *Vancouver Sun* Ottawa correspondent. Compare Joe McGinniss, *The Selling of the President 1968* (Richmond Hill, Ontario: Simon and Schuster, 1970).

The Republican pattern of keeping reporters busy with prepared texts, many of which were never actually delivered, and stage-managed events, while also keeping them away from the leader and important issues, was clearly picked up by the Liberals. Ironically, the complaints leveled at the media by Senator George McGovern foreshadowed the Stanfield charges summarized above. McGovern commented late in the 1972 campaign that the press was failing in its responsibilities by not forcing Nixon to answer questions on the issues and by not reporting on the contrast between his open campaign and Nixon's closed one. It was up to the press, McGovern said, to restore some balance to the campaign.[70]

Was the Trudeau campaign strategy somehow improper? *Vancouver Sun* Ottawa correspondent David Ablett took the view that reporters have no constitutional right to interrogate political leaders: "It has never been my view that the Prime Minister must communicate with the press. How he communicates with the electorate is his business." *Toronto Star* correspondent Anthony Westell argued that in any case "the press likes to be manipulated. There is a natural alliance between news makers and news reporters. The news maker wants publicity and the reporter needs a steady flow of usable copy. . . . The press gets angry when politicians don't make news. . . . The non-news campaign in 1972 seems to have been disastrous for Trudeau." The Liberals' strategy was to give the press what it wanted, but in such a way as to get its message to the public with the greatest frequency and the least distortion possible.

There was, however, general concern among reporters about the lack of critical reporting of the campaign, especially of Trudeau's policy announcements. Factors such as the lack of advance notice of the statements, their complexity, and the fact that few news organizations have experts in specific policy areas—housing, transportation, and so on—were cited. Canadian Press, which provided most news outlets with the bulk of their national campaign coverage, felt handicapped by the special demands made on national wire services. "Critical reporting is not easy for CP," according to Ottawa editor Arch Mackenzie. "It must be well supported by research to provide protection against complaints." In addition, he noted, many newspapers will not print lengthy analyses, especially three or four days after the original statement. Often, succeeding announcements intervened and swept an issue off the front page before an analysis could be prepared, though CP did try to examine the various policy

---

[70] Crouse, *Boys on the Bus*, pp. 110, 114-115, 195-200, 337.

pronouncements. In the view of Clark Davey, "The real reason for the lack of analysis was that editors had their reporters already committed to other tasks." The Canadian combination of long distances and small staffs makes it difficult to adapt to a campaign that is developing differently than planners had anticipated.

Many reporters and editors also felt uneasy about the coverage of the Conservative wage and price control proposal. Anthony Westell wrote after the election, "Those of us out on the campaign trail never did get at the heart of Stanfield's economic policies. True, he held numerous press conferences and gave endless interviews, but either we did not ask the right questions or accepted too easily evasive answers." [71] Responding to charges by Conservative finance critic James Gillies that they had failed to communicate the wage and price control policy to their readers, reporters commented that they had never been able to find out precisely what it was.

The major news organizations did try to be "more than a conduit for party propaganda," as one editor put it, but they often lacked the resources to do more than report on the issues raised by the parties. Only a handful of major newspapers and the CBC national news were able to do much critical analysis, and original journalistic contributions to public discussion were relatively rare. Some issues, such as inflation, were poorly handled, primarily because of their complexity, and others, avoided by party leaders because they were too controversial, such as abortion and French-English relations, hardly surfaced in the national campaign at all. Rightly or wrongly, the journalists for the most part let the parties set the tone of the campaign.

The news organizations compounded their own problems by the way in which they approached the coverage of the campaign. As tradition requires, the major organizations all assigned reporters to travel with the major party leaders (about forty each with Trudeau and Stanfield and about twenty with Lewis) and most also posted reporters to regional centers to cover the campaign on the ground. (The parties arranged travel and accommodations for the reporters and billed the news organizations.) Although CP provided comprehensive basic coverage of the leaders from the beginning of the campaign, the country's other major news outlets felt that they had to have their own correspondents on the job. Few chose to keep one or more correspondents in Ottawa to do analysis. Pundits and correspondents who were not on a coverage team tended to float from

---

[71] "The Media Were the Really Big Losers in the Election," *Toronto Star*, 12 July 1974.

leader to leader. As a result, most outlets had little choice but to be led by the party leaders and to treat the campaign primarily as an evolving series of speeches and announcements. CBC news executive Ray Chaisson commented that "the media fall into a trap when they focus excessively on the leaders. It allows the parties to lead them too much."

The "flying consensus" which tends to emerge aboard the campaign planes was also a problem in 1974. The working conditions were such that reporters were either on the plane, where it is difficult to write, or following the candidate through a rigorous day on the hustings. There was little time to write and file stories, let alone to reflect. Reporters were forced to live in a constricted, artificial world in which they interacted primarily with their colleagues and party press agents, a situation in which it is difficult to get a clear perspective on the campaign.[72] David Ablett, Ottawa correspondent for the *Vancouver Sun*, describes meeting the Trudeau entourage at midcampaign in Winnipeg, where Ablett had been for several days:

> When the national reporters arrived, they headed for me to find out what was happening in Winnipeg. They were starved for information about what was happening on the ground. Opinion becomes homogenized and abstracted from reality on the plane. They headed for me because they knew me and what slant I was likely to take. But they regularly quizzed local reporters for background.

The reporters felt trapped into writing formula stories because they had little opportunity to do anything different.

Many editors sought to combat the problem by rotating reporters among leaders or, in a few cases, from leader coverage to other duties. But some reporters doubted the utility of the strategy. Anthony Westell commented that "rotating reporters is no real answer. When you join a new plane, you talk to the reporters already there to find out what has been going on. You integrate yourself very rapidly into the 'flying consensus.' " Clark Davey, managing editor of the *Globe and Mail*, has questioned the value of traveling with the leaders at all. In 1972 the *Globe* abandoned the practice, but in 1974, anticipating a leader-oriented campaign, reinstituted it. Davey believes that reporters tend inevitably to be "led around" by the leaders and that the group context of the tours makes it difficult for reporters to avoid the "herd instinct, to do something different from what others

---

[72] For an extended discussion of this problem in the United States, see Crouse, *Boys on the Bus*, especially pp. 51-63 and 369.

are doing." The strong temptation to "run with the wire," that is, to make certain that you have covered whatever the CP reporters are featuring to avoid queries from editors, is well known to reporters. To some extent this defeats the purpose of having staff reporters on the plane, rather than simply relying directly on CP, but few major news outlets are willing to take the risk of losing prestige or missing a chance for a big story by not assigning their own staff.

These coverage problems are much the same in Canadian federal elections as in American presidential elections, except that the U.S. campaigns are much longer and many more reporters are involved. The longer American campaigns are probably more exhausting for reporters, but they are not so intensive and reporters can take time off for analysis and reflection. In addition, the larger agencies often assign two or three reporters to a candidate, as the Associated Press does, to permit one to stay behind when the entourage moves on to write a fuller and more reflective story, or to probe local issues and then fly ahead to prepare for the arrival of the tour. In Canada such doubling up is extremely rare.

Some Final Comments

The data presented here make it quite clear that the Liberals, despite an unsympathetic press corps and a wave of Conservative endorsements, won the 1974 media campaign. And a good case can be made for the position that in doing so they won the election.[73] The means by which the victory was achieved—shrewd adaptation of campaign techniques to take advantage of the standard operating procedures of Canadian news organizations—has raised important questions about the Canadian system of campaign coverage. In their postelection post-mortems, the major news organizations were no doubt considering such questions as: How can we improve our capacity for critical reporting? How can we achieve both balanced and critical coverage? How should we handle non-news "happenings" involving leaders and their families? Should we assign more reporters to travel with the leaders—or none at all? How can we cope with the Liberals' strategy of carefully timed releases? Some were even asking if elections deserved as much attention as they get.

Broader questions also arise. Are Canadian campaigns becoming more national? Are they becoming more leader-oriented? Comparative studies of recent elections are needed. Do Canadian citizens

---

[73] For this argument, see Clarkson, "The Liberal Party and Pierre Trudeau."

think that coverage is fair or unfair? Do they think there is too much election coverage or too little? Surveys are needed. Sophisticated studies are also needed to determine more precisely the extent to which the media campaign actually influences voting.

More generally, those concerned with the functioning of representative democracy must consider the implications of election campaigns which are primarily contests for media attention. In 1974 the emphasis appeared to be on television news, which party strategists believe "is the chief means through which 10 million or more of the potential 13 million voters form their opinions. . . ." [74] The television emphasis means that presentations must be brief, simple, aphoristic, and, if possible, have a significant visual component. Increasingly in recent years, Canadian political commentators have urged an end to the media attention contest, to the "phoney romping over the country with advance men, manufactured and processed incidents, all designed primarily to get a good slice of the leader on to the national TV news . . . ," [75] in favor of a "rational" campaign using television in a variety of formats to provide a full airing of each party's proposals and credentials. Such developments are most unlikely, however. Politics, like journalism, is slow to change.

[74] Fisher, "PC Complaint about CBC."

[75] Ibid.; a similar proposal has been made by Walter Pitman. See *Toronto Star*, 28 May 1974.

APPENDIX

A Summary of Canadian General Election Results, 1968–74

Compiled by Richard M. Scammon

1968 HOUSE OF COMMONS ELECTION RESULTS

	Total	Liberal	Progressive Conservative	New Democratic	Social Credit	Other
CANADA						
Alberta	563,835	201,045	283,987	52,720	—	26,083
% of total vote		35.7	50.4	9.4	—	4.6
Seats	19	4	15	—	—	—
British Columbia	798,742	333,949	155,101	260,989	—	48,703
% of total vote		41.8	19.4	32.7	—	6.1
Seats	23	16	—	7	—	—
Manitoba	400,393	166,025	125,713	99,974	949	7,732
% of total vote		41.5	31.4	25.0	0.2	1.9
Seats	13	5	5	3	—	—
New Brunswick	251,979	111,843	125,269	12,277	1,769	821
% of total vote		44.4	49.7	4.9	0.7	0.3
Seats	10	5	5	—	—	—
Newfoundland	160,200	68,549	84,483	7,042	—	126
% of total vote		42.8	52.7	4.4	—	0.1
Seats	7	1	6	—	—	—
Nova Scotia	336,957	127,962	186,026	22,676	—	293
% of total vote		38.0	55.2	6.7	—	0.1
Seats	11	1	10	—	—	—
Ontario	2,948,492	1,372,903	942,979	607,011	—	25,599
% of total vote		46.6	32.0	20.6	—	0.9
Seats	88	64	17	6	—	1
Prince Edward Island	50,766	22,854	26,276	1,636	—	—
% of total vote		45.0	51.8	3.2	—	—
Seats	4	—	4	—	—	—

Quebec	2,184,292	1,170,417	466,492	164,466	358,327	24,590
% of total vote		53.6	21.4	7.5	16.4	1.1
Seats	74	56	4	—	14	—
Saskatchewan	414,425	112,332	153,233	147,941	—	919
% of total vote		27.1	37.0	35.7	—	0.2
Seats	13	2	5	6	—	—
Yukon-N.W. Territories	15,915	9,066	5,321	1,528	—	—
% of total vote		57.0	33.4	9.6	—	—
Seats	2	1	1	—	—	—
TOTAL	8,125,996	3,696,945	2,554,880	1,378,260	361,045	134,866 [a]
% of total vote		45.5	31.4	17.0	4.4	1.7
Seats	264	155	72	22	14	1

ONTARIO [b]

Central	633,559	277,060	258,141	97,305		1,053
% of total vote		43.7	40.7	15.4		0.2
Seats	20	10	9	1		—
East	246,641	134,705	70,252	24,670		17,014
% of total vote		54.6	28.5	10.0		6.9
Seats	7	6	—	—		1
Lakeside	422,645	188,885	133,767	99,297		696
% of total vote		44.7	31.7	23.5		0.2
Seats	11	10	1	—		—
North	291,063	136,886	65,804	87,317		1,056
% of total vote		47.0	22.6	30.0		0.4
Seats	12	11	—	1		—
Southwest	604,951	258,242	228,045	118,000		664
% of total vote		42.7	37.7	19.5		0.1
Seats	18	10	7	1		—
Toronto	749,633	377,125	186,970	180,422		5,116
% of total vote		50.3	24.9	24.1		0.7
Seats	20	17	—	3		—

1968 ELECTION RESULTS (continued)

	Total	Liberal	Progressive Conservative	New Democratic	Social Credit	Other
TOTAL	2,948,492	1,372,903	942,979	607,011	—	25,599
% of total vote		46.6	32.0	20.6	—	0.9
Seats	88	64	17	6	—	1
QUEBEC c						
Bellechasse-Gaspe	148,939	68,661	42,031	2,732	34,835	680
% of total vote		46.1	28.2	1.8	23.4	0.5
Seats	7	5	—		2	—
Central	324,904	164,560	91,452	15,869	50,932	2,091
% of total vote		50.6	28.1	4.9	15.7	0.6
Seats	11	9	1	—	1	—
East	498,574	234,690	121,937	26,197	114,246	1,504
% of total vote		47.1	24.5	5.3	22.9	0.3
Seats	16	9	1	—	6	—
Montreal	792,719	518,467	128,893	104,054	21,947	19,358
% of total vote		65.4	16.3	13.1	2.8	2.4
Seats	25	24	1	—	—	—
North	199,454	85,916	40,651	8,859	64,028	—
% of total vote		43.1	20.4	4.4	32.1	—
Seats	9	4	1	—	4	—
Quebec	219,702	98,123	41,528	6,755	72,339	957
% of total vote		44.7	18.9	3.1	32.9	0.4
Seats	6	5	—	—	1	—
TOTAL	2,184,292	1,170,417	466,492	164,466	358,327	24,590
% of total vote		53.6	21.4	7.5	16.4	1.1
Seats	74	56	4	—	14	—

a 62,956 Social Credit (none elected); 36,141 independent (one elected); 16,785 independent Liberal (none elected); 18,984 miscellaneous parties (none elected).

b Regionalization for Province of Ontario, electing eighty-eight members:

Central: Twenty constituencies—central Ontario is *not* included in the following groupings.

East: Seven constituencies—from the Ottawa area and Grenville-Carleton eastward.

Lakeside: Eleven constituencies—from Peel South (renamed Mississauga for 1974), just west of Toronto area, around Lake Ontario (including Hamilton) to include Niagara Falls.

North: Twelve constituencies—Nipissing, Nickel Belt, Algoma and areas north of these seats.

Southwest: Eighteen constituencies—from (and including) Huron, Perth, Waterloo, Wellington, Brant, and Norfolk-Haldimand southwestward to include the Windsor area.

Toronto: Twenty constituencies—the Toronto metropolitan area.

c Regionalization for Province of Quebec, electing seventy-four members:

Bellechasse-Gaspe: Seven constituencies—south of the St. Lawrence River from Bellechasse eastward.

Central: Eleven constituencies—central Quebec not included in the other five regional groupings—the area north of the St. Lawrence River and the Montreal area from Champlain west to Pontiac.

East: Sixteen constituencies—south of the St. Lawrence River from the American border eastward to include Beauce.

Montreal: Twenty-five constituencies—the island of Montreal and Ile Jesus.

North: Nine constituencies—Temiscamingue eastward to Manicouagan, including Abitibi, Charlevoix, Chicoutimi, Lac-Saint-Jean, Lapointe, Roberval, and Villeneuve.

Quebec: Six constituencies—the three city constituencies plus Lévis, Montmorency, and Portneuf.

1972 HOUSE OF COMMONS ELECTION RESULTS

	Total	Liberal	Progressive Conservative	New Democratic	Social Credit	Other
CANADA						
Alberta	710,952	177,599	409,857	89,811	31,689	1,996
% of total vote		25.0	57.6	12.6	4.5	0.3
Seats	19	—	19	—	—	—
British Columbia	948,289	274,468	313,253	332,345	25,107	3,116
% of total vote		28.9	33.0	35.0	2.6	0.3
Seats	23	4	8	11	—	—
Manitoba	443,154	136,906	184,363	116,474	3,228	2,183
% of total vote		30.9	41.6	26.3	0.7	0.5
Seats	13	2	8	3	—	—
New Brunswick	292,491	125,935	131,455	16,703	16,450	1,948
% of total vote		43.1	44.9	5.7	5.6	0.7
Seats	10	5	5	—	—	—
Newfoundland	175,046	78,505	85,857	8,165	266	2,253
% of total vote		44.8	49.0	4.7	0.2	1.3
Seats	7	3	4	—	—	—
Nova Scotia	383,087	129,738	204,460	47,072	1,316	501
% of total vote		33.9	53.4	12.3	0.3	0.1
Seats	11	1	10	—	—	—
Ontario	3,578,052	1,366,922	1,399,148	768,076	12,937	30,969
% of total vote		38.2	39.1	21.5	0.4	0.9
Seats	88	36	40	11	—	1
Prince Edward Island	56,653	22,950	29,419	4,229	55	—
% of total vote		40.5	51.9	7.5	0.1	—
Seats	4	1	3	—	—	—

Quebec					
% of total vote	2,625,036	457,418	168,910	639,207	70,362
Seats	49.1	17.4	6.4	24.4	2.7
	74	2	—	15	1
Saskatchewan					
% of total vote	432,504	159,629	155,195	7,717	621
Seats	25.3	36.9	35.9	1.8	0.1
	13	7	5	1	—
Yukon-N.W. Territories					
% of total vote	22,225	8,671	6,548	—	252
Seats	30.4	39.0	29.5	—	1.1
	2	1	1	—	—
TOTAL					
% of total vote	9,667,489	3,383,530	1,713,528	737,972	114,201[a]
Seats	38.5	35.0	17.7	7.6	1.2
	264	107	31	15	2
ONTARIO [b]					
Central					
% of total vote	791,080	372,635	133,371	1,209	580
Seats	35.8	47.1	16.9	0.2	0.1
	20	14	1	—	—
East					
% of total vote	312,014	115,715	50,598	4,260	20,349
Seats	38.8	37.1	16.2	1.4	6.5
	7	2	—	—	1
Lakeside					
% of total vote	528,074	218,308	111,161	1,854	1,413
Seats	37.0	41.3	21.1	0.4	0.3
	11	9	—	—	—
North					
% of total vote	333,232	77,429	103,835	4,464	900
Seats	44.0	23.2	31.2	1.3	0.3
	12	—	3	—	—
Southwest					
% of total vote	732,968	294,626	162,223	482	698
Seats	37.5	40.2	22.1	0.1	0.1
	18	9	2	—	—
Toronto					
% of total vote	880,684	320,435	206,888	668	7,029
Seats	39.2	36.4	23.5	0.1	0.8
	20	6	5	—	—
TOTAL					
% of total vote	3,578,052	1,399,148	768,076	12,937	30,969
Seats	38.2	39.1	21.5	0.4	0.9
	88	40	11	—	1

1972 ELECTION RESULTS (continued)

	Total	Liberal	Progressive Conservative	New Democratic	Social Credit	Other
QUEBEC c						
Bellechasse-Gaspe	176,002	76,541	32,461	3,126	63,874	—
% of total vote		43.5	18.4	1.8	36.3	—
Seats	7	4	—	—	3	—
Central	397,442	189,777	54,550	18,861	113,400	20,854
% of total vote		47.7	13.7	4.7	28.5	5.2
Seats	11	9	—	—	1	1
East	621,399	266,339	123,327	28,050	194,162	9,521
% of total vote		42.9	19.8	4.5	31.2	1.5
Seats	16	9	2	—	5	—
Montreal	929,974	522,243	169,240	99,978	110,427	28,086
% of total vote		56.2	18.2	10.8	11.9	3.0
Seats	25	25	—	—	—	—
North	238,597	104,253	40,500	4,907	86,637	2,300
% of total vote		43.7	17.0	2.1	36.3	1.0
Seats	9	4	—	—	5	—
Quebec	261,622	129,986	37,340	13,988	70,707	9,601
% of total vote		49.7	14.3	5.3	27.0	3.7
Seats	6	5	—	—	1	—
TOTAL	2,625,036	1,289,139	457,418	168,910	639,207	70,362
% of total vote		49.1	17.2	6.4	24.4	2.7
Seats	74	56	2	—	15	1

a All "other" vote was for independent candidates with two elected.
b See note b for the 1968 election results table, above.
c See note c for the 1968 election results table, above.

1974 HOUSE OF COMMONS ELECTION RESULTS

	Total	Liberal	Progressive Conservative	New Democratic	Social Credit	Other
CANADA						
Alberta	682,569	168,973	417,422	63,310	22,909	9,955
% of total vote		24.8	61.2	9.3	3.4	1.5
Seats	19	—	19	—	—	—
British Columbia	1,010,881	336,435	423,954	232,547	12,433	5,512
% of total vote		33.3	41.9	23.0	1.2	0.5
Seats	23	8	13	2	—	—
Manitoba	446,731	122,470	212,990	104,829	4,750	1,692
% of total vote		27.4	47.7	23.5	1.1	0.4
Seats	13	2	9	2	—	—
New Brunswick	287,350	135,723	94,934	24,869	8,407	23,417
% of total vote		47.2	33.0	8.7	2.9	8.1
Seats	10	6	3	—	—	1
Newfoundland	173,945	81,299	75,816	16,445	143	242
% of total vote		46.7	43.6	9.5	0.1	0.1
Seats	7	4	3	—	—	—
Nova Scotia	386,864	157,582	183,897	43,470	1,457	458
% of total vote		40.7	47.5	11.2	0.4	0.1
Seats	11	2	8	1	—	—
Ontario	3,565,537	1,609,786	1,252,082	680,113	6,575	16,981
% of total vote		45.1	35.1	19.1	0.2	0.5
Seats	88	55	25	8	—	—
Prince Edward Island	58,253	26,932	28,578	2,666		77
% of total vote		46.2	49.1	4.6		0.1
Seats	4	1	3	—	—	—
Quebec	2,458,675	1,330,337	520,632	162,080	420,018	25,608
% of total vote		54.1	21.2	6.6	17.1	1.0
Seats	74	60	3	—	11	—

	Total	Liberal	Progressive Conservative	New Democratic	Social Credit	Other
Saskatchewan	413,934	127,282	150,846	130,391	4,539	876
% of total vote		30.7	36.4	31.5	1.1	0.2
Seats	13	3	8	2	—	—
Yukon-N.W. Territories	21,169	5,957	8,184	7,028	—	—
% of total vote		28.1	38.7	33.2	—	—
Seats	2	—	1	1	—	—
TOTAL	9,505,908	4,102,776	3,369,335	1,467,748	481,231	84,818[a]
% of total vote		43.2	35.4	15.4	5.1	0.9
Seats	264	141	95	16	11	1
ONTARIO [b]						
Central	800,354	324,856	340,114	132,472	1,774	1,138
% of total vote		40.6	42.5	16.6	0.2	0.1
Seats	20	6	13	1	—	—
East	319,467	158,476	121,603	36,281	1,307	1,800
% of total vote		49.6	38.1	11.4	0.4	0.6
Seats	7	6	1	—	—	—
Lakeside	525,577	238,622	192,663	91,080	1,733	1,479
% of total vote		45.4	36.7	17.3	0.3	0.3
Seats	11	8	3	—	—	—
North	337,138	161,171	61,823	111,166	96.4	2,014
% of total vote		47.8	18.3	33.0	0.3	0.6
Seats	12	9	—	3	—	—
Southwest	729,934	330,369	242,898	153,531	379	2,757
% of total vote		45.3	33.3	21.0	0.1	0.4
Seats	18	10	6	2	—	—

Toronto	853,067	396,292	292,981	155,583	418	7,793
% of total vote		46.5	34.3	18.2	—	0.9
Seats	20	16	2	2	—	—
TOTAL	3,565,537	1,609,786	1,252,082	680,113	6,575	16,981
% of total vote		45.1	35.1	19.1	0.2	0.5
Seats	88	55	25	8	—	—
QUEBEC c						
Bellechasse-Gaspe	164,292	81,396	33,091	3,720	44,701	1,384
% of total vote		49.5	20.1	2.3	27.2	0.8
Seats	7	4	—	—	3	—
Central	388,035	210,658	90,677	18,842	65,307	2,451
% of total vote		54.3	23.4	4.9	16.8	0.6
Seats	11	9	1	—	1	—
East	606,856	290,003	142,887	31,911	134,627	7,428
% of total vote		47.8	23.5	5.3	22.2	1.2
Seats	16	11	2	—	3	—
Montreal	833,946	507,712	180,571	75,824	59,298	10,541
% of total vote		60.9	21.7	9.1	7.1	1.3
Seats	25	25	—	—	—	—
North	223,244	102,506	32,836	10,393	76,139	1,370
% of total vote		45.9	14.7	4.7	34.1	0.6
Seats	9	5	—	—	4	—
Quebec	242,302	138,062	40,570	21,290	39,946	2,434
% of total vote		57.0	16.7	8.8	16.5	1.0
Seats	6	6	—	—	—	—
TOTAL	2,458,675	1,330,337	520,632	162,080	420,018	25,608
% of total vote		54.1	21.2	6.6	17.1	1.0
Seats	74	60	3	—	11	—

a 56,457 independent (one elected); 16,261 Marxist-Leninist (none elected); 12,100 Communist (none elected).
b See note b for the 1968 election results table, above.
c See note c for the 1968 election results table, above.

CONTRIBUTORS

STEPHEN CLARKSON is associate professor in the Department of Political Economy at the University of Toronto. He has published in the area of comparative politics, both on Soviet development theory and on Canadian politics at the municipal, provincial, and federal levels.

FREDERICK J. FLETCHER, assistant professor of political science at York University, Toronto, is a former reporter and editorial writer. He has done research on the mass media in Nigeria and in Canada and has recently completed an article on news coverage of provincial politics in Ontario.

WILLIAM P. IRVINE is associate professor of political studies at Queen's University, Kingston, Ontario. He is presently working on a book on Canadian voting behavior and has published articles in this area and in the areas of methodology and nationalism.

LAWRENCE LeDUC is associate professor of political science at the University of Windsor, Ontario. He was co-director of the 1974 Canadian national election survey and has published articles on Canadian federal and provincial politics and on research methods.

JOHN MEISEL is Hardy professor of political science at Queen's University. Among his studies of parties and elections in Canada are *The Canadian General Election of 1957*, *Papers on the 1962 Election* (editor), *Working Papers on Canadian Politics*, and *Cleavages, Parties and Values in Canada*. He is past president of the Canadian Political Science Association.

KHAYYAM Z. PALTIEL is professor of political science at Carleton University, Ottawa. He served as research director of the Canadian government's Advisory Committee on Election Expenses. Author of *Political Party Financing in Canada* and numerous related articles, he has also written extensively on Israeli and Middle Eastern politics.

GEORGE PERLIN is associate professor of political studies at Queen's University, Kingston, Ontario. His study of leadership conflict in the Progressive Conservative party will be published early in 1976.

MICHAEL STEIN is an associate professor of political science at McGill University in Montreal. He is the author of *The Dynamics of Right-Wing Protest: A Political Analysis of Social Credit in Quebec* and of several articles on Quebec and Canadian politics. He is also coauthor (with Robert J. Jackson) of *Issues in Comparative Politics: A Text with Readings.*

RICHARD M. SCAMMON, the coauthor of *This U.S.A.* and *The Real Majority,* is director of the Elections Research Center in Washington, D. C. He has edited the biennial statistical series, *America Votes,* since 1956.

Jo SURICH lectures in the Department of Political Science at the University of Waterloo. He has conducted several studies of Canadian provincial politics and published articles on various aspects of Ontario politics. In his nonacademic life he has been a provincial NDP candidate, finance chairman of the Ontario NDP, and is currently chairman of the Ontario NDP Election Planning Committee.

INDEX

news distribution among parties: 265–271
party strategy for: 46–47, 143, 253–256
possible political bias by: 282–285
Matte, René: 161, 164
Meisel, John: 68–69, 228
Mercier, Thérèse: 171
Minorities, treatment of: 9
Minority governments:
  1972–74: 133
  legislative program: 18–19
  opinion polls on: 233–237
  problems of: 33
Molgat, Gil: 231
Montreal Star: 261, 271
Munro, John: 93, 245, 270

Nationalism: 127, 129
Nationalization of industry: 11, 123, 129
National Liberal Federation of Canada: 11
New Brunswick:
  Conservative party: 98
  party alignment: 51, 54, 66
  Social Credit party: 157, 171, 176
New Democratic party (NDP): 11, 13, 15, 16, 18, 27
  in 1972 election: 32–38, 131–132
  1974 campaign issues: 89–90, 135–139
  campaign financing: 135–136, 141, 143, 183, 188, 189, 190, 194–197
  decentralization of: 136, 138, 144
  ideological differences in: 127, 132, 145
  leadership conflict: 146–148
  Liberal party and: 33–35, 157, 160
  media coverage of: 267, 270
  media strategy: 143, 255–256, 280, 281
  policies: 17, 133–134
  in provinces: 142–144
  Regina Manifesto: 123, 146
  votes: 121, 122, 213
  Waffle movement and: 125, 128–131
Newfoundland: 51, 52, 66
Newspapers: 112, 143, 182
  campaign coverage: 257, 260–261, 264–265
  candidate endorsements: 271–272
  concentration of ownership: 248
  national news in: 245–246

news distribution among parties: 265–267
parliamentary press gallery: 248, 251
problems relating to campaign-assigned reporters: 286–288
role in 1974 campaign: 83, 84, 91–92
surveys: 215–216
Nova Scotia: 51, 54, 66, 98
Nystrom, Lorne: 147, 148

Official Languages Act: 44
Oliver, Craig: 265
Ontario:
  1974 Liberal vote: 92, 93
  Conservative party: 98
  NDP: 136, 145
  party alignment: 53, 54, 67
  regional loyalty: 9–10
  Waffle movement: 128–130
Opinion polls:
  accuracy: 216–217
  on confederation: 210
  cost of: 191, 193
  forecasting from: 212–213, 217
  on inflation: 41, 78–79, 220–223
  on leadership image: 226–232
  on majority versus minority governments: 233–237
  pre-1974 election: 48–49, 80, 89, 91, 237
  regional differences: 210–211
  techniques used: 216
  types of: 215–216
  see also Gallup poll
Organization for Economic Cooperation and Development (OECD): 47
Ottawa Citizen: 271

Parliament: 29–30, 39
Parti Québécois: 21, 28, 146, 148, 163, 168, 267
Party system:
  evaluation of: 20–25
  factors influencing: 1–7, 26
  one-party dominant: 18, 19–20
  organization: 72
  role of federal and provincial parties in: 11
  U.S. influence on: 23–25
Pearson, Lester: 59–60, 71, 72, 73
Pensions: 34
Petrie, Dorothy: 86, 89